Decisions
of the
United States
Supreme Court

2003-04 TERM

---

by
The Editorial Staff
United States Supreme Court Reports,
Lawyers' Edition

LexisNexis®

LexisNexis and the Knowledge Burst logo are registered trademarks of Reed Elsevier
Properties Inc., used under license. Matthew Bender is a registered trademark of Matthew
Bender Properties Inc.

Copyright © 2004
Matthew Bender & Company, Inc., a member of the LexisNexis® Group.
All rights reserved.

No copyright is claimed in the text of statutes, regulations, and excerpts from court opinions quoted
within this work. Permission to copy material exceeding fair use, 17 U.S.C. § 107, may be licensed
for a fee of $1 per page per copy from the Copyright Clearance Center, 222 Rosewood Drive,
Danvers, MA, 01923, telephone (978) 750-8400.

ISBN 0-327-12376-1

Editorial Office

701 East Water Street, Charlottesville, VA 22902-7587
(800) 446-3410

www.lexisnexis.com

Customer Service: 800/833-9844

Publication Number 7683516

(Pub. 76800)

CONTENTS

	PAGE
Preface	v
The Court's Personnel	vii
Survey of the 2003-04 Term	xxi
Summaries of Decisions	1
Glossary of Common Legal Terms	293
Table of Cases	303
Index	Ind-1

PREFACE

This volume is designed to serve as a quick-reference guide to the work of the United States Supreme Court during its 2003–2004 Term. Its important features are described below.

The Court's Personnel. A list of the Justices of the Supreme Court is accompanied by photographs and biographical sketches of each Justice serving during the Term.

Survey of the Term. A succinct narrative statement outlines the high spots of the Term.

Summaries of Decisions. Every important decision of the Supreme Court is individually summarized. These summaries (reprinted from Vols. 157–159, Part 2 L Ed 2d) describe the manner in which the case came before the Court, the facts involved and issues presented, the holding of the Court and the reasons supporting that holding, the name of the Justice who wrote the opinion of the majority, and the names and views of those of the Justices who concurred or dissented.

The Summaries are printed in the order in which the cases were decided by the Court. Notations to Summaries indicate the volume and page at which the full opinion of the Court may be found in the official reports (US) published by the Federal Government, and the privately published United States Supreme Court Reports, Lawyers' Edition (L Ed 2d), and Supreme Court Reporter (S Ct).

Following each Summary is a listing of the attorneys who argued in behalf of the litigants.

Glossary. A glossary of common legal terms defines, in simple, nontechnical language, various legal words and phrases frequently used in the Supreme Court's decisions.

Table of Cases. A complete Table of Cases makes possible the location of the Summary of any case through the name of a party litigant.

Index. A detailed, alphabetical word index makes possible the location of the Summary of any case by consulting the index entries for appropriate factual and conceptual terms.

THE COURT'S PERSONNEL

JUSTICES

OF THE

SUPREME COURT OF THE UNITED STATES

2003–04 Term

Chief Justice

HON. WILLIAM H. REHNQUIST

Associate Justices

HON. JOHN P. STEVENS

HON. SANDRA DAY O'CONNOR

HON. ANTONIN SCALIA

HON. ANTHONY M. KENNEDY

HON. DAVID H. SOUTER

HON. CLARENCE THOMAS

HON. RUTH BADER GINSBURG

HON. STEPHEN BREYER

BIOGRAPHIES OF THE JUSTICES

Chief Justice Rehnquist was born in Milwaukee, Wisconsin, on October 1, 1924, the son of William B.  and Margery P. Rehnquist. He married Natalie Cornell in 1953. They have three children, James, Janet, and Nancy.

Chief Justice Rehnquist attended public schools in Shorewood, Wisconsin, and received his B.A. degree, with great distinction, and an M.A. degree from Stanford University in 1948. He also earned an M.A. degree from Harvard University in 1950, and then returned to Stanford University, where he received his LL.B. degree in 1952.

From 1952 to 1953, he served as law clerk for Justice Robert H. Jackson, Supreme Court of the United States. From 1953 to 1969, Chief Justice Rehnquist engaged in private practice in Phoenix, Arizona, and in 1969, he was appointed Assistant Attorney General, Office of Legal Counsel, by President Nixon.

Chief Justice Rehnquist served in the United States Army Air Corps in this country and overseas from 1943 to 1946, and was discharged with the rank of sergeant.

Chief Justice Rehnquist was nominated to the position of Associate Justice of the United States Supreme Court by President Nixon on October 21, 1971, and took office on January 7, 1972. On June 17, 1986, he was nominated Chief Justice by President Reagan, and on September 26, 1986, he was sworn in as Chief Justice.

Chief Justice Rehnquist's professional activities have included membership in the American Bar Association, the Arizona Bar Association, the Maricopa County (Arizona) Bar Association (President, 1963), the National Conference of Lawyers and Realtors, the National Conference of Commissioners of Uniform State Laws, and the Council of the Administrative Conference of the United States.

Justice Stevens was born in Chicago, Illinois, on April 20, 1920. He is married to Maryan Mulholland Stevens  and has four children, John Joseph, Kathryn Stevens Tedlicka, Elizabeth Jane, and Susan Roberta.

Justice Stevens received an A.B. degree from the University of Chicago in 1941 and a J.D. degree, magna cum laude, from Northwestern University School of Law in 1947.

During the 1947–1948 Term of the United States Supreme Court, he was a law clerk to Justice Wiley Rutledge, and in 1949, he was admitted to practice law in Illinois. In 1951 and 1952, Justice Stevens was Associate Counsel to the Subcommittee on the Study of Monopoly Power of the Judiciary Committee of the United States House of Representatives, and from 1953 to 1955 he was a member of the Attorney General's National Committee to Study Anti-trust Law. From 1970 to 1975 he served as a Judge of the United States Court of Appeals for the Seventh Circuit.

Justice Stevens served in the United States Navy from 1942 to 1945.

Justice Stevens was appointed to the position of Associate Justice of the United States Supreme Court by President Ford on December 1, 1975, and took his seat on December 19, 1975.

Justice Stevens is a member of the Illinois Bar Association, Chicago Bar Association, Federal Bar Association, American Law Institute, and American Judicature Society.

Justice O'Connor was born in El Paso, Texas, on March 26, 1930, the daughter of Harold A. Day and Ada  Mae Wilkey Day. She married John Jay O'Connor III in 1952. They have three children, Scott, Brian, and Jay.

Justice O'Connor graduated from Stanford University in 1950 with a B.A. degree, magna cum laude. She earned her LL.B. degree at Stanford in 1952.

Justice O'Connor served as a deputy county attorney in San Mateo County, California, from 1952 to 1953, and as a civilian attorney for the Quartermaster Market Center in Frankfurt, Germany, from 1954 to 1957. She was in the private practice of law in Maryvale, Arizona, from 1958 to 1960, and served as an Assistant Attorney General in Arizona from 1965 to 1969.

Justice O'Connor was a member of the Arizona State Senate from 1969 to 1975. She was a judge of the Maricopa County Superior Court in Phoenix, Arizona, from 1975 to 1979, and served on the Arizona Court of Appeals from 1979 to 1981.

Justice O'Connor was appointed to the position of Associate Justice of the United States Supreme Court by President Reagan on July 7, 1981, and took office on September 25, 1981.

Justice Scalia was born on March 11, 1936 in Trenton, New Jersey. He married Maureen McCarthy, September 10, 1960. They have nine children: Ann Forrest, Eugene, John Francis, Catherine Elisabeth, Mary Clare, Paul David, Matthew, Christopher James, and Margaret Jane.

Justice Scalia attended Georgetown University and University of Fribourg (Switzerland), receiving his A.B. degree in 1957. He earned his LL.B. degree in 1960 from Harvard University.

Justice Scalia was admitted to the Ohio Bar, 1962, and the Virginia Bar, 1970. He was in private practice with Jones, Day, Cockley and Reavis, Cleveland, Ohio, from 1961 to 1967.

He served as general counsel, Office of Telecommunications Policy, Executive Office of the President, 1971 to 1972; chairman, Administrative Conference of the United States, 1972 to 1974; Assistant Attorney General, Office of Legal Counsel, U. S. Department of Justice, 1974 to 1977.

Justice Scalia was a professor of law at the University of Virginia from 1967 to 1974, a scholar in residence at the American Enterprise Institute in 1977, visiting professor of law at Georgetown University in 1977, professor of law at the University of Chicago from 1977 to 1982, and visiting professor of law at Stanford University from 1980 to 1981.

From 1982 to 1986, Justice Scalia served as a Judge of the United States Court of Appeals for the District of Columbia Circuit. He was nominated by President

Reagan as Associate Justice of the United States Supreme Court, and he took the oath of office on September 26, 1986.

Justice Kennedy was born in Sacramento, California, on July 23, 1936. He married Mary Davis on June 29,  1963, and they have three children, Justin Anthony, Gregory Davis, and Kristin Marie.

Justice Kennedy attended Stanford University and the London School of Economics, receiving a B.A. from Stanford in 1958. He then earned an LL.B. from Harvard Law School in 1961. From 1960 to 1961, he was on the board of student advisors, Harvard Law School.

Justice Kennedy was admitted to the California bar in 1962 and the United States Tax Court bar in 1971. From 1961 to 1963, he was an associate at Thelen, Marrin, Johnson & Bridges, San Francisco, then practiced as a sole practitioner in Sacramento from 1963 to 1967, and was a partner in Evans, Jackson & Kennedy, Sacramento, from 1967 to 1975. He was nominated to be a judge of the United States Court of Appeals for the Ninth Circuit by President Ford, and took the oath of office on May 30, 1975. In addition, Justice Kennedy has been a professor of constitutional law at McGeorge School of Law, University of the Pacific, from 1965 to 1988.

He has served in the California Army National Guard, 1961; the Judicial Conference of the United States Advisory Panel on Financial Disclosure Reports and Judicial Activities (subsequently renamed the Advisory Committee on Codes of Conduct), 1979 to 1987; and the board of the Federal Judicial Center, 1987 to 1988. He has been on the Committee on Pacific Territories, 1979 to 1988, and was named chairman 1982. He is a member of the American Bar Association,

Sacramento County Bar Association, State Bar of California, and Phi Beta Kappa.

Justice Kennedy was nominated by President Reagan as an Associate Justice of the Supreme Court, and took the oath of office on February 18, 1988.

Justice Souter was born in Melrose, Massachusetts on September 17, 1939, the son of Joseph Alexander and Helen Adams Hackett Souter.

He graduated from Harvard College in 1961 with an A.B. degree. After two years as a Rhodes Scholar, Justice Souter received an A.B. in Jurisprudence from Oxford University in 1963. He earned an LL.B. degree from Harvard Law School in 1966 and an M.A. degree from Oxford University in 1989.

Justice Souter was an associate at the law firm of Orr and Reno in Concord, New Hampshire from 1966 to 1968. He then became an Assistant Attorney General of New Hampshire. In 1971, he became Deputy Attorney General, and in 1976, Attorney General of New Hampshire. Justice Souter was named Associate Justice of the Superior Court of New Hampshire in 1978. In 1983, he was appointed as an Associate Justice of the Supreme Court of New Hampshire.

On May 25, 1990, Justice Souter became a Judge of the United States Court of Appeals for the First Circuit. He was nominated by President Bush as an Associate Justice of the United States Supreme Court, and he took his seat on October 9, 1990.

Justice Souter is a member of the National Association of Attorneys General, the New Hampshire Bar Association, and the American Bar Association.

Justice Thomas was born in Pinpoint, Georgia on June 23, 1948. He married Virginia Lamp on May 30,  1987, and has one child, Jamal Adeen.

Justice Thomas attended Conception Seminary and Holy Cross College, receiving an A.B. degree, cum laude, from Holy Cross in 1971. He earned a J.D. degree from Yale Law School in 1974.

He was admitted to the Missouri Bar in 1974, and after serving as Assistant Attorney General of Missouri from 1974 to 1977, he was an attorney for the Monsanto Company from 1977 to 1979.

Justice Thomas served as a legislative assistant to Senator John C. Danforth of Missouri from 1979 to 1981, before serving as Assistant Secretary for Civil Rights for the United States Department of Education from 1981 to 1982 and Chairman of the United States Equal Employment Opportunity Commission from 1982 to 1990.

On March 12, 1990, Justice Thomas became a Judge of the United States Court of Appeals for the District of Columbia Circuit. He was nominated by President Bush as Associate Justice of the United States Supreme Court, and he took the oath of office on October 23, 1991.

Justice Ginsburg was born in Brooklyn, New York, on March 15, 1933, the daughter of Nathan Bader and  Celia Amster Bader. She married Martin D. Ginsburg in 1954, and they have two children, Jane and James.

She received a B.A. degree, with high honors in Government and distinction in all subjects, from Cornell University in 1954. She attended Harvard Law School and Columbia Law School, receiving her L.L.B. degree from Columbia in 1959.

Justice Ginsburg was admitted to the New York Bar in 1959 and the District of Columbia Bar in 1975. She served as a law clerk for Judge Edmund L. Palmieri of the United States District Court for the Southern District of New York from 1959 to 1961.

Justice Ginsburg was a professor at the Rutgers University School of Law from 1963 to 1972 and at Columbia Law School from 1972 to 1980. In addition, she served the American Civil Liberties Union as general counsel from 1973 to 1980 and as a member of the national board of directors from 1974 to 1980.

On June 30, 1980, Justice Ginsburg became a Judge of the United States Court of Appeals for the District of Columbia Circuit. She was nominated by President Clinton as an Associate Justice of the United States Supreme Court, and she took the oath of office on August 10, 1993.

Justice Breyer was born in San Francisco, California, on August 15, 1938. He married Joanna Hare on  September 4, 1967, and they have three children, Chloe, Nell, and Michael.

Justice Breyer received an A.B. degree, with Great Distinction, from Stanford University in 1959. He attended Oxford University as a Marshall Scholar and received a B.A. degree, with 1st Class Honors, in 1961. He earned his LL.B. degree from Harvard Law School, magna cum laude, in 1964.

During the 1964-1965 Term of the United States Supreme Court, he served as clerk to Justice Arthur Goldberg. He served as Special Assistant to the Assistant Attorney General (Antitrust), Department of Justice, 1965 to 1967; Assistant Special Prosecutor, Watergate Special Prosecution Force, 1973; Special Counsel to the U.S. Senate Judiciary Committee, 1974 to 1975; and Chief Counsel to the U.S. Senate Judiciary Committee, 1979 to 1980.

At Harvard University, Justice Breyer was an assistant professor from 1967 to 1970, a professor of law from 1970 to 1980, a professor at the Kennedy School of Government from 1977 to 1980, and a lecturer since 1980. He was a visiting professor at the College of Law, Sydney, Australia, in 1975, and the University of Rome in 1993.

He was appointed to the United States Court of Appeals for the First Circuit in 1980, and served as Chief Judge of that Court from 1990 to 1994. He was nominated by President Clinton as Associate Justice of the United States Supreme Court and took office on August 4, 1994.

SURVEY OF THE 2003-2004 TERM

by

Gary Knapp, M.B.A., J.D.

§ 1. Generally; statistics
§ 2. Landmark decisions
§ 3. Abduction from Mexico
§ 4. Adult businesses
§ 5. Age discrimination
§ 6. Airlines
§ 7. Attorneys' fees
§ 8. Bankruptcy
§ 9. Bribery
§ 10. Child Online Protection Act
§ 11. Disability discrimination
§ 12. Double jeopardy
§ 13. Elections
§ 14. Environmental law
§ 15. Evidence—admissibility
§ 16. —Destruction
§ 17. Discovery
§ 18. Federal court jurisdiction—District Court
§ 19. —Supreme Court
§ 20. Foreign sovereign immunity
§ 21. Guilty plea
§ 22. Habeas corpus—generally
§ 23. —Death sentence
§ 24. —Ineffective assistance of counsel
§ 25. Medicaid benefits
§ 26. Pensions and retirement funds
§ 27. Postal Service
§ 28. Price fixing
§ 29. Prisoners—generally
§ 30. —Enemy combatants
§ 31. Privacy
§ 32. Public land grants
§ 33. Race discrimination

§ 34. Religion in schools
§ 35. Right to counsel
§ 36. Search and seizure—generally
§ 37. —Automobiles
§ 38. —Homes
§ 39. Securities regulation
§ 40. Sentencing by judge
§ 41. Sex discrimination
§ 42. Social Security benefits
§ 43. Standing to bring suit
§ 44. State borders
§ 45. Taxes—federal
§ 46. —State
§ 47. Telecommunications
§ 48. Truth in Lending Act

§ 1. Generally; statistics

The Supreme Court's 2003-2004 Term began on October 6, 2003 and adjourned on October 4, 2004.

Statistics released by the Office of the Clerk of the Supreme Court show that, as of the court's beginning its summer recess in late June 2004, (1) 8,882 cases appeared on the Supreme Court's docket for the 2003-2004 Term; and (2) of these, 1,068 were carried over from the prior term, and 7,814 were docketed during the 2003-2004 Term.

Of the 8,882 cases on the docket during the 2003-2004 Term, 7,646 nonoriginal cases were disposed of by (1) the court's denial of review, (2) the court's dismissal, or (3) withdrawal. Another 50 nonoriginal cases were summarily decided. In addition, 2 original cases were disposed of. A total of 1,046 cases, including 4 original cases, were not acted upon, or remained undisposed of.

There were 140 cases available for argument during the 2003-2004 Term, of which 91 cases were argued and 2 were dismissed or remanded without argument, leaving 47 cases still available for argument. Of the 91 cases that were argued, 89 were disposed of by signed opinion, and 2 were disposed of by per curiam opinion.

§ 2. Landmark decisions

During the 2003-2004 Term, the United States Supreme Court issued a number of well-publicized decisions. In one such case, where three opinions, supported by varying majorities of Justices, together constituted the opinion of the court, the court held that many parts of the Bipartisan Campaign Reform Act of 2002—including provisions that regulated the use of "soft money" by political parties, officeholders, and candidates (2 USCS § 441i)—were valid under the Federal Constitution's First Amendment (McConnell v FEC (2003, US) 157 L Ed 2d 491, 124 S Ct 619, infra § 13).

The Supreme Court determined that the Age Discrimination in Employment Act of 1967 (29 USCS §§ 621 et seq.), which protects from discrimination because of age employees who are at least 40 years old, does not prohibit discrimination against younger protected employees in favor of older protected employees (Gen. Dynamics Land Sys. v Cline (2004, US) 157 L Ed 2d 1094, 124 S Ct 1236, infra § 5). In another discrimination case, which involved two paraplegics—a criminal defendant and a certified court reporter—the court held that Title II of the Americans with Disabilities Act (42 USCS §§ 12131 et seq.), as applied to cases implementing the right of access to courts, was a valid exercise of Congress' authority, under § 5 of the Federal Constitution's Fourteenth Amendment, to enforce the amendment's guarantees (Tennessee v Lane (2004, US) 158 L Ed 2d 820, 124 S Ct 1978, infra § 11).

Two cases concerning religion in schools attracted national attention. The court decided that a postsecondary-education scholarship program that had been established by the state of Washington, under which program students were not permitted to use a scholarship to pursue "a degree in theology," did not violate the free exercise of religion clause of the Federal Constitution's First Amendment (Locke v Davey (2004, US) 158 L Ed 2d 1, 124 S Ct 1307, infra § 34). Also, the court held that a public elementary school student's father—who sought to challenge Congress' addition, in 1954, of the words "under God" to the Pledge of Allegiance (codified at 4 USCS § 4) as violating the religion clauses of the Federal Constitution's First Amendment—lacked prudential standing to bring suit against the school district in federal court, where the student's mother asserted that, according to a California state court's custody order, the mother had the right to make final decisions about the student's education if the mother and father could not agree. (Elk Grove Unified Sch. Dist. v Newdow (2004, US) 159 L Ed 2d 98, 124 S Ct 2301, infra § 43).

The Supreme Court decided that a business owner who worked in the business qualified as a participant in the business' pension plan covered by the Employee Retirement Income Security Act (ERISA) (29 USCS §§ 1001 et seq.) if the plan covered one or more employees other than the owner or the owner's spouse, where an ERISA provision (29 USCS § 1002(7)) defined a plan "participant" as any employee eligible to receive a benefit from an employee benefit plan (Raymond B. Yates, M.D., P.C. Profit Sharing Plan v Hendon (2004, US) 158 L Ed 2d 40, 124 S Ct 1330, infra § 26).

Two noteworthy cases decided by the Supreme Court during the court's 2003-2004 Term involved sentencing decisions made by judges. In one case, the court held that a state judge's imposition—on the basis of the judge's determination that an accused, who had pleaded guilty to kidnapping, had acted with deliberate cruelty—of a sentence exceeding the general state statutory maximum violated the accused's right, under the Federal Constitution's Sixth Amendment, to a jury trial, where the purported facts supporting the finding of deliberate cruelty had been neither admitted by the accused nor found by a jury (Blakely v Washington (2004, US) 159 L Ed 2d 403, 124 S Ct 2531, infra § 40). In the other case, the court concluded that a new rule that the court had announced in Ring v Arizona (2002) 536 US 584, 153 L Ed 2d 556, 122 S Ct 2428—requiring that aggravating factors necessary for imposition of the death penalty be found by a jury—was not retroactively applicable to cases that already were final on direct review (Schriro v Summerlin (2004, US) 159 L Ed 2d 442, 124 S Ct 2519, infra § 40).

During the 2003-2004 Term, the court issued decisions in three particularly well-publicized cases that involved purported "enemy combatants." In one case, the court—without reaching the merits of a petition for federal habeas corpus relief filed on the purported behalf of an American citizen who was being detained, as an asserted enemy combatant, in a United States Navy brig in South Carolina—held that the petition had improperly been filed in the United States District Court for the Southern District of New York and should have been filed in the United States District Court for the District of South Carolina (Rumsfeld v Padilla (2004, US) 159 L Ed 2d 513, 124 S Ct 2711, infra § 30). In another case, it was decided that the United States District Court for the District of Columbia had jurisdiction, under a federal habeas corpus provision (28 USCS § 2241(c)(3))—which authorized Federal District Courts to entertain federal habeas corpus applications by persons claiming to be held in custody "in violation of the Constitution or laws or treaties of the United States"—to review the legality of executive detention of some foreign nationals who were incarcerated at Guantanamo Bay Naval Base in Cuba after being captured during hostilities between the United States and the Taliban regime in Afghanistan (Rasul v Bush (2004, US) 159 L Ed 2d 548, 124 S Ct 2686, infra § 30). Finally, two different majorities of Justices concluded that (1) the Authorization for Use of Military Force resolution (115 Stat 224, note following 50 USCS § 1541)—in which Congress authorized the President of the United States to use all necessary and appropriate force against nations, organizations, or persons associated with the September 11, 2001 attacks—provided the executive branch with some authority to detain American citizens as "enemy combatants"; but (2) one such detainee had a right to a hearing with, at least, an opportunity to present evidence that he was not an enemy combatant (Hamdi v Rumsfeld (2004, US) 159 L Ed 2d 578, 124 S Ct 2633, infra § 30).

§ 3. Abduction from Mexico

The Supreme Court held that a Mexican individual who alleged that the United States Drug Enforcement Administration had instigated his abduction from Mexico for criminal trial in the United States (at which he had been acquitted) was not entitled to a remedy for the abduction under (1) the Federal Tort Claims Act (28 USCS §§ 1346(b)(1), 2671 et seq.), which removes the sovereign inmmunity of the United States from certain tort suits but, in 28 USCS § 2680(k), excepts from this removal any claim arising in a foreign country; or (2) the Alien Tort Statute (28 USCS § 1350), which grants Federal District Courts original jurisdiction of any civil action by an alien for a tort committed in violation of the "law of nations" or a treaty of the United States. [Sosa v Alvarez-Machain (2004, US) 159 L Ed 2d 718, 124 S Ct 2739.]

§ 4. Adult businesses

The court determined that a Colorado city's ordinance—that (1) required businesses such as adult bookstores to have "adult business" licenses, (2) listed specific circumstances under which the city would deny a license application, (3) imposed time limits within which city officials were to make a final licensing decision, and (4) provided that a final decision could be appealed to a state court—facially met the requirement, under the Federal Constitution's First Amendment, that such a licensing scheme assure prompt judicial review of administrative decision denying a license. [City of Littleton v Z. J. Gifts D-4, L.L.C. (2004, US) 159 L Ed 2d 84, 124 S Ct 2219.]

§ 5. Age discrimination

According to the Supreme Court, the Age Discrimination in Employment Act of 1967 (29 USCS §§ 621 et seq.), which protects from discrimination because of age employees who are at least 40 years old, does not prohibit discrimination against younger protected employees in favor of older protected employees. [Gen. Dynamics Land Sys. v Cline (2004, US) 157 L Ed 2d 1094, 124 S Ct 1236.]

§ 6. Airlines

The Supreme Court held that the refusal, by a flight attendant on an airplane flight from Europe to the United States, of a request by a passenger's wife to move the passenger, who had asthma, farther from the plane's smoking section constituted an "accident" within the meaning of the Warsaw Convention's Article 17 (49 Stat 3000 et seq.)—which provides that an air carrier may be liable for a passenger's death or bodily injury caused by an accident on an international flight—where the wife alleged that the passenger's death during the flight had resulted from a severe asthma attack caused by inhaling secondhand smoke. [Olympic Airways v Husain (2004, US) 157 L Ed 2d 1146, 124 S Ct 1221.]

§ 7. Attorneys' fees

The court held that a Bankruptcy Code provision (11 USCS § 330(a)(1)), in authorizing compensation awards from estate funds, did not authorize awards to debtors' attorneys, unless the attorneys were employed as authorized by another Bankruptcy Code provision (11 USCS § 327). [Lamie v United States Tr. (2004, US) 157 L Ed 2d 1024, 124 S Ct 1023.]

With respect to an Equal Access to Justice Act provision (28 USCS § 2412(d)(1)(A))—which, in authorizing the payment of attorneys' fees to a prevailing party in an action against the United States, allows the Federal Government to defeat this entitlement by showing that the government's position in the underlying litigation was substantially justified—the court held that a prevailing party's timely application for attorneys' fees properly could be amended, after the 30-day filing period, to cure an initial failure to allege that the government's position lacked substantial justification. [Scarborough v Principi (2004, US) 158 L Ed 2d 674, 124 S Ct 1856.]

§ 8. Bankruptcy

In a unanimous decision, it was held that a debtor had forfeited the right to rely on time constraints, under Bankruptcy Rules 4004 and 9006(b)(3), for a creditor's objecting to the debtor's discharge from bankruptcy under 11 USCS § 727(a), where the debtor had not raised this time issue before a federal bankruptcy court had reached merits of the creditor's objection. [Kontrick v Ryan (2004, US) 157 L Ed 2d 867, 124 S Ct 906.]

The Supreme Court decided that a Bankruptcy Code provision (11 USCS § 330(a)(1)), in authorizing compensation awards from estate funds, did not authorize awards to debtors' attorneys, unless the attorneys were employed as authorized by another Bankruptcy Code provision (11 USCS § 327). [Lamie v United States Tr. (2004, US) 157 L Ed 2d 1024, 124 S Ct 1023.]

According to the Supreme Court, a proceeding instituted by an individual, in federal bankruptcy court, to determine the dischargeability of her student-loan debt—of which a Tennessee governmental corporation was an assignee holder—pursuant to 11 USCS § 523(a)(8) was not a suit against the state within the meaning of the Federal Constitution's Eleventh Amendment, which generally prohibits private suits against states in federal court. [Tenn. Student Assistance Corp. v Hood (2004, US) 158 L Ed 2d 764, 124 S Ct 1905.]

Although unable to agree on an opinion, 5 of the 9 Supreme Court Justices agreed that a Federal Court of Appeals had erred in calculating, and ought to recalculate on remand, the interest rate to be paid in installment payments to a creditor, under a "cram down" bankruptcy provision (11 USCS § 1325(a)(5)(B)(ii))—which allows a federal bankruptcy court to approve certain debt-adjustment plans, despite a secured creditor's objections—where the Court of Appeals had concluded that the original 21-percent interest rate in a contract ought to serve as the "presumptive" cram-down rate. [Till v SCS Credit Corp. (2004, US) 158 L Ed 2d 787, 124 S Ct 1951.]

§ 9. Bribery

The Supreme Court determined that 18 USCS § 666(a)(2), which criminalized bribery of a state, local, or Indian tribal official of a government entity that receives in any 1-year period more than $10,000 in federal funds was a valid exercise of congressional authority under Article I of the Federal Constitution, notwithstanding that the statute did not require proof of a connection between the federal funds and the alleged bribe as an element of the crime. [Sabri v United States (2004, US) 158 L Ed 2d 891, 124 S Ct 1941.]

§ 10. Child Online Protection Act

It was held, in a 5-to-4 decision, that a Federal District Court had not abused its discretion in granting a preliminary injunction against enforcement of the Child Online Protection Act (47 USCS § 231)—which prohibited any person from knowingly, in interstate or foreign commerce by means of the World Wide Web, making any communication for commercial purposes that was available to any minor and that included any material that was harmful to minors—as there remained several disputes as to the effectiveness of less restrictive alternatives. [Ashcroft v ACLU (2004, US) 159 L Ed 2d 690, 124 S Ct 2783.]

§ 11. Disability discrimination

In an opinion expressing the view of all seven participating members of the court, it was held that a Federal Court of Appeals had improperly applied disparate-impact analysis to a disparate-treatment claim of disability discrimination brought under the Americans with Disabilities Act (42 USCS §§ 12101 et seq.) by a purportedly recovering drug addict who was seeking to be rehired by the employer that, in a prior year, had forced him to resign, in lieu of termination, after he had tested positive for cocaine use. [Raytheon Co. v Hernandez (2003) 540 US 44, 157 L Ed 2d 357, 124 S Ct 513.]

In a case involving two paraplegics—a criminal defendant and a certified court reporter—the Supreme Court held that Title II of the Americans with Disabilities Act (42 USCS §§ 12131 et seq.), as applied to cases implementing the right of access to courts, was a valid exercise of Congress' authority, under § 5 of the Federal Constitution's Fourteenth Amendment, to enforce the amendment's guarantees. [Tennessee v Lane (2004, US) 158 L Ed 2d 820, 124 S Ct 1978.]

§ 12. Double jeopardy

The court held that (1) Congress was authorized under the Federal Constitution to permit Indian tribes, as an exercise of their inherent authority, to prosecute nonmember Indians, as Congress had done by amending a provision of the Indian Civil Rights Act of 1968 (25 USCS § 1301(2)); and (2) therefore, federal prosecution of an Indian—who had struck a federal police officer on the reservation of an Indian tribe of which the Indian was not a member—for assaulting a federal officer after the Indian had pleaded guilty in a tribal court to a charge of violence to a policeman was not barred by the double jeopardy clause of the Federal Constitution's Fifth Amendment. [United States v Lara (2004, US) 158 L Ed 2d 420, 124 S Ct 1628.]

§ 13. Elections

In a case in which three opinions, supported by varying majorities of Justices, together constituted the opinion of the court, it was held that many parts of the Bipartisan Campaign Reform Act of 2002—including provisions regulating the use of "soft money" by parties, officeholders, and candidates (2 USCS § 441i)—were valid under the Federal Constitution's First Amendment. [McConnell v FEC (2003, US) 157 L Ed 2d 491, 124 S Ct 619.]

Although unable to agree on an opinion, five members of the Supreme Court agreed that some claims, by some registered Pennsylvania voters, that Pennsylvania's reapportionment plan for congressional election districts constituted a political gerrymander in violation of the Federal Constitution's Article I and the equal protection clause of the Constitution's Fourteenth Amendment, ought not to be adjudicated. [Vieth v Jubelirer (2004, US) 158 L Ed 2d 546, 124 S Ct 1769.]

§ 14. Environmental law

The court held that the Environmental Protection Agency (EPA) (1) generally had supervisory authority under the Clean Air Act (42 USCS §§ 7401 et seq.), subject to review by a federal court, to rule on reasonableness of best-available-control-technology (BACT) decisions by state permitting agencies concerning pollution-emitting facilities, and could issue a stop-construction order concerning such a facility under 42 USCS §§ 7413(a)(5) and 7477, if a BACT selection approved by a state agency was not reasonable; and (2) properly had issued orders stopping construction that had been permitted by the Alaska department of environmental conservation at such a facility. [Alaska Dep't of Envtl. Conservation v EPA (2004, US) 157 L Ed 2d 967, 124 S Ct 983.]

The Supreme Court determined that, for purposes of a Clean Water Act (CWA) provision (33 USCS § 1342) that required a permit for the discharge of pollutants into the nation's waters, such discharges included point sources that did not themselves generate pollutants, where (1) one CWA provision (33 USCS § 1362(12)) defined "discharge of a pollutant" to mean any addition of any pollutant to navigable waters from any point source; and (2) another CWA provision (33 USCS § 1362(14)) defined "point source" as any discernible, confined and discrete conveyance, such as a pipe, ditch, channel, or tunnel, from which pollutants were or might be discharged. [S. Fla. Water Mgmt. Dist. v Miccosukee Tribe of Indians (2004, US) 158 L Ed 2d 264, 124 S Ct 1537.]

Rules enacted by a California air-quality management district that was responsible for air pollution control in counties that included the Los Angeles metropolitan area—which rules imposed emission requirements on motor vehicles purchased or leased by public and private fleet operators—were held by the Supreme Court not to escape pre-emption under § 209(a) of Clean Air Act (42 USCS § 7543(a)), which generally prohibited states and their political subdivisions from adopting or attempting to enforce any standard relating to the control of emissions from new motor vehicles or new motor vehicle engines. [Engine Mfrs. Ass'n v S. Coast Air Quality Mgmt. Dist. (2004, US) 158 L Ed 2d 529, 124 S Ct 1756.]

The court unanimously held that the National Environmental Policy Act of 1969 (42 USCS §§ 4321 et seq.)—which generally required a federal agency to prepare an Environmental Impact Statement for a proposed "major Federal action"—and the Clean Air Act (CAA) (42 USCS §§ 7401 et seq.)—which, in 42 USCS § 7506(c)(1), included some safeguards intended to prevent the Federal Government from interfering with the states' abilities to comply with the CAA's requirements—did not require the Federal Motor Carrier Safety Administration to evaluate the environmental effects of some cross-border operations by Mexican-domiciled motor carriers. [DOT v Pub. Citizen (2004, US) 159 L Ed 2d 60, 124 S Ct 2204.]

The Supreme Court, in a unanimous opinion, held that a federal court's general authority, under an Administrative Procedure Act provision (5 USCS

§ 706(1)), to compel federal agency action that was unlawfully withheld or unreasonably delayed did not to extend to remedying some asserted failures by the United States Bureau of Land Management, in its stewardship of public lands in Utah, to take certain actions concerning the use of off-road vehicles. [Norton v S. Utah Wilderness Alliance (2004, US) 159 L Ed 2d 137, 124 S Ct 2373.]

§ 15. Evidence—admissibility

Although unable to agree on an opinion, five Justices agreed that an incriminating statement, made by an accused after she had received Miranda warnings, was inadmissible at the accused's murder trial in a Missouri state court, where, prior to receiving the warnings, the accused had confessed after being questioned by a police officer for 30 to 40 minutes. [Missouri v Seibert (2004, US) 159 L Ed 2d 643, 124 S Ct 2601.]

In another case that lacked a majority opinion, five members of the court agreed that police officers' failure to finish giving an accused Miranda warnings did not to require suppression, at the accused's federal trial for possession of a firearm by a convicted felon, of a pistol that one officer had found at the accused's home as result of the accused's voluntary statement, where, when the officer had attempted to give the Miranda warnings, the accused had interrupted and had asserted that he knew his rights. [United States v Patane (2004, US) 159 L Ed 2d 667, 124 S Ct 2620.]

In a case in which an accused, having been indicted for conspiracy to distribute methamphetamine, had made several inculpatory statements at his home concerning methamphetamine distribution before being taken to a county jail and then, for the first time being advised of his rights under Miranda and under another earlier Supreme Court case—in which case the court had determined that the Federal Constitution's Sixth Amendment does not bar postindictment questioning of an accused in the absence of counsel if the accused waives the right to counsel—the Supreme Court unanimously held that a Federal Court of Appeals, in inquiring solely whether the accused's inculpatory statements made at the jail after he had signed a Miranda waiver form had been knowing and voluntary, had wrongly used a Fifth Amendment standard in ruling that the statements made at the jail were not inadmissible as fruits of the statements that the accused had made at home, where the Court of Appeals had not reached the question whether the Sixth Amendment required suppression of the statements made at the jail. [Fellers v United States (2004, US) 157 L Ed 2d 1016, 124 S Ct 1019.]

The playing, at an accused's trial in a Washington state court for assault and attempted murder, of a tape-recorded statement in which the accused's wife—who, because of the state marital privilege that generally barred one spouse from testifying against the other without the other's consent, did not testify at trial—had described to police the accused's stabbing of the victim, was held to violate the accused's right under the Federal Constitution's Sixth Amendment to be confronted by the witnesses against him. [Crawford v Washington (2004, US) 158 L Ed 2d 177, 124 S Ct 1354.]

For cases involving the obtaining of evidence as a result of an allegedly illegal search or seizure, see §§ 36-38, infra.

§ 16. —Destruction

The court held that the due process clause of the Federal Constitution's Fourteenth Amendment did not require dismissal of a cocaine-possession charge against an accused who, after failing to appear for trial, had been a fugitive for over 10 years before being apprehended, where the police, acting according to established procedure two months before the accused was apprehended, had destroyed the substance seized from the accused during his original arrest. [Illinois v Fisher (2004, US) 157 L Ed 2d 1060, 124 S Ct 1200.]

§ 17. —Discovery

The Supreme Court determined that 28 USCS § 1782(a)—which authorized Federal District Courts to order some discovery for use in a proceeding in a foreign or international tribunal upon the application of any interested person—authorized, but did not require, a Federal District Court to order some discovery requested by a private complainant for use in an antitrust proceeding before the Commission of the European Communities. [Intel Corp. v Advanced Micro Devices, Inc. (2004, US) 159 L Ed 2d 355, 124 S Ct 2466.]

A Federal Court of Appeals was held to have prematurely terminated a mandamus inquiry without reaching separation-of-powers objections raised, by federal-official defendants including the Vice President of the United States, to a Federal District Court's civil discovery orders in a dispute involving the National Energy Policy Development Group, which had been established to advise and make policy recommendations to the President of the United States. [Cheney v United States Dist. Court (2004, US) 159 L Ed 2d 459, 124 S Ct 2576.]

§ 18. Federal court jurisdiction—District Court

In a 5-to-4 decision, the Supreme Court held that party's change in citizenship after the party—alleging that a Federal District Court had diversity-of-citizenship jurisdiction pursuant to 28 USCS § 1332(a)—had filed a state-law diversity action in the District Court was unable to cure the lack of subject-matter jurisdiction that had existed at the time of filing. [Grupo Dataflux v Atlas Global Group, L.P. (2004, US) 158 L Ed 2d 866, 124 S Ct 1920.]

§ 19. —Supreme Court

The Supreme Court unanimously held that a case lacked the final state-court judgment required by 28 USCS § 1257 for Supreme Court jurisdiction, where an intermediate state court, in reversing a murder conviction, had not determined whether the accused's evidentiary and prosecutorial-misconduct claims would have independently supported reversal. [Johnson v California (2004, US) 158 L Ed 2d 696, 124 S Ct 1833.]

§ 20. Foreign sovereign immunity

The court determined that the Foreign Sovereign Immunities Act of 1976 (28 USCS §§ 1330, 1602 et seq.)—including 28 USCS § 1605(a)(3), providing that foreign states are not immune from jurisdiction in the United States in cases of illegal expropriation—is applicable to pre-1976 conduct. [Republic of Aus. v Altmann (2004, US) 159 L Ed 2d 1, 124 S Ct 2240.]

§ 21. Guilty plea

According to the Supreme Court, a federal criminal defendant—who had entered into a plea agreement (including terms that (1) he would plead guilty to a drug charge, and (2) the government would make a nonbinding sentence recommendation) was entitled to plain-error relief from the guilty plea, on an unpreserved claim that the Federal District Court in which the defendant had entered the plea had failed to give him the warning, then required under Federal Crimi-

nal Procedure Rule 11(e)(2) (later under Rule
11(c)(3)(B))—that he could not withdraw his plea if
the District Court did not accept the government's
recommendation—only if he could show reasonable
probability that, but for the lack of warning, he would
not have entered the plea. [United States v Dominguez
Benitez (2004, US) 159 L Ed 2d 157, 124 S Ct 2333.]

§ 22. Habeas corpus—generally

It was held that a Federal District Court intending to
recharacterize a pro se litigant's motion as a first
motion for postconviction relief under 28 USCS § 2255
was required to (1) notify the litigant that the District
Court intended to recharacterize the pleading, (2)
warn the litigant that this recharacterization meant that
that any subsequent motion under § 2255 would be
subject to § 2255's restrictions on "second or successive" motions, and (3) provide the litigant an opportunity to withdraw the motion or to amend it so that it
contained all the § 2255 claims that the litigant believed
the litigant had. [Castro v United States (2003, US) 157
L Ed 2d 778, 124 S Ct 786.]

The Supreme Court decided that for purposes of the
requirement, under 28 USCS § 2254(b)(1), that a state
prisoner must exhaust available state remedies before
seeking federal habeas corpus relief, ordinarily, the
prisoner has not fairly presented a federal-law claim to
a state court if the state court had to read beyond
uninformative petition, brief, or similar document to
be alerted to the federal-law claim. [Baldwin v Reese
(2004, US) 158 L Ed 2d 64, 124 S Ct 1347.]

The Supreme Court decided two cases involving both
California state courts and 28 USCS § 2254(d)(1),
which generally authorized a federal court to grant
habeas corpus relief to a state prisoner on a federal
constitutional claim, if a state court's prior adjudication

of the claim had been contrary to, or had involved an unreasonable application of, clearly established federal law, as determined by the United States Supreme Court. In one case, a unanimous decision, it was held that a California appellate court had not unreasonably applied federal law, for purposes of § 2254(d)(1), in concluding that a jury in a murder case had not likely been misled about the state's "imperfect self-defense" doctrine [Middleton v McNeil (2004, US) 158 L Ed 2d 701, 124 S Ct 1830.] In the other case, a 5-to-4 decision, it was held that a California state court had reasonably applied federal law in holding that a 17-year-old suspect concerning a shooting and attempted robbery had not been in custody during a 2-hour interrogation at a county sheriff's station outside the presence of the suspect's parents, where (1) the suspect had not been given Miranda warnings; and (2) the questioning focused not on the suspect's alleged crimes, but rather on those of another person who allegedly had done the shooting. [Yarborough v Alvarado (2004, US) 158 L Ed 2d 938, 124 S Ct 2140.]

The Supreme Court held that a Federal District Court's failure to give a California state prisoner two particular warnings concerning the District Court's procedures had not made improper a Federal District Court's dismissals of two "mixed" habeas corpus petitions—containing both unexhausted and exhausted claims—that the prisoner had filed pro se. [Pliler v Ford (2004, US) 159 L Ed 2d 338, 124 S Ct 2441.]

For cases involving applications for habeas corpus relief for purported "enemy combatants," see § 30, infra.

§ 23. —Death sentence

The Supreme Court decided unanimously that (1) a death sentence imposed by an Ohio state court for aggravated murder, where the indictment had not charged the accused as a "principal offender"—as required, by an Ohio statute, for imposition of the death penalty for aggravated murder—was not contrary to, and did not involve unreasonable application of, established federal law, as determined by the United States Supreme Court; and (2) therefore, the accused was not entitled to habeas corpus relief under 28 USCS § 2254(d)(1). [Mitchell v Esparza (2003) 540 US 12, 157 L Ed 2d 263, 124 S Ct 7.]

A Texas prisoner was determined by the Supreme Court to be entitled to federal habeas corpus relief from his state death sentence, on the basis of the prisoner's allegation that the prosecution had violated the due process clause of the Federal Constitution's Fourteenth Amendment by concealing from the prisoner impeachment evidence that a key prosecution witness had been a paid police informant [Banks v Dretke (2004, US) 157 L Ed 2d 1166, 124 S Ct 1256.]. In another Texas case, a state prisoner seeking federal habeas corpus relief from his death sentence was held to be held entitled to a certificate of appealability under 28 USCS § 2253(c)(2), as reasonable jurists would have found the state-court disposition of the prisoner's low-IQ mitigation claim debatable or wrong, where the trial had not instructed the jury to consider the prisoner's asserted IQ of 67. [Tennard v Dretke (2004, US) 159 L Ed 2d 384, 124 S Ct 2562.]

The Supreme Court held that the rule that it had announced in Mills v Maryland (1988) 486 US 367, 100 L Ed 2d 384, 108 S Ct 1860—that the Federal Constitution's Eighth Amendment forbids states from imposing a requirement that a jury find a potential mitigating factor unanimously before that factor may be considered in a capital sentencing decision—was a new constitutional rule that could not be applied retroactively on federal habeas corpus review. [Beard v Banks (2004, US) 159 L Ed 2d 494, 124 S Ct 2504.]

§ 24. —Ineffective assistance of counsel

The Supreme Court held unanimously that a state prisoner was not entitled to federal habeas corpus relief, as it was reasonable to conclude that defense counsel's trial summation had not been so flawed as to deprive the prisoner of the right to effective counsel under Federal Constitution's Sixth Amendment, where even if some arguments omitted from the summation unquestionably would have supported the defense, the omitted issues were not so clearly more persuasive than those that counsel discussed that their omission could be attributed to only a professional error of constitutional magnitude. [Yarborough v Gentry (2003) 540 US 1, 157 L Ed 2d 1, 124 S Ct 1.]

In a case in which the court, with respect to a state prisoner's application for federal habeas corpus relief, declined to decide whether, for the purpose of excusing state-court procedural default, the "actual innocence" exception, to federal courts' general practice of not entertaining procedurally defaulted claims in habeas corpus petitions, was applicable to noncapital sentencing, the court remanded the case for consideration of an ineffective-assistance-of-counsel claim, which a state official had conceded was "significant." [Dretke v Haley (2004, US) 158 L Ed 2d 659, 124 S Ct 1847.]

According to the Supreme Court, a Federal Court of Appeals, in reviewing a request for habeas corpus relief under 28 USCS § 2254(d), had in erred in finding a state-court decision rejecting the accused's ineffective-assistance-of-counsel claim to be an unreasonable application of clearly established federal law, where the accused alleged that his trial counsel had failed to conduct an adequate investigation. [Holland v Jackson (2004, US) 159 L Ed 2d 683, 124 S Ct 2736.]

§ 25. Medicaid benefits

The Federal Constitution's Eleventh Amendment—which generally provides states with sovereign immunity from suit by private parties in state court—was held not to bar enforcement of federal consent decree entered into by Texas officials who were defending a suit, brought by private parties, asserting that the Texas Medicaid program had failed to provide children with the health-care benefits allegedly required under 42 USCS §§ 1396a(a)(43) and 1396d(r). [Frew v Hawkins (2004, US) 157 L Ed 2d 855, 124 S Ct 899.]

§ 26. Pensions and retirement funds

The Supreme Court held that a business owner who worked in the business qualified as a participant in the business' pension plan covered by the Employee Retirement Income Security Act (ERISA) (29 USCS §§ 1001 et seq.) if the plan covered one or more employees other than the owner or the owner's spouse, where an ERISA provision (29 USCS § 1002(7)) defined a plan "participant" as any employee eligible to receive a benefit from an employee benefit plan. [Raymond B. Yates, M.D., P.C. Profit Sharing Plan v Hendon (2004, US) 158 L Ed 2d 40, 124 S Ct 1330.]

It was held, in a unanimous opinion, that the "anti-cutback" provision of the Employee Retirement Income Security Act (ERISA) (29 USCS § 1054(g)), which prohibited any pension-plan amendment that would reduce a participant's "accrued benefit," prohibited an amendment that expanded the types of postretirement employment that would trigger suspension of a participant's early-retirement benefits already accrued. [Cent. Laborers' Pension Fund v Heinz (2004, US) 159 L Ed 2d 46, 124 S Ct 2230.]

In another unanimous opinion, the court held that some state-court actions alleging that the failure of a health maintenance organization (HMO) to cover certain medical services violated a state statute (1) were pre-empted by § 502(a)(1)(B) of the Employee Retirement Income Security Act (ERISA) (29 USCS § 1132(a)(1)(B)), which authorized certain actions by allegedly wronged beneficiaries of employee welfare benefit plans; and (2) thus were removable from state court to a Federal District Court. [Aetna Health Inc. v Davila (2004, US) 159 L Ed 2d 312, 124 S Ct 2488.]

§ 27. Postal Service

The court held, in a unanimous opinion, that the United States Postal Service was not a "person" subject to antitrust liability under the Sherman Act (15 USCS §§ 1 et seq.). [United States Postal Serv v Flamingo Indus. (USA) Ltd. (2004, US) 158 L Ed 2d 19, 124 S Ct 1321.]

§ 28. Price fixing

Alleged price-fixing activity was held to excluded from the reach of Sherman Act (15 USCS §§ 1 et seq.) by the Foreign Trade Antitrust Improvements Act of 1982 (15 USCS § 6a)—which excluded from the reach of the Sherman Act much anticompetitive conduct that caused only foreign injury—where the plaintiff's claim under the Sherman Act rested solely on independent foreign harm. [F. Hoffmann-La Roche Ltd. v Empagran S.A. (2004, US) 159 L Ed 2d 226, 124 S Ct 2359.]

§ 29. Prisoners—generally

The court issued two unanimous opinions involving a civil rights action filed by a state prisoner under 42 USCS § 1983. In one case, the court held—with respect to the court's determination in an earlier case that, where success in a state prisoner's § 1983 damages action would implicitly question the validity of the prisoner's conviction or the duration of the prisoner's sentence, the prisoner first had to achieve favorable termination of the prisoner's available state opportunities or federal habeas corpus opportunities—that the favorable-termination requirement did not apply to a Michigan prisoner's challenge that had been found to threaten no consequence to his conviction or the duration of his sentence [Muhammad v Close (2004, US) 158 L Ed 2d 32, 124 S Ct 1303.]. In the other case, the court decided that an action under § 1983 was an appropriate vehicle for a condemned Alabama prisoner's action, pursuant to the cruel-and-unusual-punishment prohibition of the Federal Constitution's Eighth Amendment, seeking (1) a temporary stay of execution; and (2) a permanent injunction against the "cut down" procedure that the state intended to use to access the prisoners veins for lethal injection. [Nelson v Campbell (2004, US) 158 L Ed 2d 924, 124 S Ct 2117.]

§ 30. —Enemy combatants

Without reaching the merits of a petition for federal habeas corpus relief filed on the purported behalf of an American citizen who was being detained, as an asserted "enemy combatant," in a United States Navy brig in South Carolina, the Supreme Court, in a 5-to-4 decision, held that the petition had improperly been filed in the United States District Court for the Southern District of New York and should have been filed in the United States District Court for the District of South Carolina. [Rumsfeld v Padilla (2004, US) 159 L Ed 2d 513, 124 S Ct 2711.]

The United States District Court for the District of Columbia was held to have jurisdiction, under a federal habeas corpus provision (28 USCS § 2241(c)(3))—which authorized Federal District Courts to entertain federal habeas corpus applications by persons claiming to be held in custody "in violation of the Constitution or laws or treaties of the United States"—to review the legality of executive detention of some foreign nationals who were incarcerated at Guantanamo Bay Naval Base in Cuba after being captured during hostilities between the United States and the Taliban regime in Afghanistan. [Rasul v Bush (2004, US) 159 L Ed 2d 548, 124 S Ct 2686.]

It was held, by two different majorities of Justices, that (1) the Authorization for Use of Military Force resolution (115 Stat 224, note following 50 USCS § 1541)—in which Congress authorized the President of the United States to use all necessary and appropriate force against nations, organizations, or persons associated with the September 11, 2001 attacks—provided the executive branch with some authority to detain American citizens as "enemy combatants"; but (2) one such detainee had a right to a hearing with, at least, an opportunity to present evidence that he was not an enemy combatant. [Hamdi v Rumsfeld (2004, US) 159 L Ed 2d 578, 124 S Ct 2633.]

§ 31. Privacy

A plaintiff, in seeking to recover from the United States under a Privacy Act provision (5 USCS § 552a(g)(4)(A))—which provided for a minimum award of $1,000 for various types of privacy violations by federal agencies—was held to be required to prove some "actual damages" in order to qualify for the minimum award. [Doe v Chao (2004, US) 157 L Ed 2d 1122, 124 S Ct 1204.]

The court unanimously held that four official-investigation photographs showing the death scene of a person who had been deputy counsel to the then President of the United States were exempted from public disclosure by a Freedom of Information Act provision (5 USCS § 552(b)(7)(C)) that exempted law-enforcement records if their production could reasonably be expected to constitute an unwarranted invasion of personal privacy. [Nat'l Archives & Records Admin. v Favish (2004, US) 158 L Ed 2d 319, 124 S Ct 1570.]

§ 32. Public land grants

Although unable to agree on an opinion, six members of the Supreme Court agreed that sand and gravel were not "valuable minerals" for purposes of the Pittman Act (43 USCS §§ 351 et seq., later repealed), which required some land patents granted by the United States to private entities to reserve to the United States all coal and other valuable minerals in the land in question. [BedRoc Ltd., LLC v United States (2004, US) 158 L Ed 2d 338, 124 S Ct 1587.]

§ 33. Race discrimination

The court, in a unanimous opinion, held that a class action filed by some former employees who—alleging a racially hostile work environment, wrongful termination, and failure to transfer in connection with a plant closing—asserted violations of their rights to make and enforce contracts under 42 USCS § 1981, as amended by the Civil Rights Act of 1991 (PL 102-166), was governed by 28 USCS § 1658(a)'s catchall 4-year statute of limitations for actions arising under federal statutes enacted after December 1, 1990, that did not include a limitations provision. [Jones v R. R. Donnelley & Sons Co. (2004, US) 158 L Ed 2d 645, 124 S Ct 1836.]

§ 34. Religion in schools

The court determined that a postsecondary-education scholarship program established by the state of Washington, under which program students were not permitted to use a scholarship to pursue "a degree in theology," did not violate the free exercise of religion clause of the Federal Constitution's First Amendment. [Locke v Davey (2004, US) 158 L Ed 2d 1, 124 S Ct 1307.]

For a case in which a public elementary school student's father who sought to challenge, on the basis of the Federal Constitution's First Amendment, Congress' addition, in 1954, of the words "under God" to the Pledge of Allegiance was held to lack standing to bring suit against the school district in federal court, see § 43, infra.

§ 35. Right to counsel

According to a unanimous opinion of the Supreme Court, a trial court is not required by the Federal Constitution's Sixth Amendment to warn an accused that waiving the accused's right to counsel at a plea hearing (1) entails a risk that viable a defense will be overlooked, and (2) deprives the accused of an independent opinion as to whether to plead guilty. [Iowa v Tovar (2004, US) 158 L Ed 2d 209, 124 S Ct 1379.]

§ 36. Search and seizure—generally

The court decided, in a 5-to-4 decision, that the conviction of an assault suspect, under Nevada law, for refusing to disclose his name to a deputy sheriff during a valid investigative stop did not violate (1) the prohibition, under the Federal Constitution's Constitution's Fourth Amendment, against unreasonable searches and seizures; or (2) the Fifth Amendment's privilege against compelled self-incrimination. [Hiibel v Sixth Judicial Dist. Court (2004, US) 159 L Ed 2d 292, 124 S Ct 2451.]

§ 37. —Automobiles

In the unanimous view of the court, a warrantless arrest of an automobile passenger by a county police officer in Maryland during a stop for speeding did not contravene the Federal Constitution's Fourth Amendment, where the officer, having seized $763 from the automobile's glove compartment and cocaine from behind the back-seat armrest, arrested all three occupants after each had denied ownership of the cash and the cocaine. [Maryland v Pringle (2003, US) 157 L Ed 2d 769, 124 S Ct 795.]

The court held that police stops of motorists, by local police officers at an Illinois highway checkpoint that had been set up at the location of a recent hit-and-run accident, to ask for information about the accident did not violate the prohibition, under the Federal Constitution's Fourth Amendment, against unreasonable seizures. [Illinois v Lidster (2004, US) 157 L Ed 2d 843, 124 S Ct 885.]

The Supreme Court, in a unanimous opinion, held that, in view of the Federal Government's "paramount" interest in protecting the nation's borders, the Federal Government's authority, under the Federal Constitution's Fourth Amendment, to conduct suspicionless inspections at the international border included the authority to remove, disassemble, and reassemble a motor vehicle's fuel tank. [United States v Flores-Montano (2004, US) 158 L Ed 2d 311, 124 S Ct 1582.]

A police officer who had made a lawful custodial arrest of an automobile occupant was held by the Supreme Court to be allowed, under the Federal Constitution's Fourth Amendment, to contemporaneously search the automobile's passenger compartment even when officer first had made contact with the arrestee after the arrestee had left the automobile. [Thornton v United States (2004, US) 158 L Ed 2d 905, 124 S Ct 2127.]

§ 44. —Homes

According to the court, federal and local law-enforcement officers' 15-to-20 second wait, after calling out "police search warrant" and knocking on an apartment door, before breaking open the door satisfied (1) the Federal Constitution's Fourth Amendment; and (2) 18 USCS § 3109, which authorized a federal law-enforcement officer to break open any outer or inner door or window of a house, or any part of a house, or anything therein, to execute a search warrant, if, after notice of the officer's authority and purpose, the officer was refused admittance. [United States v Banks (2003) 540 US 31, 157 L Ed 2d 343, 124 S Ct 521.]

In a 5-to-4 decision, the Supreme Court held that (1) a warrant to search a home that failed to describe the persons or things to be seized was invalid; (2) the search performed pursuant to the warrant was unreasonable, in violation of the Federal Constitution's Fourth Amendment; and (3) the federal agent who had led the search was not entitled to qualified immunity from suit with respect to the violation. [Groh v Ramirez (2004, US) 157 L Ed 2d 1068, 124 S Ct 1284.]

§ 39. Securities regulation

The court unanimously held that, for purposes of some federal securities provisions (15 USCS

§§ 77b(a)(1), 78c(a)(10)), an investment scheme was not excludible from the term "investment contract"—a scheme that involved an investment of money in a common enterprise with profits to come solely from the efforts of others§ simply because the scheme promised a fixed rather than a variable return. [SEC v Edwards (2004, US) 157 L Ed 2d 813, 124 S Ct 892.]

§ 40. Sentencing by judge

It was held, in a 5-to-4 decision, that a state judge's imposition—on the basis of the judge's determination that an accused, who had pleaded guilty to kidnapping, had acted with deliberate cruelty—of a sentence exceeding the general state statutory maximum violated the accused's right, under the Federal Constitution's Sixth Amendment, to a jury trial, where the purported facts supporting the finding of deliberate cruelty had been neither admitted by the accused nor found by a jury. [Blakely v Washington (2004, US) 159 L Ed 2d 403, 124 S Ct 2531.]

In another 5-to-4 decision, the court held that a new rule that the court had announced in Ring v Arizona (2002) 536 US 584, 153 L Ed 2d 556, 122 S Ct 2428—requiring that aggravating factors necessary for imposition of the death penalty be found by a jury—was not retroactively applicable to cases that already were final on direct review. [Schriro v Summerlin (2004, US) 159 L Ed 2d 442, 124 S Ct 2519.]

§ 41. Sex discrimination

The Supreme Court decided that in suits under Title VII of the Civil Rights Act of 1964 (42 USCS §§ 2000e et seq.) alleging constructive discharge resulting from sexual harassment by a supervisor, the affirmative defense that the plaintiff had failed to make use of the employer's remedial policy was (1) available to the employer only where a supervisor's official act—or, in other words, a tangible employment action—did not underlie the alleged constructive discharge; and (2) not available if the plaintiff had quit in reasonable response to an employer-sanctioned adverse action that had officially changed the plaintiff's employment status or situation. [Pa. State Police v Suders (2004, US) 159 L Ed 2d 204, 124 S Ct 2342.]

§ 42. Social Security benefits

According to a unanimous opinion of the court, the Social Security Administration was allowed to determine that a claimant was not disabled, for purposes of 42 USCS § 423(d)(1)(A)—which described how to make a disability determination concerning an individual claiming disability insurance benefits under the Social Security Act's Title II (42 USCS §§ 401 et seq.)—where the claimant could do his or her previous work, regardless of whether such work existed in the national economy. [Barnhart v Thomas (2003) 540 US 20, 157 L Ed 2d 333, 124 S Ct 376.]

§ 43. Standing to bring suit

The court held that a public elementary school student's father—who sought to challenge Congress' addition, in 1954, of the words "under God" to the Pledge of Allegiance (codified at 4 USCS § 4) as violating the religion clauses of the Federal Constitution's First Amendment—lacked prudential standing to bring suit against the school district in federal court, where the student's mother asserted that, according to a California state court's custody order, the mother had the right to make final decisions about the student's education if the mother and father could not agree. [Elk Grove Unified Sch. Dist. v Newdow (2004, US) 159 L Ed 2d 98, 124 S Ct 2301.]

§ 44. State borders

The Supreme Court held that Maryland, whose boundary along the Potomac River extended to the low-water mark on the Virginia shore, lacked authority to require Virginia, Virginia's governmental subdivisions, or Virginia's citizens to obtain a permit to (1) construct improvements appurtenant to the Virginia shore, or (2) draw water from the river. [Virginia v Maryland (2003) 540 US 56, 157 L Ed 2d 461, 124 S Ct 598.]

§ 45. Taxes—federal

The Supreme Court unanimously held that under § 6501(a) of the Internal Revenue Code (26 USCS § 6501(a))—which generally provided that the amount of any tax imposed by the Code was to be assessed within 3 years after the tax return was filed—the United States was authorized to collect a partnership's unpaid federal employment taxes, from some individuals who had been general partners in the partnership, in these individuals' bankruptcy proceedings, where those taxes had been timely assessed against the partnership. [United States v Galletti (2004, US) 158 L Ed 2d 279, 124 S Ct 1548.]

§ 46. —State

In a 5-to-4 decision, the court held that the Tax Injunction Act (28 USCS § 1341)—which prohibited federal courts from restraining "the assessment, levy or collection" of any tax under state law where a "plain, speedy and efficient remedy" could be had in state court—did not bar a federal-court seeking to enjoin operation of an Arizona statute that authorized state income tax credits for payments funding scholarships to private schools, where the statute did not prohibit such scholarships from covering tuition at schools that provided religious instructions or that gave religion-based admission preference. [Hibbs v Winn (2004, US) 159 L Ed 2d 172, 124 S Ct 2276.]

For cases involving religion in schools generally, see § 34, supra.

§ 47. Telecommunications

It was held that a complaint—alleging, as to local telephone service, that the incumbent local exchange carrier had breached its duty, under the Telecommunications Act of 1996, to share the incumbent's network with competitors—did not state a valid antitrust claim under 15 USCS § 2, which prohibited monopolizing or attempting to monopolize. [Verizon Communs., Inc. v Law Offices of Curtis V. Trinko (2004, US) 157 L Ed 2d 823, 124 S Ct 872.]

The Supreme Court decided that the authorization, in 47 USCS § 253, of federal pre-emption of state and local laws that prohibited the ability of "any entity" to provide telecommunications services did not include entities that were state subdivisions. [Nixon v Mo. Mun. League (2004, US) 158 L Ed 2d 291, 124 S Ct 1555.]

§ 48. Truth in Lending Act

The court unanimously held that the Federal Reserve Board's Regulation Z—in specifically excluding (in 12 CFR § 226.4(c)(2)) fees imposed for exceeding a credit limit from the definition of the disclosure term "finance charge"—provided a binding interpretation of the Truth in Lending Act (15 USCS §§ 1601 et seq.), which regulated creditors' disclosures to debtors concerning finance charges. [Household Credit Servs. v Pfennig (2004, US) 158 L Ed 2d 450, 124 S Ct 1741.]

SUMMARIES OF DECISIONS

MICHAEL YARBOROUGH, WARDEN, et al., Petitioners

v

LIONEL E. GENTRY

540 US 1, 157 L Ed 2d 1, 124 S Ct 1

[No. 02-1597]

Decided October 20, 2003.

Decision: State prisoner held not entitled to federal habeas corpus relief, as it was reasonable to conclude that defense counsel's trial summation had not been so flawed as to deprive prisoner of right to effective counsel under Federal Constitution's Sixth Amendment.

SUMMARY

A defendant was tried in a California trial court on a charge of assault with a deadly weapon. The theme of the defense counsel's closing summation was that the jury, like the prosecutor and defense counsel himself, had not been at the scene of the crime and so could only speculate about what had happened and who was lying. In the summation, counsel (1) did not highlight various potentially exculpatory pieces of evidence; (2) argued that the jury had to acquit if the defendant was telling the truth, even though the defendant was a "bad person, lousy drug addict, stinking thief, jail bird"; (3) did not make an express demand for acquittal, but

1

rather requested only that the jury reach some verdict; and (4) did not argue explicitly that the government had failed to prove the defendant's guilt beyond a reasonable doubt. After his conviction, the prisoner alleged that the summation had been so flawed as to deprive the prisoner of the right to effective assistance of counsel under the Federal Constitution's Sixth Amendment.

The Court of Appeal of California affirmed the prisoner's conviction and sentence, and the Supreme Court of California denied review. The prisoner's petition for federal habeas corpus relief under 28 USCS § 2254(d)(1) was denied by the United States District Court for the Central District of California. However, the United States Court of Appeals for the Ninth Circuit, in reversing and ordering a remand, concluded that (1) there was a reasonable probability that the result of the trial would have been different in the absence of defense counsel's assertedly deficient performance during closing argument, and (2) the California Court of Appeal's decision to the contrary was an objectively unreasonable application of federal law (320 F3d 891).

Granting certiorari and granting leave to proceed in forma pauperis, the United States Supreme Court reversed. In a per curiam opinion expressing the unanimous view of the court, it was held that:

(1) Even if some of the omitted arguments would unquestionably have supported the defense, it did not follow that counsel was incompetent for failing to include such arguments, for the issues that counsel omitted were not so clearly more persuasive than those that counsel discussed that their omission could be attributed only to a professional error of constitutional magnitude.

(2) Notwithstanding these omissions and the other

alleged flaws in counsel's presentation, the California Court of Appeal's conclusion that counsel's performance was not ineffective (a) was supported by the record, and (b) was not an objectively unreasonable application of governing federal law.

BETTY MITCHELL, WARDEN, Petitioner

v

GREGORY ESPARZA

540 US 12, 157 L Ed 2d 263, 124 S Ct 7, reh den
(US) 157 L Ed 2d 956, 124 S Ct 1124

[No. 02-1369]

Decided November 3, 2003.

Decision: Death sentence for aggravated murder on
charge not literally complying with Ohio's requirements for indictment held not contrary to, or to
involve unreasonable application of, established
federal law, as required for habeas corpus relief
under 28 USCS § 2254(d)(1).

SUMMARY

A federal statute (28 USCS § 2254) describing the
circumstances under which a state prisoner may be
entitled to federal habeas corpus relief provides, in 28
USCS § 2254(d)(1), that a federal court may grant such
relief for a claim that was adjudicated on the merits in
state court if that adjudication resulted in a decision
that was contrary to, or involved an unreasonable
application of, clearly established federal law, as determined by the United States Supreme Court.

A state prisoner whose conviction—of aggravated
murder during the commission of an aggravated
robbery—and death sentence by a state trial court in
Ohio had been upheld by the Ohio Supreme Court (39
Ohio St 3d 8, 529 NE2d 192), argued on state postconviction review that the prisoner's death sentence was
invalid because the indictment that had charged the

prisoner with aggravated murder had not charged him as a "principal offender," as required, by an Ohio statute, for imposition of the death penalty for aggravated murder. After the Ohio Court of Appeals' rejection of the claim for postconviction relief—on the basis that literal compliance with the principal-offender requirement was not necessary where, as in the case at hand, only one defendant was named in the indictment in question—was upheld by the Ohio Supreme Court (65 Ohio St 3d 1453, 602 NE2d 650), the Ohio Supreme Court, referring to its previous decision in the case at hand, denied the prisoner's petition for state postconviction relief on other grounds (70 Ohio St 3d 1473, 640 NE2d 845).

Having exhausted his avenues for relief under state law, the prisoner sought habeas corpus relief in the United States District Court for the Northern District of Ohio. Concluding that the Ohio Court of Appeals had unreasonably applied clearly established federal law, as determined by the United States Supreme Court, the District Court issued a writ of habeas corpus as to the death sentence. The United States Court of Appeals for the Sixth Circuit (1) held that the Federal Constitution's Eighth Amendment, which prohibits cruel and unusual punishment, precluded the prisoner's death sentence, and that harmless-error review was inappropriate; and (2) affirmed the Federal Court of Appeals' judgment (310 F3d 414).

Granting certiorari and granting leave to proceed in forma pauperis, the United States Supreme Court reversed and remanded. In a per curiam opinion expressing the unanimous view of the court, it was held that the Ohio Court of Appeals' decision could not be set aside on federal habeas corpus review under § 2254(d)(1), for:

(1) The decision was not contrary to clearly established

federal law, as the Supreme Court's precedents did not support the Federal Court of Appeals' conclusion that the state's failure to charge in the indictment that the prisoner was a "principal" was the functional equivalent of dispensing with the reasonable doubt requirement.

(3) The Ohio Court of Appeals' conclusion that the prisoner had been convicted of a capital offense was not an objectively unreasonable application of clearly established federal law.

JO ANNE B. BARNHART, COMMISSIONER OF SO-
CIAL SECURITY, Petitioner

v

PAULINE THOMAS

540 US 20, 157 L Ed 2d 333, 124 S Ct 376

[No. 02-763]

Argued October 14, 2003.
Decided November 12, 2003.

Decision: Social Security Administration held allowed
to determine that claimant is not disabled, for
purposes of 42 USCS § 423(d)(1)(A), where claimant can do his or her previous work, regardless of
whether such work exists in national economy.

SUMMARY

Under a provision of the Social Security Act (42
USCS § 423(d)(1)(A)), an individual claiming disability insurance benefits under Title II of the Act (42
USCS §§ 401 et seq.) or Supplemental Security Income
under Title XVI of the Act (42 USCS §§ 1381 et seq.)
could be determined to be under a disability only if the
individual's physical or mental impairment or impairments were of such severity that the individual was not
only unable to do his or her previous work, but also
could not—considering the individual's age, education,
and work experience—engage in any other kind of
substantial gainful work existing in the national
economy.

The Social Security Administration (SSA) promulgated parallel regulations establishing a five-step se-
quential process to evaluate claims for disability insur-

7

ance benefits (20 CFR § 404.1520) and for Supplemental Security Income (20 CFR § 416.920). Under this process, the fourth step required the SSA to assess whether the claimant could do his or her previous work. If a claim survived the fourth step, then the fifth step required the SSA to consider various so-called vocational factors and to determine whether the claimant was capable of performing other jobs existing in significant numbers in the national economy.

A former elevator operator, allegedly suffering from heart disease and other medical problems, claimed eligibility for disability insurance benefits and Supplemental Security Income. The Commissioner of Social Security denied the claimant's application. After a hearing, an Administrative Law Judge (ALJ) concluded that the claimant was not under a disability, as her impairments did not prevent her from performing her past work as an elevator operator. The SSA's Appeals Council denied the claimant's request for review.

The United States District Court for the District of New Jersey, in affirming the ALJ's ruling, rejected the claimant's argument that she was unable to do her previous work due to the fact that such work no longer existed in significant numbers in the national economy. However, the United States Court of Appeals for the Third Circuit reversed and ordered a remand, on the ground that § 423(d)(1)(A) was to be read as providing that the ability to perform prior work disqualified a claimant from benefits only if such work was substantial gainful work which existed in the national economy (294 F3d 568).

On certiorari, the United States Supreme Court reversed. In an opinion by SCALIA, J., expressing the unanimous view of the court, it was held that the SSA may properly determine that a disability claimant is not disabled, for purposes of § 423(d)(1)(A), where the

8

claimant remains physically and mentally able to do his or her previous work, regardless of whether that previous work exists in significant numbers in the national economy, for:

(1) A reading of § 423(d)(1)(A) under which "previous work" is a species of "work which exists in the national economy" is contrary to the grammatical rule of the last antecedent, according to which a limiting clause or phrase (here, the relative clause "which exists in the national economy") should ordinarily be read as modifying only the noun or phrase that it immediately follows (here, "any other kind of substantial gainful work").

(2) In enacting § 423(d)(1)(A), Congress could have determined that an analysis of a claimant's physical and mental capacity to do the claimant's previous work would—in the vast majority of cases—serve as an effective and efficient administrative proxy for the claimant's ability to do some work that does exist in the national economy.

(3) Although the SSA's interpretation of § 423(d)(1)(A)—as well as the other reading—could give rise to undesirable results in some instances, the SSA's interpretation was at least a reasonable construction of the text and therefore had to be given effect.

COUNSEL

Jeffrey A. Lamken argued the cause for petitioner.
Abraham S. Alter argued the cause for respondent.

_____

UNITED STATES, Petitioner

v

LASHAWN LOWELL BANKS

540 US 31, 157 L Ed 2d 343, 124 S Ct 521

[No. 02-473]

Argued October 15, 2003.
Decided December 2, 2003.

Decision: Law-enforcement officers' 15-to-20 second wait, after calling out "police search warrant" and knocking on apartment door, before breaking door open held to satisfy Federal Constitution's Fourth Amendment and 18 USCS § 3109.

SUMMARY

At about 2 p.m. on a Wednesday, federal and local law-enforcement officers, who had a warrant to search for cocaine in an accused's two-bedroom apartment, called out "police search warrant" and knocked on the apartment's front door. After waiting 15 to 20 seconds with no response, the officers broke open the door with a battering ram. The accused, who was in the shower at the time, testified that he had heard nothing until the crash of the door. The search produced weapons, crack cocaine, and other evidence of dealing in illegal drugs.

The accused, who was charged with drug and firearms crimes, argued that the officers who had executed the search had, by waiting an unreasonably short time before forcing entry, violated (1) the Federal Constitution's Fourth Amendment; and (2) 18 USCS § 3109, which authorized a federal law-enforcement officer to break open any outer or inner door or window of a
10

house, or any part of a house, or anything therein, to execute a search warrant, if, after notice of the officer's authority and purpose, the officer was refused admittance. After a Federal District Court denied the accused's motion to suppress the evidence produced by the search, the accused pleaded guilty but reserved his right to challenge the search on appeal.

On appeal, the United States Court of Appeals for the Ninth Circuit, using a four-part scheme for vetting knock-and-announce entries, (1) held that the officers' 15-to-20 second delay before knocking down the apartment door was insufficient to satisfy constitutional safeguards, (2) reversed the accused's conviction, and (3) ordered suppression of the evidence produced by the search (282 F3d 699).

On certiorari, the United States Supreme Court reversed. In an opinion by SOUTER, J., expressing the unanimous view of the court, it was held that officers' 15-to-20 second wait, after calling out "police search warrant" and knocking on the door, before breaking open the door satisfied:

(1) The Fourth Amendment, as (a) after 15 or 20 seconds without a response, the officers could fairly have suspected that cocaine would be gone if the officers were reticent any longer; and (b) the exigent need of law enforcement trumped a resident's interest in avoiding all property damage.

(2) § 3109, as the officers had forcibly entered the apartment after a reasonable suspicion of exigency had ripened.

COUNSEL

David B. Salmons argued the cause for petitioner.
Randall J. Roske argued the cause for respondent.

RAYTHEON COMPANY, Petitioner

v

JOEL HERNANDEZ

540 US 44, 157 L Ed 2d 357, 124 S Ct 513

[No. 02-749]

Argued October 8, 2003.
Decided December 2, 2003.

Decision: Federal Court of Appeals held to have improperly applied disparate-impact analysis to worker's disparate-treatment claim of disability discrimination under Americans with Disabilities Act (42 USCS §§ 12101 et seq.).

SUMMARY

In 1991, a worker who had tested positive for cocaine use was forced to resign from his company, in lieu of termination, for violating the company's workplace-conduct rules. In 1994, the worker applied to be rehired and attached to his application letters of reference from (1) a pastor who stated that the worker was a faithful and active church member, and (2) an Alcoholics Anonymous counselor who stated that the worker was in recovery. Nevertheless, the company rejected the application.

The worker, alleging that he had been discriminated against in violation of the Americans with Disabilities Act of 1990 (ADA) (42 USCS §§ 12101 et seq.), filed a charge with the Equal Employment Opportunity Commission, which issued a right-to-sue letter. The worker brought suit under the ADA against the company in the United States District Court for the District of Arizona

13

on a disparate-treatment theory, that is, on an allegation that the company had rejected his application because of his record of drug addiction and/or because he was regarded as being a drug addict. However, the company asserted that the refusal to rehire the worker had been based on the company's neutral policy of not rehiring employees who were terminated for violating the company's code of conduct.

In response to the company's motion for summary judgment, the worker for the first time argued in the alternative that even if the company had applied a neutral no-rehire policy in his case, the company had still violated the ADA, as such a policy allegedly had a disparate impact on recovering drug addicts. The District Court (1) ruled that the worker had not timely raised the disparate-impact claim, and (2) granted the company summary judgment with respect to the worker's disparate-treatment claim.

The United States Court of Appeals for the Ninth Circuit, in reversing and ordering a remand, (1) acknowledged that the worker's case was limited to a disparate-treatment theory; and (2) granted the company's motion to strike the portions of the worker's reply brief that discussed his disparate-impact claim; but (3) concluded that as a matter of law, the company's no-rehire policy—at least as applied to employees who were lawfully forced to resign for illegal drug use but were since rehabilitated—contravened the ADA (298 F3d 1030).

On certiorari, the United States Supreme Court vacated and remanded. In an opinion by THOMAS, J., expressing the unanimous view of all seven participating members of the court, it was held that the Court of Appeals had improperly applied a disparate-impact analysis to the worker's claim, for:

(1) The company's proffer of a neutral no-rehire policy
14

had satisfied the company's obligation to provide a
legitimate nondiscriminatory reason for refusing to
rehire the worker.

(2) Thus, the only remaining relevant question before
the Court of Appeals—given that the worker had not
timely pursued a disparate-impact claim—was whether
there was sufficient evidence from which a jury could
conclude that the company had made its employment
decision based on the worker's status as disabled,
despite the company's proffered explanation.

(3) In holding that the company's no-rehire policy
contravened the ADA, the Court of Appeals had erred
by conflating the analytical framework for disparate-
impact and disparate-treatment claims.

SOUTER and BREYER, JJ., did not participate.

COUNSEL

Carter G. Phillips argued the cause for petitioner.

Paul D. Clement argued the cause for the United
States, as amicus curiae, by special leave of court.

Stephen G. Montoya argued the cause for respondent.

COMMONWEALTH OF VIRGINIA, Plaintiff

v

STATE OF MARYLAND

540 US 56, 157 L Ed 2d 461, 124 S Ct 598

[No. 129, Orig.]

Argued October 7, 2003.
Decided December 9, 2003.

Decision: Maryland held to lack authority to require Virginia, Virginia's governmental subdivisions, or Virginia's citizens to obtain permit (1) to construct improvements appurtenant to Virginia's shore of Potomac River, or (2) to draw water from river.

SUMMARY

With respect to the Potomac River between Maryland and Virginia, Article Seventh of a binding 1785 compact between Maryland and Virginia, which compact had been ratified by the states' legislatures, provided that "The citizens of each state respectively shall have full property in the shores of Potowmack river adjoining their lands, with all emoluments and advantages thereunto belonging, and the privilege of making and carrying out wharves and other improvements, so as not to obstruct or injure the navigation of the river."

The Black-Jenkins Award, which was issued in 1877 as a result of the submission to binding arbitration of a boundary dispute between Maryland and Virginia, (1) placed the boundary at the low-water mark on the Virginia shore of the Potomac River; (2) provided, in the Award's Article Fourth, that "Virginia is entitled not only to full dominion over the soil to low-water

16

mark on the south shore of the Potomac, but has a right to such use of the river beyond the line of low-water mark as may be necessary to the full enjoyment of her riparian ownership, without impeding the navigation or otherwise interfering with the proper use of it by Maryland, agreeably to the compact of seventeen hundred and eighty-five" (20 Stat 482); (3) was ratified by the states' legislatures; and (4) pursuant to the Federal Constitution's interstate-compact provision (in Art I, § 10, cl 3), was approved by Congress (20 Stat 481).

Pursuant to Maryland's establishment of a permitting system for water withdrawal and waterway construction taking place within Maryland territory, Maryland (1) beginning in 1957, had issued, without objection, at least 29 water-withdrawal permits to Virginia entities; and (2) since 1968, had issued numerous waterway-construction permits to Virginia entities. In 1996, the water authority of Virginia's Fairfax County sought permits from Maryland for construction of a water-intake structure extending 725 feet from the Virginia shore above the tidal reach of the Potomac River, in order to improve water quality for Fairfax County residents. In 1997, Maryland's department of the environment, concluding that Virginia had not demonstrated a sufficient need for the offshore intake, for the first time refused a permit request concerning the river from a Virginia entity.

Virginia, after unsuccessfully pursuing Maryland administrative appeals for more than 2 years, sought leave to file in the United States Supreme Court a bill of complaint that sought a declaratory judgment that Maryland could not require Virginia, its governmental subdivisions, or its citizens to obtain a permit in order to construct improvements appurtenant to the Virginia shore of the river or to withdraw water from the river. The court (1) granted such leave (530 US 1201, 147 L

Ed 2d 230, 120 S Ct 2213); and (2) subsequently, while Virginia's permit request was still pending, referred the bill of complaint to a Special Master (531 US 922, 148 L Ed 2d 236, 121 S Ct 294).

Maryland, although not disputing that Virginia had rights to withdraw water and construct improvements under the compact and the Award, asserted that (1) as sovereign over the river to the low-water mark, Maryland was entitled to regulate Virginia's exercise of these rights; and (2) even if the compact and the Award had granted Virginia unrestricted rights of waterway construction and water withdrawal, Virginia had lost those rights by acquiescing in Maryland's regulation of activities on the river. The Special Master filed a report recommending that the court grant the relief sought by Virginia.

On exceptions to the report of the Special Master, the Supreme Court (1) overruled Maryland's exceptions, (2) granted the relief sought by Virginia, and (3) entered the decree proposed by the Special Master. In an opinion by REHNQUIST, Ch. J., joined by O'CONNOR, SCALIA, SOUTER, THOMAS, GINSBURG, and BREYER, JJ., it was held that:

(1) The Black-Jenkins Award gave Virginia sovereign authority, free from regulation by Maryland, to build improvements appurtenant to the Virginia shore and to withdraw water from the river, subject to the constraints of federal common law and the Award.

(2) Maryland had not carried its burden of showing that Virginia had lost its sovereign riparian rights by acquiescing in Maryland's regulation of Virginia's waterway-construction and water-withdrawal activities.

STEVENS, J., joined by KENNEDY, J., dissenting, expressed the view that (1) although riparian owners could withdraw water for domestic and agricultural purposes, the Federal Government and—in the ab-

18

sence of conflict with federal action or policy—the states could exercise their police powers by controlling the initiation and conduct of riparian and nonriparian uses of water; (2) under Virginia law, the use of the waters of a stream to supply inhabitants with water for domestic purposes was not a riparian right; and (3) therefore, such a use could be made only with the consent of the sovereign, Maryland, that owned the river.

KENNEDY, J., joined by STEVENS, J., dissenting, expressed the view that (1) the 1785 compact's Article Seventh had not abrogated Maryland's sovereign right to exercise its police power, and the regulatory authority that such power implied, over Maryland's river territory; (2) the citizen-landowner rights created by Article Seventh, as a consequence, remained subject to Maryland's sovereign powers insofar as they were consistent with Virginia's guaranteed access; and (3) the Supreme Court's interpretation—that Virginia's right was whole, sovereign, and unobstructed—led to the conclusion that Virginia, if it so chose, could build all the way across the river, as long as Virginia concluded that the construction was an improvement appurtenant to the Virginia shoreline and not an obstruction to the river's navigability.

COUNSEL

Stuart A. Raphael argued the cause for plaintiff.
Andrew H. Baida argued the cause for defendant.

MITCH McCONNELL, UNITED STATES SENATOR,
et al., Appellants

v

FEDERAL ELECTION COMMISSION, et al. (No. 02-
1674)

NATIONAL RIFLE ASSOCIATION, et al., Appellants

v

FEDERAL ELECTION COMMISSION, et al. (No. 02-
1675)

FEDERAL ELECTION COMMISSION, et al., Appellants

v

MITCH McCONNELL, UNITED STATES SENATOR,
et al. (No. 02-1676)

JOHN McCAIN, UNITED STATES SENATOR, et al.,
Appellants

v

MITCH McCONNELL, UNITED STATES SENATOR,
et al. (No. 02-1702)

REPUBLICAN NATIONAL COMMITTEE, et al., Appellants

v

FEDERAL ELECTION COMMISSION, et al. (No. 02-
1727)

NATIONAL RIGHT TO LIFE COMMITTEE, INC., et
al., Appellants

v

FEDERAL ELECTION COMMISSION, et al. (No. 02-1733)

AMERICAN CIVIL LIBERTIES UNION, Appellant

v

FEDERAL ELECTION COMMISSION, et al. (No. 02-1734)

VICTORIA JACKSON GRAY ADAMS, et al., Appellants

v

FEDERAL ELECTION COMMISSION, et al. (No. 02-1740)

RON PAUL, UNITED STATES CONGRESSMAN, et al., Appellants

v

FEDERAL ELECTION COMMISSION, et al. (No. 02-1747)

CALIFORNIA DEMOCRATIC PARTY, et al., Appellants

v

FEDERAL ELECTION COMMISSION, et al. (No. 02-1753)

AMERICAN FEDERATION OF LABOR AND CONGRESS OF INDUSTRIAL ORGANIZATIONS, et al., Appellants

v

FEDERAL ELECTION COMMISSION, et al. (No. 02-1755)

CHAMBER OF CONGRESS OF THE UNITED STATES, et al., Appellants

v

FEDERAL ELECTION COMMISSION, et al. (No. 02-1756)

540 US —, 157 L Ed 2d 491, 124 S Ct 619

Argued September 8, 2003.
Decided December 10, 2003.

Decision: Many parts of Bipartisan Campaign Reform Act of 2002—including provisions regulating use of "soft money" by parties, officeholders, and candidates (2 USCS § 441i)—held valid under Federal Constitution's First Amendment.

SUMMARY

In enacting the Bipartisan Campaign Reform Act of 2002 (BCRA)—which amended the Federal Election Campaign Act of 1971 (FECA) (2 USCS §§ 431 et seq.), a Communications Act of 1934 provision (47 USCS § 315), and other federal statutory provisions—Congress primarily sought to address perceived problems associated with (1) "soft money," that is, contributions to political parties for such purposes as (a) activities intended to influence state or local elections, (b) mixed-purpose activities, such as get-out-the-vote drives and generic party advertising, and (c) legislative advocacy advertisements that did not expressly advocate a candidate's election or defeat; and (2) "issue ads," that is, political advertisements that were specifically intended to affect election results, but did not contain certain "magic words," such as "Elect John Smith" or "Vote Against Jane Doe," which would have subjected the ads to FECA's existing restrictions.

Title I of BCRA regulated the use of soft money by political parties, officeholders, and candidates. The
22

core of Title I was new FECA § 323(a) (2 USCS § 441i(a)), which made it illegal for a political party's national committee to solicit, receive, direct, or spend any funds that were not subject to FECA's limitations, prohibitions, and reporting requirements. BCRA's Title II primarily prohibited corporations and unions from using general treasury funds for communications that were intended to, or had the effect of, influencing federal election outcomes. Among Title II's provisions was an amendment to FECA § 304 (2 USCS § 434), which specified significant disclosure and expenditure requirements for persons who funded "electioneering communications," that is, any broadcast, cable, or satellite communications (1) referring to a clearly identified candidate for federal office, (2) made within a specified time before an election, and (3) targeted to the relevant electorate.

Titles III, IV, and V set out various other requirements, including (1) "millionaire provisions" (in amended FECA § 315 and new FECA § 315A) (2 USCS §§ 441a, 441a-1), which provided for a series of staggered increases in otherwise applicable contribution-to-candidate limits if the candidate's opponent spent a triggering amount of personal funds; (2) new FECA § 324 (2 USCS § 441k), prohibiting individuals 17 years old or younger from making contributions to candidates or political parties; and (3) "candidate request" requirements (47 USCS § 315(e)(1)(A)), which called for broadcasters to keep records of broadcast requests made by or on behalf of any candidate.

Eleven actions challenging BCRA's constitutionality were filed by various individuals and organizations in the United States District Court for the District of Columbia against the Federal Election Commission (FEC) and other parties. A three-judge panel of the

District Court held some parts of BCRA unconstitutional and upheld others (251 F Supp 2d 176; 251 F Supp 2d 948).

On direct appeal, the United States Supreme Court affirmed in part and reversed in part. Three opinions, supported by varying majorities of Justices, together constituted the opinion of the court.

In an opinion by STEVENS and O'CONNOR, JJ., which constituted the opinion of the court with respect to BCRA Titles I and II, and which was joined by SOUTER, GINSBURG, and BREYER, JJ., it was held that:

(1) The soft-money provisions of new FECA § 323 were not facially invalid under the Federal Constitution's First Amendment.

(2) Title I did not (a) exceed Congress' authority under the Constitution's elections clause (in Article I, § 4) to make or alter rules governing federal elections, (b) violate constitutional federalism principles by impairing the states' authority to regulate their own elections, or (c) violate the equal protection component of the due process clause of the Constitution's Fifth Amendment by discriminating against political parties in favor of special interest groups.

(3) Amended FECA § 304 did not violate the First Amendment.

(4) New FECA § 315(a)(7)(B)(ii) (2 USCS § 441a(a)(7)(B)(ii)), providing that expenditures coordinated with political parties were to be treated as contributions to such parties, was not unconstitutional.

(5) There was no basis for finding unconstitutional the amended FECA § 315(a)(7)(C) (2 USCS § 441a(a)(7)(C)), which provided that disbursements for electioneering communications that were coordinated with a candidate or party were to be treated as contributions to, and expenditures by, that candidate or party.

24

(6) Amended FECA § 315(d)(4) (2 USCS § 441a(d)(4)), purporting to require political parties to choose between coordinated and independent expenditures during the postnomination pre-election period, placed an unconstitutional burden on the parties' right to make unlimited independent expenditures.

(7) New FECA § 316(b)(2) (2 USCS § 441b(b)(2)), extending certain restrictions on the use of corporate and union general treasury funds to all electioneering communications, was constitutional.

(8) New FECA § 316(c)(6) (2 USCS § 441b(c)(6)), extending to nonprofit corporations the prohibition on the use of general treasury funds to pay for electioneering communications, was valid as limited to nonprofit entities that were not "MCFL organizations," that is, certain organizations formed for the express purpose of promoting political ideas.

In an opinion by REHNQUIST, Ch. J., which constituted the opinion of the court with respect to miscellaneous BCRA Title III and IV provisions, and which was joined by O'CONNOR, SCALIA, KENNEDY, and SOUTER, JJ., and joined in part (except with respect to holding 1 below) by STEVENS, GINSBURG, and BREYER, JJ., and joined in part (with respect to holdings 1-3 and 6 below) by THOMAS, J., it was held that:

(1) The plaintiffs who had challenged an amendment to a Communications Act provision (47 USCS § 315(b))—which denied a candidate the benefit of broadcast stations' "lowest unit charge" for air time in specified circumstances—lacked standing.

(2) The plaintiffs who had challenged the amended FECA § 315(a)(1) (2 USCS § 441a(a)(1))—which increased and indexed for inflation certain contribution limits—lacked standing.

(3) The plaintiffs who had challenged the "millionaire provisions" lacked standing.

(4) The expansion of FECA § 318(a) (2 USCS § 441d(a)) to include mandatory electioneering-communications-disbursements disclosure was valid.

(5) New FECA § 324's ban on political contributions by individuals 17 years old or younger violated the First Amendment rights of minors.

(6) The Supreme Court did not need to address whether some intervenor-defendants—whose position was identical to that of the FEC—had standing, for the FEC itself had standing.

In an opinion by BREYER, J., which constituted the opinion of the court with respect to BCRA Title V, and which was joined by STEVENS, O'CONNOR, SOUTER, and GINSBURG, JJ., it was held that no facial violation of the First Amendment was presented by (1) the "candidate request" requirements of 47 USCS § 315(e)(1)(A); (2) the "election message" requirements of 47 USCS §§ 315(e)(1)(B)(i), (ii), which required broadcasters to keep records of requests made by anyone to broadcast messages referring to a "legally qualified candidate" or to "any election to Federal office"; or (3) the "issue request" requirements of 47 USCS § 315(e)(1)(B)(iii), which called for broadcasters to keep records of requests made by anyone to broadcast messages related to a "national legislative issue of public importance" or a "political matter of national importance."

SCALIA, J., concurred with respect to BCRA Titles III and IV, dissented with respect to Titles I and V, and concurred in the judgment in part and dissented in part with respect to Title II.

THOMAS, J., joined in part by SCALIA, J., (1) concurred with respect to Titles III and IV, except for BCRA § 311 (amending FECA § 318(a)) and BCRA § 318 (adding FECA § 324); (2) concurred in the result with respect to BCRA § 318; (3) concurred in the

26

judgment in part and dissented in part with respect to Title II; and (4) dissented with respect to Titles I and V and BCRA § 311.

KENNEDY, J., joined by REHNQUIST, Ch. J., and joined by SCALIA, J., except to the extent that the opinion upheld new FECA § 323(e) and BCRA § 202 (amending FECA § 315(a)(7)(C)), and joined by THOMAS, J., with respect to BCRA § 213 (amending FECA § 315(d)(4)), (1) dissented with respect to BCRA Titles I and II, (2) concurred in the judgment with respect to BCRA § 213 and FECA § 323(e), and (3) concurred in the judgment in part and dissented in part with respect to BCRA §§ 201 (amending FECA § 304), 202, and 214 (adding FECA § 315(a)(7)(B)(ii)).

REHNQUIST, Ch. J., joined by SCALIA and KENNEDY, JJ., dissented with respect to BCRA Titles I and V.

STEVENS, J., joined by GINSBURG and BREYER, JJ., (1) dissented with respect to the issue of standing to challenge BCRA § 305 (amending 47 USCS § 315(b)), and (2) would have upheld § 305 on the merits.

COUNSEL

Kenneth W. Starr argued the cause for the McConnell, et al. plaintiffs.

Bobby R. Burchfield argued the cause for the Political Party plaintiffs.

Floyd Abrams argued the cause for the McConnell, et al. plaintiffs.

Laurence E. Gold argued the cause for the AFL-CIO plaintiffs.

Jay Alan Sekulow argued the cause for the Echols, et al. plaintiffs.

Theodore B. Olson argued the cause for the Federal defendants.

Paul D. Clement argued the cause for the Federal defendants.

Seth P. Waxman argued the cause for the Intervenor-defendants.

MARYLAND, Petitioner

v

JOSEPH JERMAINE PRINGLE

540 US —, 157 L Ed 2d 769, 124 S Ct 795

[No. 02-809]

Argued November 3, 2003.
Decided December 15, 2003.

Decision: Warrantless arrest of automobile passenger
during stop for speeding held not to contravene
Fourth Amendment, where police officer, having
seized $763 from glove compartment and cocaine
from behind back-seat armrest, arrested all three
occupants after each denied ownership of cash and
cocaine.

SUMMARY

During a 3:16 a.m. stop, by a county police officer in
Maryland, of a relatively small car for speeding, the
officer (1) observed a large amount of rolled-up money
in the glove compartment when the driver-owner
opened the compartment to retrieve the car's registration; and (2) performed, with the owner's consent, a
search of the car that yielded $763 from the glove
compartment and cocaine from behind the back-seat
armrest. After none of the car's three occupants, when
questioned by the officer, offered any information
regarding ownership of the cocaine or the money, the
officer arrested all three occupants and transported
them to a police station. At the station, the accused,
who had been the car's front-seat passenger, admitted
that the cocaine belonged to him and stated that the

other two occupants of the car had not known about the cocaine. The other occupants were released.

In a Maryland court, the accused was (1) convicted of possession with intent to distribute cocaine and possession of cocaine, and (2) sentenced to 10 years' incarceration without the possibility of parole. The Maryland Court of Special Appeals affirmed (141 Md App 292, 785 A2d 790). However, the Court of Appeals of Maryland reversed, holding that the officer had lacked probable cause to arrest the accused for possession of cocaine (370 Md 525, 805 A2d 1016).

On certiorari, the United States Supreme Court reversed and remanded. In an opinion by REHNQUIST, Ch. J., expressing the unanimous view of the court, it was held that:

(1) A reasonable officer could have concluded that there was probable cause to believe that the accused had committed the crime of possession of cocaine, which was then a felony under Maryland law, either solely or jointly.

(2) Therefore, the warrantless arrest of the accused did not contravene the Federal Constitution's Fourth Amendment.

COUNSEL

Gary E. Bair argued the cause for petitioner.

Sri Srinivasan argued the cause for the United States, as amicus curiae, by special leave of the Court.

Nancy S. Forster argued the cause for respondent.

HERNAN O'RYAN CASTRO, Petitioner

v

UNITED STATES

540 US —, 157 L Ed 2d 778, 124 S Ct 786

[No. 02-6683]

Argued October 15, 2003.

Decided December 15, 2003.

Decision: Federal District Court intending to recharacterize pro se litigant's motion as first motion for postconviction relief under 28 USCS § 2255 held required (1) to notify litigant of intended recharacterization and its consequences, and (2) to provide opportunity to withdraw or amend motion.

SUMMARY

In 1994, a federal prisoner attacked his federal drug conviction by filing, in a Federal District Court, a pro se motion that the prisoner called a motion for a new trial under Rule 33 of the Federal Rules of Criminal Procedure. The District Court denied the motion on the merits, referring to it as both a Rule 33 motion and a motion for relief under 28 USCS § 2255, which restricted a litigant's right to file a "second or successive motion" under § 2255. The prisoner, on his pro se appeal, did not challenge the District Court's recharacterization of the motion as a § 2255 motion. The United States Court of Appeals for the Eleventh Circuit summarily affirmed (82 F3d 429).

Subsequently, in 1997, the prisoner filed a pro se motion that the prisoner called a § 2255 motion, which motion raised new claims, including a claim of ineffec-

31

tive assistance of counsel, that had not been raised in the 1994 motion. After the District Court denied the motion, the Court of Appeals, on appeal, remanded for the District Court to consider, among other matters, whether the 1997 motion was the prisoner's second § 2255 motion. The District Court (1) determined that the 1997 motion was the prisoner's second § 2255 motion (the 1994 motion having been his first); and (2) dismissed the 1997 motion for failure to comply with § 2255's requirement that the prisoner obtain the Court of Appeals' permission to file a "second or successive" motion. The Court of Appeals affirmed (290 F3d 1270).

On certiorari, the United States Supreme Court vacated and remanded. In an opinion by BREYER, J., expressing the unanimous view of the court with respect to the court's judgment, and joined by REHNQUIST, Ch. J., and STEVENS, O'CONNOR, KENNEDY, SOUTER, and GINSBURG, JJ., with respect to the holdings below, it was held that:

(1) A District Court could not recharacterize a pro se litigant's motion as a first motion for postconviction relief under § 2255, unless the court (a) notified the litigant that the court intended to recharacterize the pleading, (b) warned the litigant that this recharacterization meant that any subsequent § 2255 motion would be subject to § 2255's restrictions on "second or successive" motions, and (c) provided the litigant an opportunity to withdraw the motion or to amend it so that it contained all the § 2255 claims that the litigant believed that the litigant had.

(2) Because of the absence of the required warnings, the prisoner's 1994 motion could not be considered a first § 2255 motion.

(3) Thus, the prisoner's 1997 motion could not be considered "second or successive" for § 2255 purposes.

32

SCALIA, J., joined by THOMAS, J., concurring in part and concurring in the judgment, (1) agreed that the Supreme Court had the power to review the prisoner's claim; but (2) expressed the view that (a) because of the risk involved, pleadings never ought to be recharacterized as § 2255 motions, and (b) even if this were not so, running the risk was unjustified where, as in the case at hand, there was nothing to be gained by recharacterization.

COUNSEL

Michael G. Frick argued the cause for petitioner.
Dan Himmelfarb argued the cause for respondent.

SECURITIES AND EXCHANGE COMMISSION, Petitioner

v

CHARLES E. EDWARDS

540 US —, 157 L Ed 2d 813, 124 S Ct 892

[No. 02-1196]

Argued November 4, 2003.
Decided January 13, 2004.

Decision: Investment scheme held not excludible from term "investment contract"—for purposes of federal securities provisions (15 USCS §§ 77b(a)(1), 78c(a)(10))—simply because scheme promises fixed rather than variable return.

SUMMARY

In SEC v W. J. Howey Co. (1946) 328 US 293, 90 L Ed 1244, 66 S Ct 1100, the United States Supreme Court held that the test for determining whether a particular moneymaking scheme is an "investment contract" for purposes of § 2(a)(1) of the Securities Act of 1933 (1933 Act) (15 USCS § 77b(a)(1)) and § 3(a)(10) of the Securities Exchange Act of 1934 (1934 Act) (15 USCS § 78c(a)(10))—and thus a "security" subject to the federal securities laws—is whether the scheme involves an investment of money in a common enterprise with profits to come solely from the efforts of others.

A company sold payphones to the public via independent distributors. The payphones were offered with an agreement under which the company leased back the payphones from the purchasers for a fixed monthly payment representing a 14 percent annual return. Purchasers were not involved in the day-to-day operation of the payphones they owned, as the company (1) selected the site for the phone, (2) installed the equipment, (3) arranged for connection and long-distance service, (4) collected coin revenues, and (5) maintained and repaired the phones. However, the payphones did not generate enough revenue for the company to make the payments required by the lease-back agreements, and the company depended on funds from new investors to meet its obligations. Eventually, the company filed for bankruptcy protection.

The Securities and Exchange Commission (SEC) brought a civil enforcement action against the company and the company's chairman in the United States District Court for the Northern District of Georgia. The SEC alleged that the defendants had violated various federal securities provisions, including the antifraud provisions of § 17(a) of the 1933 Act (15 USCS § 77q(a)) and § 10(b) of the 1934 Act (15 USCS § 78j(b)). The District Court (1) concluded that the payphone sale-and-leaseback arrangement was an investment contract within the meaning of the federal securities laws; and (2) granted the SEC relief that included a preliminary injunction to prevent the company from engaging in future securities violations (123 F Supp 2d 1349).

The United States Court of Appeals for the Eleventh Circuit—in reversing with directions to dismiss the complaint for lack of subject matter jurisdiction—concluded that the company's scheme was not an investment contract, on the grounds that (1) an investment contract must offer either capital appreciation or a participation in the earnings of the enterprise; (2) such a definition excluded schemes offering a fixed rate of return; and (3) the requirement that the return on the investment be derived solely from the efforts of others was not satisfied when the purchasers had a contractual entitlement to the return (300 F3d 1281, reh den 54 Fed Appx 687).

On certiorari, the Supreme Court reversed and remanded. In an opinion by O'CONNOR, J., expressing the unanimous view of the court, it was held that an investment scheme offering a contractual entitlement to a fixed rather than variable rate of return could properly be considered an "investment contract" for purposes of the federal securities laws, for:

(1) There was no reason to distinguish between promises of fixed returns and promises of variable returns for purposes of the Howey test for investment contracts, as (a) in both cases, the investing public was attracted by representations of investment income; (b) investments pitched as low-risk—such as those offering a "guaranteed" fixed return—were particularly attractive to individuals who were more vulnerable to investment fraud; and (c) the fact that investors bargained for a fixed return on their investment did not mean that the return was not also expected to come solely from the efforts of others.

(2) The inclusion among investment contracts of investment schemes that promised a fixed return (1) did not conflict with Supreme Court precedent, and (2) was in keeping with the position that the SEC had consistently taken.

COUNSEL

Theodore B. Olson argued the cause for petitioner.

Michael K. Wolensky argued the cause for respondent.

VERIZON COMMUNICATIONS INC., Petitioner

v

LAW OFFICES OF CURTIS V. TRINKO, LLP

540 US —, 157 L Ed 2d 823, 124 S Ct 872

[No. 02-682]

Argued October 14, 2003.
Decided January 13, 2004.

Decision: Complaint—alleging, as to local telephone service, that incumbent local exchange carrier had breached its duty, under Telecommunications Act of 1996, to share incumbent's network with competitors—held not to state valid antitrust claim under 15 USCS § 2.

SUMMARY

With respect to local telephone service, the Telecommunications Act of 1996, in 47 USCS § 251(c), required each incumbent local exchange carrier to share its network with competitors, including, under 47 USCS § 251(c)(3), the provision of access to individual "unbundled" network elements (UNEs). These § 251(c) requirements were beyond the basic responsibilities which the 1996 Act, in provisions such as 47 USCS § 251(b), imposed upon all carriers. Also, the 1996 Act, in 47 USCS § 252, required such incumbents to sign interconnection agreements with rivals, with compulsory arbitration if the terms could not be completely agreed upon. Moreover, in order for an incumbent to enter the potentially lucrative market for long-distance service, the 1996 Act, under 47 USCS § 271, required satisfaction of a competitive checklist, which included

37

such an incumbent's nondiscriminatory provision of access to the UNEs offered pursuant to § 251(c). In addition, the 1996 Act contained an antitrust-specific saving clause (47 USCS § 152 note), which provided that "nothing in this Act or the amendments made by this Act [would] be construed to modify, impair, or supersede the applicability of any of the antitrust laws."

The incumbent local exchange carrier for New York state had, as one of the incumbent's § 251(c)(3) obligations, the provision of access to operations support systems (OSS), used to provide services to customers and to insure quality. Also, after this incumbent applied to provide long-distance service in the state, an eventual § 271 authorization by the Federal Communications Commission (FCC) discussed the incumbent's commitments to provide access to UNEs, including the provision of OSS. Moreover, the incumbent subjected itself to oversight by the state's public service commission (PSC). When several competitors complained about alleged deficiencies in the incumbent's OSS-related servicing of local-telephone orders, the FCC and PSC responded by (1) imposing substantial financial penalties, and (2) establishing measurements and reporting requirements to gauge the incumbent's remediation.

The day after the incumbent had entered into a consent decree with the FCC on this subject, a New York City law firm, which was assertedly a local-telephone-service customer of another company, filed a complaint in the United States District Court for the Southern District of New York, on the purported behalf of the law firm and a class of similarly situated customers. As later amended, the complaint (1) asserted claims under various state and federal laws, including an antitrust claim under § 2 of the Sherman Act (15 USCS § 2), which prohibited monopolizing or attempting to monopolize; (2) sought damages and injunctive relief; (3) alleged that the incumbent had breached its 1996 Act duty to share the incumbent's network with competitors; and (4) set forth, as the complaint's single example of the incumbent's alleged failure to provide adequate access, the OSS failure that had resulted in the FCC consent decree and some PSC orders.

However, the District Court (1) dismissed the complaint in its entirety; and (2) as to the antitrust portion, concluded that the law firm's allegations of the incumbent's deficient assistance to rivals failed to satisfy the requirements of § 2 (123 F Supp 2d 738).

On appeal, the United States Court of Appeals for the Second Circuit—in vacating in part and in ordering a remand—(1) effectively reinstated the law firm's complaint in part, including the antitrust claim; and (2) expressed the view that the complaint's allegations described conduct that might support a § 2 antitrust claim "under a number of theories" (305 F3d 89).

The United States Supreme Court granted certiorari limited to the antitrust issue (538 US 905, 155 L Ed 2d 224, 123 S Ct 1480).

Then, on certiorari, the Supreme Court reversed and remanded. In an opinion by SCALIA, J., joined by REHNQUIST, Ch. J., and O'CONNOR, KENNEDY, GINSBURG, and BREYER, JJ., it was held that the law firm, in alleging that the incumbent had breached its 1996 Act duty to share the incumbent's network with competitors, failed to state a valid antitrust claim under § 2 of the Sherman Act, for among other factors:

(1) Just as the 1996 Act, through its antitrust-specific saving clause, preserved claims that satisfied existing antitrust standards, the 1996 Act did not create new claims that went beyond existing antitrust standards.

(2) The allegations in the law firm's complaint did not fit within the existing refusal-to-deal exceptions already

recognized by the Supreme Court, whereby the incumbent's alleged refusal to cooperate with the incumbent's rivals could properly constitute anticompetitive conduct violating § 2.

(3) Moreover, the allegations in the law firm's complaint did not provide a basis, under traditional antitrust principles, for the Supreme Court to recognize a new refusal-to-deal exception, whereby the incumbent's alleged refusal to cooperate with the incumbent's rivals could properly constitute anticompetitive conduct violating § 2.

STEVENS, J., joined by SOUTER and THOMAS, JJ., concurring in the judgment, expressed the view that (1) even if the allegations in the law firm's complaint were assumed to be true, the law firm was not a covered "person," under the Supreme Court's precedents, within the meaning of § 4 of the Clayton Act (15 USCS § 15), which provided for the treble-damages remedy which the law firm sought; and (2) the Supreme Court ought not to go beyond this threshold question in the case at hand.

COUNSEL

Richard G. Taranto argued the cause for petitioner.

Theodore B. Olson argued the cause for the United States, as amicus curiae, by special leave of court.

Donald B. Verrilli, Jr. argued the cause for respondent.

ILLINOIS, Petitioner

v

ROBERT S. LIDSTER

540 US —, 157 L Ed 2d 843, 124 S Ct 885

[No. 02-1060]

Argued November 5, 2003.
Decided January 13, 2004.

Decision: Police stops of motorists, at highway checkpoint set up at location of recent hit-and-run accident, to ask for information about accident held valid under Fourth Amendment.

SUMMARY

About 1 week after a hit-and-run accident in which a bicyclist in Illinois had been killed, local police set up a highway checkpoint, at about the same location and time of night at which the accident had occurred, to obtain information from motorists about the accident. Officers stopped each vehicle for 10 to 15 seconds, asked the occupants whether they had seen anything happen there the previous weekend, and handed each driver a flyer requesting information about the accident. As one driver approached the checkpoint, his van swerved, nearly hitting an officer. The officer (1) smelled alcohol on the driver's breath; and (2) directed the driver to a side street where another officer administered a sobriety test and then arrested the driver.

In the Circuit Court of DuPage County, Illinois, (1) the driver was convicted of driving under the influence of alcohol; and (2) the driver's challenge to his arrest and conviction, on the ground that the government had obtained evidence through the use of a checkpoint stop that allegedly violated the Federal Constitution's Fourth Amendment, was rejected.

However, the Appellate Court of Illinois, Second District, reversed (319 Ill App 3d 825, 747 NE2d 419). The Supreme Court of Illinois then (1) held that the United States Supreme Court's decision in City of Indianapolis v Edmond (2000) 531 US 32, 148 L Ed 2d 333, 121 S Ct 447—that the Fourth Amendment had been violated by a highway checkpoint program under which police, without individualized suspicion, had stopped vehicles for the primary purpose of discovering and interdicting illegal narcotics—required a finding the stop in question in the case at hand was unconstitutional; and (2) affirmed the Appellate Court's judgment (202 Ill 2d 1, 779 NE2d 855).

On certiorari, the United States Supreme Court reversed. In an opinion by BREYER, J., joined in pertinent part by REHNQUIST, Ch. J., and O'CONNOR, SCALIA, KENNEDY, and THOMAS, JJ., it was held that the stops at the highway checkpoint in question did not violate the Fourth Amendment's prohibition against unreasonable seizures, for in the case at hand (1) the relevant public concern was grave; (2) the stops advanced this grave public concern to a significant degree; and (3) most importantly, the stops interfered only minimally with liberty of the sort that the Fourth Amendment sought to protect.

STEVENS, J., joined by SOUTER and GINSBURG, JJ., concurring in part and dissenting in part, (1) agreed with the Supreme Court that the decision in City of Indianapolis v Edmond, supra, did not control the instant case; but (2) expressed the view that the case ought to be remanded to the Illinois courts, which were

42

more familiar with local conditions and practices, to undertake initial analysis of the Fourth Amendment issue.

COUNSEL

Gary Feinerman argued the cause for petitioner.

Donald J. Ramsell argued the cause for respondent.

Patricia A. Millett argued the cause for the United States, as amicus curiae, by special leave of court.

LINDA FREW, on behalf of her daughter, CARLA
FREW, et al., Petitioners

v

ALBERT HAWKINS, COMMISSIONER, TEXAS
HEALTH AND HUMAN SERVICES COMMISSION,
et al.

540 US —, 157 L Ed 2d 855, 124 S Ct 899

[No. 02-628]

Argued October 7, 2003.
Decided January 14, 2004.

Decision: Eleventh Amendment held not to bar enforcement of federal consent decree entered into
by Texas officials defending suit asserting that
Texas Medicaid program failed to provide children
with health-care benefits allegedly required under
42 USCS §§ 1396a(a)(43) and 1396d(r).

SUMMARY

A state's participation in Medicaid—a cooperative
federal-state program that provides federal funding for
state medical services to the poor—which participation
is voluntary, requires the state to meet certain federal
requirements. One requirement, under 42 USCS §§
1396a(a)(43) and 1396d(r), is that the state maintain
an Early and Periodic Screening, Diagnosis, and Treatment (EPSDT) program for children. Some mothers of
children eligible for EPSDT services in Texas—a Medicaid participant—brought, under 42 USCS § 1983, an
action asserting that the Texas EPSDT program did not
meet federal requirements. The action, which was
brought against the Texas department of health, the
Texas health and human services commission, the

commissioners of these two agencies, and some other employees of the department of health, sought injunctive relief. The individuals were sued in their official capacities.

After the United States District Court for the Eastern District of Texas dismissed the claims against the state agencies on the ground of the state's sovereign immunity, under the Federal Constitution's Eleventh Amendment, from suit by individuals in federal court, (1) the state officials remained in the suit, and (2) the District Court certified a class of children in Texas who were entitled to EPSDT services. The remaining parties agreed to a consent decree that was approved and entered by the District Court. In contrast with the federal statute's brief and general mandate, the decree required state officials to implement many specific procedures.

Two years after the consent decree was entered, the mothers filed, in District Court, an action to enforce the decree. The District Court (1) rejected the state officials' argument that the Eleventh Amendment rendered the decree unenforceable, (2) concluded that certain provisions of the decree had been violated, and (3) directed the parties to submit proposals outlining possible remedies (109 F Supp 2d 579).

On interlocutory appeal, the United States Court of Appeals for the Fifth Circuit reversed, holding that the Eleventh Amendment prevented enforcement of the decree, because the violations of the decree were not violations of the Medicaid Act that imposed a clear and binding obligation on the state (300 F3d 530).

On certiorari, the United States Supreme Court reversed and remanded. In an opinion by KENNEDY, J., expressing the unanimous view of the court, it was held that the Eleventh Amendment did not bar judicial enforcement of the decree under the doctrine of Ex parte Young (1908) 209 US 123, 52 L Ed 714, 28 S Ct 441—which had held proper, under the Eleventh Amendment, a federal court's prospective injunctive relief against a state official—as:

(1) In the case at hand, the decree was a federal court order that sprang from a federal dispute and furthered the objectives of federal law.

(2) The motion to enforce the decree sought enforcement of a remedy that was consistent with Ex parte Young and with Local Number 93, International Asso. of Firefighters, etc. v Cleveland (1986) 478 US 501, 92 L Ed 2d 405, 106 S Ct 3063, which had held valid a consent decree requiring prospective relief against a city in favor of some individuals.

(3) The order to be enforced in the case at hand was a federal decree entered to implement a federal statute.

(4) The decree reflected a choice among various ways that a state could implement the Medicaid Act and, as a result, enforcing the decree vindicated an agreement that the state officials had reached to comply with federal law.

COUNSEL

Susan F. Zinn argued the cause for petitioners.

Irving L. Gornstein argued the cause for the United States, as amicus curiae, by special leave of court.

R. Edward Cruz argued the cause for respondents.

ANDREW J. KONTRICK, Petitioner

v

ROBERT A. RYAN

540 US —, 157 L Ed 2d 867, 124 S Ct 906

[No. 02-819]

Argued November 3, 2003.
Decided January 14, 2004.

Decision: Debtor held to forfeit right to rely upon time constraints, under Bankruptcy Rules 4004 and 9006(b)(3), for creditor's objecting to debtor's discharge under 11 USCS § 727(a), where debtor did not raise this time issue before federal bankruptcy court reached merits of creditor's objection.

SUMMARY

With respect to proceedings under Chapter 7 of the Bankruptcy Code (11 USCS §§ 701 et seq.), Rules 4004 and 9006(b)(3) of the Federal Rules of Bankruptcy Procedure imposed some time constraints for a creditor's objecting to a debtor's discharge, under 11 USCS § 727(a), from bankruptcy. In relevant part, (1) Rule 4004(a) provided that a complaint objecting to such a discharge had to be filed no later than 60 days after the first date set for the meeting of creditors; (2) Rule 4004(b) provided that a court could "for cause" extend Rule 4004(a)'s deadline if a motion was filed before the time had expired; and (3) Rule 9006(b)(3) effectively provided that an enlargement of the Rule 4004(a) time would occur only as permitted by Rule 4004(b).

After a doctor had filed a Chapter 7 bankruptcy petition in 1997, it was not until 1998 that a major creditor filed, in the United States Bankruptcy Court for the Northern District of Illinois, an amended complaint which for the first time asserted a particular claim—the "family-account" claim—concerning an allegedly fraudulent transfer that, according to the creditor, ought to disqualify the doctor from a § 727(a) discharge. It was uncontested that with respect to the family-account claim, the amended complaint had been filed outside the time constraints of Rules 4004 and 9006(b)(3). However, the doctor was later found not to have asserted this time issue (1) in his answer to the amended complaint, or (2) when he later responded to a motion by the creditor for summary judgment.

In 2000, the Bankruptcy Court in pertinent part (1) awarded summary judgment to the creditor on the merits of the family-account claim, and (2) held that the doctor did not qualify for a discharge from bankruptcy. The doctor then moved for reconsideration, in effect arguing that because the family-account claim had been filed outside the rules' time constraints—which the doctor asserted to be "mandatory" and "unalterable"—the Bankruptcy Court had lacked jurisdiction over the family-account claim. However, the Bankruptcy Court denied the doctor's motion, expressing the view that (1) these time constraints were not "jurisdictional"; and (2) the doctor had waived the right to assert the untimeliness of the amended complaint, by failing squarely to raise the point before the court had reached the merits of the creditor's objection.

The United States District Court for the Northern District of Illinois sustained the Bankruptcy Court's decision denying the doctor's discharge (2001 US Dist

LEXIS 7473), and the United States Court of Appeals for the Seventh Circuit affirmed (295 F3d 724). Both these courts used reasoning similar to the Bankruptcy Court's with respect to the time constraints.

On certiorari, the United States Supreme Court affirmed. In an opinion by GINSBURG, J., expressing the unanimous view of the court, it was held that:

(1) With respect to a creditor's objecting to a debtor's § 727(a) discharge from bankruptcy, the time constraints under Rules 4004 and 9006(b)(3) were not "jurisdictional," in the sense that these time constraints were not always dispositive.

(2) Thus, even if it were assumed for the purposes of argument that a debtor would have prevailed if the debtor had timely asserted the untimeliness of such an objection to discharge, the debtor forfeited the right, or defense, of relying upon the time constraints under Rules 4004 and 9006(b)(3), where—as had been found to be the situation in the case at hand—the debtor did not raise this time issue before a federal bankruptcy court reached the merits of the creditor's objection.

COUNSEL

E. King Poor argued the cause for petitioner.

James R. Figliulo argued the cause for respondent.

Kent L. Jones argued the cause for the United States, as amicus curiae, by special leave of court.

ALASKA DEPARTMENT OF ENVIRONMENTAL
CONSERVATION, Petitioner

v

ENVIRONMENTAL PROTECTION AGENCY et al.

540 US —, 157 L Ed 2d 967, 124 S Ct 983

[No. 02-658]

Argued October 8, 2003.
Decided January 21, 2004.

Decision: EPA held to (1) have authority to rule on
reasonableness of best-available-control-technology decisions by state permitting agencies concerning pollution-emitting facilities; and (2) properly
have blocked construction permitted by Alaska
agency at such facility.

SUMMARY

Under the Prevention of Significant Deterioration
(PSD) program of the Clean Air Act (CAA), as
amended (42 USCS §§ 7401 et seq.), § 165(a)(4) of the
CAA (42 USCS § 7475(a)(4)) provided that no major
air pollutant-emitting facility could be constructed unless the facility was equipped with the best available
control technology (BACT). In addition, § 113(a)(5) of
the CAA (42 USCS § 7413(a)(5)) authorized the
United States Environmental Protection Agency (EPA),
when it found that a state was not complying with a
CAA requirement governing construction of a pollutant source, to issue an order prohibiting construction,
to prescribe an administrative penalty, or to commence
a civil action for injunctive relief. Moreover, § 167 of the
CAA (42 USCS § 7477) instructed the EPA to take

measures, including issuance of an order, or seeking injunctive relief, necessary to prevent the construction of a major pollutant-emitting facility that did not conform to the PSD requirements of the CAA.

The Alaska department of environmental conservation made a BACT decision under which the department issued a permit that would have allowed a company to construct, in the state on some diesel-electric generators at a zinc mine, pollution-control devices that had a less-polluting alternative. The EPA issued orders, purportedly under §§ 113(a)(5) and 167, that (1) prohibited the department from issuing a PSD permit to the company without satisfactorily documenting why the less-polluting alternative was not BACT, and (2) generally prohibited the company from beginning construction or modification activities at the mine.

In response to challenges to the EPA orders by the department and the company, the United States Court of Appeals for the Ninth Circuit concluded that the court had jurisdiction over the challenges (244 F3d 748). Subsequently, the Court of Appeals concluded that the EPA (1) had the authority under §§ 113(a)(5) and 167 to determine the reasonableness or adequacy of the department's justification for its BACT decision, and (2) properly had exercised the EPA's discretion in issuing the orders (298 F3d 814).

On certiorari, the United States Supreme Court affirmed. In an opinion by GINSBURG, J., joined by STEVENS, O'CONNOR, SOUTER, and BREYER, JJ., it was held that:

(1) The EPA generally had supervisory authority under the CAA, subject to federal-court review, to rule on the reasonableness of BACT decisions by state permitting agencies and could issue a stop-construction order, under §§ 113(a)(5) and 167, if a BACT selection approved by a state agency was not reasonable.

51

(2) In the case at hand, the EPA validly had issued orders stopping installation of the more-polluting devices, because (a) the department's BACT designation did not qualify as reasonable in light of the CAA guides; and (b) the EPA, in exercising its supervisory authority under the CAA, had not acted arbitrarily or capriciously in finding that the department's decision to permit installation of the more-polluting devices lacked evidentiary support.

KENNEDY, J., joined by REHNQUIST, Ch. J., and SCALIA and THOMAS, JJ., dissenting, expressed the view that (1) the court's reasoning in the case at hand conflicted with (a) the express language of the CAA, (b) sound rules of administrative law, and (c) principles that preserved the integrity of states in the nation's federal system; (2) Alaska (a) had in place procedures that were in full compliance with the governing statute and accompanying regulations promulgated by the EPA, and (b) had followed these procedures to determine BACT in the case at hand; and (3) the EPA, on the basis of nothing more than its substantive disagreement with Alaska's discretionary judgment, had exceeded its powers in setting aside Alaska's BACT determination.

COUNSEL

Jonathan S. Franklin argued the cause for petitioner. Thomas G. Hungar argued the cause for respondents.

JOHN J. FELLERS, Petitioner

v

UNITED STATES

540 US —, 157 L Ed 2d 1016, 124 S Ct 1019

[No. 02-6320]

Argued December 10, 2003.
Decided January 26, 2004.

Decision: Federal Court of Appeals held to have wrongly used Fifth Amendment standard in ruling that accused's inculpatory statements were not inadmissible as fruits of prior statements that accused had made at home after indictment.

SUMMARY

After a grand jury had indicted an accused for conspiracy to distribute methamphetamine, two police officers went to the accused's home to arrest him. The officers, upon arriving at the home, informed the accused that their purpose in coming was to discuss his involvement in the distribution of methamphetamine and his association with certain charged coconspirators. In an ensuing discussion, the accused made several inculpatory statements.

The officers transported the accused to a county jail, where the officers advised the accused for the first time of his rights under Miranda v Arizona (1966) 384 US 436, 16 L Ed 2d 694, 86 S Ct 1602, and under Patterson v Illinois (1988) 487 US 285, 101 L Ed 2d 261, 108 S Ct 2389, which held that the Federal Constitution's Sixth Amendment does not bar the postindictment questioning of a defendant in the absence of counsel if the

53

defendant waives the right to counsel. The accused and the two officers signed a Miranda waiver form, and the accused then reiterated the inculpatory statements that he had made at home.

Before trial in the United States District Court for the District of Nebraska, the accused moved to suppress the statements that he had made at home and at the county jail. A United States Magistrate Judge conducted a hearing and recommended the suppression of (1) the at-home statements, as having been made (a) without Miranda warnings, and (b) in response to the officers' implicit questions; and (2) portions of the jailhouse statements, as fruits of the prior failure to provide Miranda warnings. The District Court (1) suppressed the at-home statements; but (2) admitted the jailhouse statements, on the ground that the accused had knowingly and voluntarily waived his Miranda rights before making those statements. The accused was subsequently convicted of conspiracy.

The United States Court of Appeals for the Sixth Circuit, in affirming on appeal, concluded that (1) the officers' failure to administer Miranda warnings at the accused's home did not violated his Sixth Amendment right to counsel, as the officers had not interrogated the accused there; and (2) the jailhouse statements had been properly admitted in light of the accused's knowing and voluntary waiver of the right to counsel (285 F3d 721, reh den 2002 US App LEXIS 8763).

On certiorari, the United States Supreme Court reversed and remanded. In an opinion by O'CONNOR, J., expressing the unanimous view of the court, it was held that the Court of Appeals had erred in holding that the absence of an "interrogation" at home foreclosed the claim that the jailhouse statements ought to have been suppressed, for:

(1) The police officers had deliberately elicited the

at-home statements from the accused, in violation of Sixth Amendment standards.

(2) The Court of Appeals had improperly conducted its "fruits" analysis under the Constitution's Fifth Amendment—inquiring solely as to whether the jailhouse statements had been knowingly and voluntarily made—without reaching the question whether the Sixth Amendment required suppression of the jailhouse statements.

COUNSEL

Seth P. Waxman argued the cause for petitioner.

Michael R. Dreeben argued the cause for respondent.

JOHN M. LAMIE, Petitioner

v

UNITED STATES TRUSTEE

540 US —, 157 L Ed 2d 1024, 124 S Ct 1023

[No. 02-693]

Argued November 10, 2003.
Decided January 26, 2004.

Decision: Bankruptcy Code provision (11 USCS
§ 330(a)(1)), in authorizing compensation awards
from estate funds, held not to authorize awards to
debtors' attorneys, unless attorneys were employed
as authorized by 11 USCS § 327.

SUMMARY

One of the ways in which the Bankruptcy Reform Act
of 1994 amended the Bankruptcy Code (11 USCS
§§ 101 et seq.) was to replace 11 USCS § 330(a)'s
provision authorizing a court to "award to a trustee, to
an examiner, to a professional person employed under
section 327 . . . , or to the debtor's attorney . . .
reasonable compensation for . . . services rendered by
such trustee, examiner, professional person, or attorney . . . ." with 11 USCS § 330(a)(1)'s provision authorizing a court to "award to a trustee, an examiner, a
professional person employed under section 327 . . .
reasonable compensation for actual, necessary services
rendered by the trustee, examiner, professional person,
or attorney . . . ." Thus, the change from the former
§ 330(a) to the new § 330(a)(1) basically consisted of
(1) deletion of "or to the debtor's attorney," which

defeated the parallelism of the statute's earlier version; and (2) an apparent legislative drafting error in omitting "or."

A bankruptcy attorney filed an application with the United States Bankruptcy Court for the Western District of Virginia, seeking attorneys' fees under § 330(a)(1) for the time that the attorney had spent working on behalf of a debtor in a proceeding under the Code's Chapter 7 (11 USCS §§ 701 et seq.). In denying the application of the attorney, who admitted that he had been not employed by the trustee and approved by the Bankruptcy Court under § 327, the Bankruptcy Court held that in a Chapter 7 proceeding, § 330(a)(1) did not authorize payment of attorneys' fees unless the attorney had been appointed under § 327 (253 BR 724). The United States District Court for the Western District of Virginia affirmed the Bankruptcy Court's judgment (260 BR 273), and the United States Court of Appeals for the Fourth Circuit affirmed the District Court's judgment (290 F3d 739).

On certiorari, the United States Supreme Court affirmed. In an opinion by KENNEDY, J., joined by REHNQUIST, Ch. J., and O'CONNOR, SOUTER, THOMAS, GINSBURG, and BREYER, JJ., and joined in pertinent part by SCALIA, J., it was held that § 330(a)(1) did not authorize compensation awards to debtors' attorneys from estate funds, unless the attorneys were employed as authorized by § 327—and thus, if an attorney was to be compensated from bankruptcy estate funds under § 330(a)(1) in a case under Chapter 7, then the attorney had to be employed by the trustee in bankruptcy and approved by the Bankruptcy Court—as

(1) The fact that § 330(a)(1) was awkward and even ungrammatical did not make it ambiguous concerning payments to attorneys.

(2) The plain meaning that § 330(a)(1) set forth did

not lead to absurd results requiring the Supreme Court to treat the text as if it were ambiguous.

(3) With a plain, nonabsurd meaning in view, the Supreme Court would not read into § 330(a)(1) language purportedly inadvertently omitted by Congress.

STEVENS, J., concurring in the judgment, joined by SOUTER and BREYER, JJ., concurring, said that (1) whenever there was such a plausible basis, as in the case at hand, for believing that a significant change in statutory law had resulted from a scrivener's error, the court had a duty to examine legislative history; and (2) evidence that the assumed drafting error had been called to Congress' attention in a timely fashion indicated that the Supreme Court's reading of the statutory text was correct.

COUNSEL

Thomas C. Goldstein argued the cause for petitioner.

Lisa S. Blatt argued the cause for respondent.

ILLINOIS, Petitioner

v

GREGORY FISHER

540 US —, 157 L Ed 2d 1060, 124 S Ct 1200

[No. 03-374]

Decided February 23, 2004.

Decision: Dismissal of cocaine-possession charge against accused who had been fugitive for over 10 years after failing to appear for trial, held not required, under Fourteenth Amendment's due process clause, by routine destruction of evidence by police 2 months before accused was apprehended.

SUMMARY

In Arizona v Youngblood (1988) 488 US 51, 102 L Ed 2d 281, 109 S Ct 333, the United States Supreme Court held that unless a criminal defendant can show bad faith on the part of the police, their failure to preserve potentially useful evidence does not constitute a violation of the due process clause of the Federal Constitution's Fourteenth Amendment.

In 1988, after four tests conducted by the Chicago police crime lab and the Illinois state police crime lab confirmed that a bag seized from an accused when he was arrested by Chicago police contained cocaine, the accused was charged, in the Circuit Court of Cook County, Illinois, with possession of cocaine. The accused filed a motion for discovery that requested all physical evidence that the state intended to use at trial, the state responded that all evidence would be made available at a reasonable time and date upon request, and the accused was released on bond pending trial. However, the accused failed to appear for trial in 1989, and the Circuit Court issued an arrest warrant to secure his presence. After the accused had remained a fugitive for over 10 years, the arrest warrant was executed in November 1999. The state then reinstated the 1988 cocaine-possession charge.

Before trial, the state informed the accused that in September 1999, the police, acting according to established procedures, had destroyed the substance seized from the accused during his arrest. The accused then filed a motion to dismiss the cocaine-possession charge on the basis of the state's destruction of evidence. The trial court denied the motion. At trial, the accused's case in chief consisted solely of his own testimony—in which he denied that he ever had possessed cocaine—and the accused was convicted of cocaine possession.

The Appellate Court of Illinois, First District, reversing the conviction, relied on a prior Illinois Supreme Court decision in concluding that the due process clause required dismissal of the charge. The Illinois Supreme Court denied leave to appeal.

Granting certiorari, the United States Supreme Court reversed and remanded. In a per curiam opinion expressing the views of REHNQUIST, Ch. J., and O'CONNOR, SCALIA, KENNEDY, SOUTER, THOMAS, GINSBURG, and BREYER, JJ., it was held that the Supreme Court's decision in Youngblood foreclosed a conclusion that destruction of the seized substance by the police required dismissal of the cocaine-possession charge under the due process clause, as:

(1) In Youngblood, the court had recognized that a due-process violation did not result from a state's failure to preserve evidentiary material of which no

more could be said than that it could have been subjected to tests, the results of which might have exonerated the defendant.

(2) It was undisputed that, in destroying the evidence, the police had acted in good faith and in accord with their normal practice.

(3) The substance seized from the accused was plainly the sort of potentially useful evidence referred to in Youngblood, not material exculpatory evidence.

STEVENS, J., concurring in the judgment, expressed the view that (1) the instant case was not one in which a defendant was unable to prove that the state had acted in bad faith but in which the loss or destruction of evidence was nonetheless so critical to the defense as to make a criminal trial fundamentally unfair; and (2) the state's certiorari petition should have been denied, as the judgment of the Illinois Appellate Court had limited precedential value, and might be reinstated on remand because the result was supported by the state-law holding in the prior Illinois Supreme Court case in question.

JEFF GROH, Petitioner

v

JOSEPH R. RAMIREZ et al.

540 US —, 157 L Ed 2d 1068, 124 S Ct 1284

[No. 02-811]

Argued November 4, 2003.
Decided February 24, 2004.

Decision: Home search pursuant to warrant that failed to describe persons or things to be seized held to violate Fourth Amendment; federal agent who led search held not entitled to qualified immunity from suit with respect to violation.

SUMMARY

A United States Bureau of Alcohol, Tobacco and Firearms agent prepared and signed an application for a warrant to search a family's Montana house. The application, which stated that the search was for specified weapons, explosives, and records, was supported by the agent's detailed affidavit setting forth his basis for believing that such items were in the house. The agent presented these documents, along with a warrant form completed by the agent, to a Federal Magistrate Judge (Magistrate), who then signed the warrant form. The warrant, rather than identifying any of the items that the agent intended to seize, (1) in the portion calling for a description of the "person or property," described only the house; and (2) did not incorporate by reference the itemized list in the application; but (3) recited that the Magistrate was satisfied that (a) the affidavit established probable cause to believe that contraband was concealed in the house, and (b) sufficient grounds existed for issuance of the warrant.

The agent led a team of federal and local law enforcement officers in a search of the house, but found no illegal weapons or explosives. The family, against whom no charges were filed, sued the agent and the other officers under Bivens v Six Unknown Named Agents of Federal Bureau of Narcotics (1971) 403 US 388, 29 L Ed 2d 619, 91 S Ct 1999, and 42 USCS § 1983, raising claims that included violation of the Federal Constitution's Fourth Amendment. The United States District Court for the District of Montana granted all of the officers summary judgment.

The United States Court of Appeals for the Ninth Circuit, affirming except as to the Fourth Amendment claim against the agent, concluded that (1) the warrant was invalid because it did not describe with particularity the place to be searched and the items to be seized; and (2) the agent was not entitled to qualified immunity from the family's suit, because the agent had been the leader of a search who had failed to read the warrant and to satisfy himself that (a) he understood its scope and limitations, and (b) it was not obviously defective (298 F3d 1022).

On certiorari, the United States Supreme Court affirmed. In an opinion by STEVENS, J., joined by O'CONNOR, SOUTER, GINSBURG, and BREYER, JJ., it was held that:

(1) The warrant was invalid, and the search was clearly unreasonable, in violation of the Fourth Amendment, for among other matters, (a) the warrant failed altogether to comply with the Fourth Amendment's unambiguous requirement that a warrant particularly describe the persons or things to be seized; (b) the fact that the application for the warrant adequately described the things to be seized did not save the warrant

from its facial invalidity; (c) by not describing the items to be seized at all, the warrant was so obviously deficient that the search had to be regarded as "warrantless"; (d) searches and seizures inside a home without a warrant were presumptively unreasonable; and (e) the presumptive rule against warrantless searches applied with equal force to searches whose only defect was a lack of particularity in the warrant.

(2) In such circumstances, the agent was not entitled to qualified immunity, for among other matters, (a) no reasonable officer could have believed that a warrant that plainly did not comply with the Fourth Amendment's particularity requirement was valid; and (b) because the agent had prepared the invalid warrant, he could not properly argue that he reasonably had relied on the Magistrate's assurance that the warrant contained an adequate description of the things to be seized.

KENNEDY, J., joined by REHNQUIST, Ch. J., dissenting, (1) agreed with the court that the search violated the Fourth Amendment; but (2) expressed the view that the agent was entitled to qualified immunity, because (a) the agent had made a clerical error that was a straightforward mistake of fact, and (b) the agent's mistaken belief that the warrant contained the proper language was reasonable.

THOMAS, J., joined by SCALIA, J., and joined as to point 2 below by REHNQUIST, Ch. J., dissenting, expressed the view that (1) the search did not violate the Fourth Amendment, because, despite the defective warrant, the search was not unreasonable; and (2) even if a constitutional violation were assumed, then the agent still ought to be entitled to qualified immunity, because, given the sheer number of warrants prepared and executed by officers each year, combined with the fact that these same officers also prepared detailed and sometimes somewhat comprehensive documents supporting the warrant applications, it was inevitable that officers acting reasonably and entirely in good faith would occasionally make errors such as the one in question.

COUNSEL

Richard A. Cordray argued the cause for petitioner.

Austin C. Schlick argued the cause for the United States, as amicus curiae, by special leave of court.

Vince Kozakiewicz argued the cause for respondents.

GENERAL DYNAMICS LAND SYSTEMS, INC., Petitioner

v

DENNIS CLINE et al.

540 US —, 157 L Ed 2d 1094, 124 S Ct 1236

[No. 02-1080]

Argued November 12, 2003.
Decided February 24, 2004.

Decision: Age Discrimination in Employment Act of 1967 (29 USCS §§ 621 et seq.) held not to prohibit discrimination against younger covered employees in favor of older covered employees.

SUMMARY

The Age Discrimination in Employment Act of 1967 (ADEA) (29 USCS §§ 621 et seq.) protects employees who are at least 40 years old. The ADEA's general antidiscrimination provision (29 USCS § 623(a)(1)) prohibits "discriminat[ion] . . . because of such individual's age."

A collective-bargaining agreement between an employer and a labor union eliminated the employer's obligation to provide health benefits to subsequently retired employees, other than then-current workers who were at least 50 years old. Some employees who were at least 40, but under 50, years old claimed, before the Equal Employment Opportunity Commission (EEOC), that the agreement violated the ADEA by discriminating against the employees because of their age. The EEOC agreed with the employees and invited the employer and the union to settle informally with the employees.

When the employer and union failed to settle, the employees brought an action against the employer under the ADEA and state law. The United States District Court for the Northern District of Ohio, relying on a decision by the United States Court of Appeals for the Seventh Circuit that the ADEA did not protect younger workers against discrimination in favor of older workers, dismissed the case (98 F Supp 2d 846).

The United States Court of Appeals for the Sixth Circuit reversed, reasoning that § 623(a)(1)'s prohibition of discrimination was so clear on its face that if Congress had meant to limit the prohibition's coverage to protect only the older worker against the younger, then Congress would have said so (296 F3d 466).

On certiorari, the United States Supreme Court reversed. In an opinion by SOUTER, J., joined by REHNQUIST, Ch. J., and STEVENS, O'CONNOR, GINSBURG, and BREYER, JJ., it was held that:

(1) The ADEA did not prohibit favoring the old over the young, as the text, structure, purpose, and history of the ADEA, along with its relationship to other federal statutes, showed that the statute did not mean to stop an employer from favoring an older employee over a younger one.

(2) An EEOC regulation (29 CFR § 1625.2(a))—providing that if two people applied for the same position, and one was 42 years old and the other 52, then the employer could not lawfully turn down either one on the basis of age—was clearly wrong.

SCALIA, J., dissenting, expressed the view that the court should have deferred to the EEOC's authoritative conclusion in the regulation, because (1) § 623(a) did

67

not unambiguously require a different interpretation, and (2) the regulation was an entirely reasonable interpretation of the ADEA's text.

THOMAS, J., joined by KENNEDY, J., dissenting, expressed the view that (1) the plain language of § 623(a)(1) mandated that the employees were able to sue for discrimination against them in favor of older workers; (2) the EEOC—the agency charged with enforcing the ADEA—had adopted a regulation and issued an opinion as an adjudicator, both of which had adopted this natural interpretation of § 623(a)(1); (3) the only portion of legislative history relevant to the question before the court was consistent with this outcome; and (4) traditional tools of statutory interpretation led inexorably to the conclusion that the employees could state a claim of discrimination against the relatively young.

COUNSEL

Donald B. Verilli, Jr. argued the cause for petitioner.

Mark W. Biggerman argued the cause for respondents.

Paul D. Clement argued the cause for the United States, as amicus curiae, by special leave of court.

BUCK DOE, Petitioner

v

ELAINE L. CHAO, SECRETARY OF LABOR

540 US —, 157 L Ed 2d 1122, 124 S Ct 1204

[No. 02-1377]

Argued December 3, 2003.

Decided February 24, 2004.

Decision: Plaintiff, in seeking to recover from United States under Privacy Act provision (5 USCS § 552a(g)(4)(A)), held required to prove some "actual damages" in order to qualify for minimum statutory award of $1,000.

SUMMARY

The Privacy Act of 1974, as amended (5 USCS § 552a), generally (1) gives federal agencies detailed instructions for managing records, and (2) provides for various sorts of civil relief to aggrieved individuals. In 5 USCS § 552a(g)(1), the Privacy Act recognizes a civil action for agency misconduct fitting in any of four categories, including (1) 5 USCS § 552a(g)(1)(C), which describes an agency's failure to maintain an adequate record on an individual, when the result is a determination "adverse" to that individual; and (2) the catchall 5 USCS § 552a(g)(1)(D), which speaks of a violation when someone suffers an "adverse effect" from any other failure to hew to the terms of the Privacy Act. Moreover, 5 USCS § 552a(g)(4) provides that in any suit brought under §§ 552a(g)(1)(C) or 552a(g)(1)(D), in which suit "the court determines that the agency acted in a manner which was intentional or willful, the United States shall be liable to the individual in an amount equal to the sum of—(A) actual damages sustained by the individual as a result of the refusal or failure, but in no case shall a person entitled to recovery receive less than the sum of $1,000; and (B) the costs of the action together with reasonable attorney fees as determined by the court" (some line breaks omitted).

A claimant for certain benefits administered by the Office of Workers' Compensation Programs, a division of the United States Department of Labor, found that the Office then had a practice of using an applicant's Social Security number to identify the applicant's claim on "multicaptioned" hearing notices sent to groups of claimants, their employers, and the lawyers involved. The claimant and some others (1) filed a Federal District Court suit against the then United States Secretary of Labor, and (2) alleged violations of provisions including the Privacy Act. The Federal Government (1) conceded that the Office's practice had led to disclosure beyond the limits set by the Privacy Act; and (2) stipulated to an order prohibiting future publication of applicants' Social Security numbers on such notices. Subsequently, on cross-motions for summary judgment, the District Court denied class certification and entered judgment against all the individual plaintiffs except the claimant in question, as the court found that the others' submissions had raised no issues of cognizable harm. However, with respect to the claimant in question, the District Court (1) accepted his uncontroverted evidence of distress on learning of the improper disclosure, (2) granted him summary judgment, and (3) awarded $1,000 in statutory damages under § 552a(g)(4).

On appeal, the United States Court of Appeals for the Fourth Circuit, in reversing in pertinent part and in ordering a remand, expressed the view that the $1,000 minimum under § 552a(g)(4)(A) was available to only plaintiffs who suffered actual damages because of a federal agency violation (306 F3d 170).

On certiorari, the United States Supreme Court affirmed. In an opinion by SOUTER, J., joined by REHNQUIST, Ch. J., and O'CONNOR, KENNEDY, and THOMAS, JJ., and joined in pertinent part by SCALIA, J., it was held that:

(1) Section 552a(g)(4)(A) did not necessarily entitle any plaintiff, adversely affected by a covered intentional or willful Privacy Act violation, to the minimum statutory award of $1,000.

(2) Instead, such a plaintiff still had to prove some "actual damages" in order to qualify under § 552a(g)(4)(A) for the $1,000 minimum award to "a person entitled to recovery."

GINSBURG, J., joined by STEVENS and BREYER, JJ., dissenting, expressed the view that the words "a person entitled to recovery," as used in § 552a(g)(4)(A)'s remedial prescription, were most sensibly read to include anyone experiencing an "adverse effect" as a consequence of a federal agency's intentional or willful commission of a Privacy Act violation of the kind described in §§ 552a(g)(1)(C) or 552a(g)(1)(D).

BREYER, J., dissenting, expressed the view that the Privacy Act, if interpreted as in the opinion of GINSBURG, J., supra, would not be likely to produce massive recoveries that Congress would not have endorsed, because the lower courts had restrictively interpreted the "intentional or willful" phrase in § 552a(g)(4).

COUNSEL

Jack W. Campbell, IV argued the cause for petitioner. Malcolm L. Stewart argued the cause for respondent.

―――――――――

OLYMPIC AIRWAYS, Petitioner

v

RUBINA HUSAIN, individually and as personal representative of the ESTATE OF ABID M. HANSON, DECEASED, et al.

540 US —, 157 L Ed 2d 1146, 124 S Ct 1221, reh den (US) 158 L Ed 2d 527, 124 S Ct 2065

[No. 02-1348]

Argued November 12, 2003.
Decided February 24, 2004.

Decision: With respect to passenger with asthma who died on airplane, flight attendant's refusal to move passenger away from airplane's smoking section held to constitute "accident" within meaning of Warsaw Convention's Article 17.

SUMMARY

Under Article 17 of the Warsaw Convention (49 Stat 3000 et seq., later amended, USCS International Agreements) an air carrier may be liable for a passenger's death or bodily injury caused by an "accident" occurring on an international flight. In Air France v Saks (1985) 470 US 392, 84 L Ed 2d 289, 105 S Ct 1338, the United States Supreme Court held that the term "accident" in Article 17 refers to an unexpected or unusual event or happening that is external to the passenger.

On an airplane flight from Europe to the United States, a passenger with asthma was seated three rows in front of a smoking section. Before takeoff, the passenger's wife asked a flight attendant to move the passenger, but the flight attendant merely told the wife to "have a seat." After all the passengers had boarded, but prior to takeoff, the wife again asked the flight attendant to reseat the passenger, but the flight attendant refused to help. After takeoff, when the passenger became surrounded by ambient cigarette smoke, the passenger's wife made a third request to move the passenger. The flight attendant, once more refusing to help, (1) claimed that the plane was full, even though there were some unoccupied seats; and (2) said that the passenger could switch seats with another passenger, but without the flight crew's assistance. The passenger subsequently moved toward the front of the plane to get some fresher air, but he died after receiving medical assistance.

The passenger's wife and other family members—alleging that the passenger had died from a severe asthma attack caused by inhaling secondhand smoke—filed a wrongful-death suit against the airline in question in California's Superior Court for Alameda County. The suit was removed to the United States District Court for the Northern District of California. The District Court, in granting judgment for the plaintiffs, determined that (1) smoke exposure during the flight was the primary cause of the passenger's death, and (2) the flight attendant's refusal to reseat the passenger constituted an "accident" within the meaning of Article 17 (116 F Supp 2d 1121). The United States Court of Appeals for the Ninth Circuit affirmed (316 F3d 829).

On certiorari, the United States Supreme Court affirmed. In an opinion by THOMAS, J., joined by REHNQUIST, Ch. J., and STEVENS, KENNEDY, SOUTER, and GINSBURG, JJ., it was held that the flight attendant's refusal to move the passenger constituted an "accident" within the meaning of Article 17, for:

74

(1) The airline's focus on the airplane's ambient cigarette smoke as the injury-producing event was misplaced, notwithstanding that the presence of such ambient smoke might have been "normal" at the time of the flight in question, as the flight attendant's refusal to move the passenger (a) was also a factual event, and (b) was a link in the chain of causes that led to the passenger's death.

(2) The airline's argument that only affirmative acts are "event[s] or happening[s]" under the Air France v Saks test—and that therefore, the flight attendant's failure to act could not have constituted an "accident"—was unavailing, as the rejection of an explicit request for assistance would be an "event" or "happening" under the ordinary and usual definitions of these terms.

(3) It was not disputed that the flight attendant's conduct was "unexpected and unusual" under the Air France v Saks test.

SCALIA, J., joined in pertinent part by O'CONNOR, J., dissenting, expressed the view that (1) the Supreme Court ought to have followed the holdings of two intermediate appellate courts of foreign countries that were Warsaw Convention signatories, to the effect that mere inaction cannot be an "accident" under Article 17; (2) the flight attendant's mere refusal to assist could not be a basis for Article 17 liability; (3) even if the flight attendant's insistence that the passenger remain seated before takeoff was an accident, it was not a proximate cause of the passenger's death; and (4) the case ought to have been remanded so that the District Court could consider in the first instance whether the flight attendant's misrepresentation about the plane's being full, independent of any failure to reseat, was an accident that caused the passenger's death.

BREYER, J., did not participate.

COUNSEL

Andrew J. Harakas argued the cause for petitioner.

H. Bartow Farr, III argued the cause for respondents.

Barbara B. McDowell argued the cause for the United States, as amicus curiae, by special leave of court.

DELMA BANKS, Jr., Petitioner

v

DOUG DRETKE, DIRECTOR, TEXAS DEPART-
MENT OF CRIMINAL JUSTICE, CORRECTIONAL
INSTITUTIONS DIVISION

540 US —, 157 L Ed 2d 1166, 124 S Ct 1256

[No. 02-8286]

Argued December 8, 2003.
Decided February 24, 2004.

Decision: Texas prisoner held entitled to federal habeas
corpus relief from his state death sentence, on
basis of due process claim that prosecution had
concealed impeachment evidence that key prosecution witness had been paid police informant.

SUMMARY

In Brady v Maryland (1963) 373 US 83, 10 L Ed 2d
215, 83 S Ct 1194, the United States Supreme Court
held that under the due process clause of the Federal
Constitution's Fourteenth Amendment, the suppression of evidence favorable to an accused, upon request
by the accused, violates due process where the evidence
is material either to guilt or to punishment, irrespective
of the prosection's good faith or bad faith.

In 1980, prior to an accused's Texas capital murder
trial, the prosecution advised the accused's attorney
that the prosecution would "without the necessity of
motions[,] provide you with all discovery to which you
are entitled." Subsequently, the accused was convicted
of murder and sentenced to death.

After the accused failed to obtain relief on direct appeal and in two state postconviction proceedings, the accused, in a third state postconviction proceeding, included Brady claims concerning two key prosecution witnesses. As supporting evidence concerning the first witness, the accused attached an unsigned affidavit, from the first witness' then sister-in-law, which asserted that the first witness "was well-connected to law enforcement people." A state postconviction court rejected the accused's claims. This denial was upheld by the Texas Court of Criminal Appeals in a January 10, 1996, order.

On March 7, 1996—prior to the enactment of the Antiterrorism and Effective Death Penalty Act of 1996 (AEDPA) (110 Stat 1214), which made various federal habeas corpus changes—the accused filed a habeas corpus petition in the United States District Court for the Eastern District of Texas. This petition alleged a Brady claim, concerning the first witness, that the state denied. However, it was eventually disclosed— assertedly contrary to prior concealment or suppression by the state—that (1) the first witness had been a paid police informant; and (2) there was a pretrial transcript revealing that the second witness' trial testimony had been intensively coached by prosecutors and law-enforcement officers. In a report, a Magistrate Judge recommended that a writ of habeas corpus ought to issue with respect to the accused's death sentence—partly on the basis of the state's failure to disclose the first witness' informant status—but not with respect to the accused's conviction.

The District Court adopted the Magistrate Judge's report and denied a motion by the accused to amend the report. With respect to the second witness, the District Court (1) concluded that the accused had not properly pleaded a Brady claim predicated on the

78

withheld transcript; and (2) rejected the accused's argument that under Rule 15(b) of the Federal Rules of Civil Procedure—which the accused contended ought to apply—this second-witness Brady claim should have been treated as if raised in the pleadings. The accused then sought, and the District Court denied, a certificate of appealability on the second-witness question.

On appeal, the United States Court of Appeals for the Fifth Circuit (1) reversed the District Court's judgment to the extent that it had granted relief on the first-witness Brady claim, as the Court of Appeals expressed the view that in the third state postconviction proceeding, the accused had not endeavored to develop the facts underpinning this claim; and (2) for substantially the District Court's reasons, denied the accused a certificate of appealability on his second-witness Brady claim (judgment order reported at 48 Fed Appx 104, 2002 US Appx LEXIS 19381).

On certiorari, the Supreme Court reversed and remanded. In an opinion by GINSBURG, J., joined by REHNQUIST, Ch. J., and STEVENS, O'CONNOR, KENNEDY, SOUTER, and BREYER, JJ., as to holding 1 below, and expressing the unanimous view of the court as to holding 2 below, it was held that:

(1) Under the applicable federal habeas corpus regime that was in place prior to AEDPA, the accused was entitled to a writ of habeas corpus granting relief from his death sentence, on the basis of his Brady claim concerning the first witness, for among other factors:

(a) The relevant suppressed evidence—concerning the witness' paid-informant status—qualified as evidence advantageous to the accused.

(b) The accused had demonstrated both (i) cause for his failure to develop the facts in the third state postconviction proceeding, by demonstrating that the reason for his failure was the state's suppression of the relevant evidence; and (ii) actual prejudice resulting from his failure.

(c) This cause-and-prejudice demonstration established that the evidence (i) had been suppressed by the state, and (ii) was material for Brady purposes.

(2) The District Court and the Court of Appeals had erred in denying the accused a certificate of appealability on his second-witness Brady claim, at least with respect to the application of Rule 15(b) to federal habeas corpus review under pre-AEDPA law.

THOMAS, J., joined by SCALIA, J., concurring in part and dissenting in part, joined the court's holding 2 above, but expressed the view that the accused's Brady claim concerning the first witness did not warrant federal habeas corpus relief, because under Supreme Court precedent—although it was a "very close question"—the nondisclosure of the first witness' informant status had not been prejudicial to the accused.

COUNSEL

George H. Kendall argued the cause for petitioner.
Gena Bunn argued the cause for respondent.

GARY LOCKE, GOVERNOR OF WASHINGTON, et
al., Petitioners

v

JOSHUA DAVEY

540 US —, 158 L Ed 2d 1, 124 S Ct 1307

[No. 02-1315]

Argued December 2, 2003.
Decided February 25, 2004.

Decision: Washington state's postsecondary-education
scholarship program, under which students were
not permitted to use scholarship to pursue degree
in devotional theology, held not to violate First
Amendment's free exercise clause.

SUMMARY

The state of Washington established a scholarship
program in order to assist students from low- and
middle-income families with the cost of postsecondary
education. In accordance with Washington's state
constitution—which included a provision that no public money or property was to be appropriated for or
applied to any religious worship, exercise, or
instruction—the scholarship program did not permit
students to use the scholarship to pursue "a degree in
theology."

A student who had been awarded a scholarship
under the program wished to pursue a degree in
pastoral ministries at a private, church-affiliated college. However, he was informed that to receive the
scholarship funds, he had to certify in writing that he
was not pursuing a degree in "devotional theology."

The student refused to so certify, and he did not receive any scholarship funds. The student then brought an action under 42 USCS § 1983 in the United States District Court for the Western District of Washington to enjoin the state from refusing to award the scholarship to a student solely because the student was pursuing a devotional-theology degree. The District Court granted summary judgment in favor of the state.

The United States Court of Appeals for the Ninth Circuit, in reversing the District Court's judgment, concluded that the denial of a scholarship to a student solely because the student decided to pursue a degree in theology from a religious perspective infringed the student's right to the free exercise of religion under the Federal Constitution's First Amendment, because (1) the state had singled out religion for unfavorable treatment, (2) the state's exclusion of theology majors thus had to be narrowly tailored to achieve a compelling state interest, and (3) the state's concerns as to the establishment of religion were not compelling (299 F3d 748).

On certiorari, the United States Supreme Court reversed. In an opinion by REHNQUIST, CH. J., joined by STEVENS, O'CONNOR, KENNEDY, SOUTER, GINSBURG, and BREYER, JJ., it was held that the scholarship program's exclusion with respect to students pursuing a degree in devotional theology did not violate the First Amendment's free exercise clause, for:

(1) The scholarship program was not presumptively unconstitutional.

(2) It was not true that because the scholarship program funded training for all secular professions, the state had to fund training for religious professions.

(3) There was nothing in the history or text of the relevant provision of the state constitution, or in the

operation of the scholarship program, that suggested animus towards religion.

(4) The state's interest in not funding the pursuit of devotional degrees was substantial.

(5) The exclusion of such funding placed a relatively minor burden on scholarship recipients.

SCALIA, J., joined by THOMAS, J., dissenting, expressed the view that (1) when a state makes a public benefit generally available, that benefit becomes part of the baseline against which burdens on religion are measured; (2) when the state withholds that benefit from some individuals solely on the basis of religion, the state violates the free exercise clause; and (3) in the case at hand, (a) no field of study but religion was singled out for disfavor, and (b) the student was seeking not a special benefit to which others were not entitled, but only the right to direct his scholarship to his chosen course of study, a right that every other scholarship recipient enjoyed.

THOMAS, J., dissenting, expressed the view that (1) the study of theology did not necessarily implicate religious devotion or faith; and (2) on the assumption that the state of Washington denied scholarships to only students who pursued a degree in devotional theology, the dissenting opinion of SCALIA, J., was correct in the case at hand.

COUNSEL

Narda Pierce argued the cause for petitioners.

Jay A. Sekulow argued the cause for respondent.

Theodore B. Olson argued the cause for the United States, as amicus curiae, by special leave of court.

UNITED STATES POSTAL SERVICE, Petitioner

v

FLAMINGO INDUSTRIES (USA) LTD. et al.

540 US —, 158 L Ed 2d 19, 124 S Ct 1321

[No. 02-1290]

Argued December 1, 2003.
Decided February 25, 2004.

Decision: United States Postal Service held not to be "person" subject to antitrust liability under Sherman Act (15 USCS §§ 1 et seq.).

SUMMARY

After a private corporation's contract to make mail sacks for the United States Postal Service was terminated, the corporation brought a suit alleging, among other matters, that the Postal Service had sought to suppress competition and create a monopoly in mail-sack production. The United States District Court for the Northern District of California, in dismissing the antitrust claims, concluded that the Postal Service was not subject to liability under federal antitrust law.

The United States Court of Appeals for the Ninth Circuit, in reversing, concluded that the Postal Service could be liable, but had a limited immunity from antitrust liability for conduct undertaken at Congress' command (302 F3d 985).

On certiorari, the United States Supreme Court reversed. In an opinion by KENNEDY, J., expressing the unanimous view of the court, it was held that the Postal Service was not a "person" subject to antitrust liability under the Sherman Act (15 USCS §§ 1 et seq.), as:
84

(1) While, in the Postal Reorganization Act (39 USCS §§ 101 et seq.), Congress had generally waived the Postal Service's sovereign immunity from suit, Congress had not stripped the Postal Service of its governmental status.

(2) A federal entity's absence of immunity did not result in liability if the substantive law in question was not intended to reach the entity.

(3) The Sherman Act, the Supreme Court's decisions interpreting it, and the statutes that had created and organized the Postal Service led to the conclusion that the Postal Service was not subject to antitrust liability.

COUNSEL

Edwin S. Kneedler argued the cause for petitioner.

Harold J. Krent argued the cause for respondents.

SHAKUR MUHAMMAD, aka JOHN E. MEASE, Petitioner

v

MARK CLOSE

540 US —, 158 L Ed 2d 32, 124 S Ct 1303

[No. 02-9065]

Argued December 1, 2003.
Decided February 25, 2004.

Decision: Favorable-termination requirement for bringing some 42 USCS § 1983 damages actions held not applicable to case at hand, where Michigan prisoner's challenge had been found to threaten no consequence to his conviction or to duration of his sentence.

SUMMARY

With respect to state prisoners, federal law opens two main avenues to relief on complaints related to imprisonment: (1) a habeas corpus petition under 28 USCS § 2254, and (2) a civil rights complaint under 42 USCS § 1983. In Heck v Humphrey (1994) 512 US 477, 129 L Ed 2d 383, 114 S Ct 2364, the United States Supreme Court held that where success in a state prisoner's § 1983 damages action would implicitly question the validity of the prisoner's conviction or the duration of the prisoner's sentence, the prisoner first had to achieve favorable termination of the prisoner's available state opportunities, or the prisoner's federal habeas corpus opportunities, in order to challenge the underlying conviction or sentence.

A Michigan state prisoner brought a § 1983 action in the United States District Court for the Eastern District of Michigan against a prison official. As amended, the prisoner's complaint alleged that (1) the official had charged the prisoner with threatening behavior—and thus had subjected the prisoner to mandatory prehearing detention—in asserted retaliation for prior lawsuits and grievance proceedings by the prisoner; and (2) at the eventual hearing, the prisoner had been (a) acquitted of the threatening-behavior charge, and (b) found guilty of only the lesser infraction of insolence. The prisoner did not seek expungement of the misconduct finding of insolence. Instead, the only relief sought was $10,000 in compensatory and punitive damages for the physical, mental, and emotional injuries allegedly sustained by the prisoner during his 6 days of prehearing detention.

Following discovery, a Magistrate Judge recommended summary judgment for the official. While the Magistrate Judge found or assumed that no good-time credits for the prisoner had been eliminated by the prehearing action which the prisoner had called in question, the Magistrate Judge expressed the view that the prisoner had failed to come forward with sufficient evidence of retaliation to raise a genuine issue of material fact as to that element. The District Court adopted the Magistrate Judge's recommendation.

The United States Court of Appeals for the Sixth Circuit, in affirming on other grounds, expressed the view that under the circumstances, the prisoner's § 1983 action was barred by Heck v Humphrey (47 Fed Appx 738, 2002 US App LEXIS 20306).

On certiorari, the United States Supreme Court reversed and remanded. In a per curiam opinion expressing the unanimous view of the court, it was held that the favorable-termination requirement of Heck v

Humphrey did not apply where, as in the case at hand, the prisoner's challenge had been found to threaten no consequence to the prisoner's conviction or the duration of the prisoner's sentence.

COUNSEL

Corinne Beckwith argued the cause for petitioner. Thomas L. Casey argued the cause for respondent.

———————

RAYMOND B. YATES, M.D., P.C. PROFIT SHARING
PLAN, and RAYMOND B. YATES, trustee, Petitioners

v

WILLIAM T. HENDON, trustee

541 US —, 158 L Ed 2d 40, 124 S Ct 1330

[No. 02-458]

Argued January 13, 2004.
Decided March 2, 2004.

Decision: Working owner of business held to qualify as
"participant" in ERISA-covered pension plan if
plan covers one or more employees other than
owner or owner's spouse.

SUMMARY

Title I of the Employee Retirement Income Security
Act of 1974 (ERISA), as amended (29 USCS §§ 1001 et
seq.), (1) in 29 USCS § 1002(3), defines an ERISA-
covered "employee benefit plan" as an employee welfare benefit plan or an employee pension benefit plan
or both; (2) in 29 USCS § 1002(7), defines a plan
"participant" as any employee eligible to receive a
benefit from an employee benefit plan; (3) in 29 USCS
§ 1002(6), defines an "employee" as any individual
employed by an employer; and (4) in 29 USCS
§ 1002(5), defines an "employer" to include any person acting as an employer, or in the interest of an
employer.

From the inception of a professional corporation's
profit-sharing plan, at least one person other than one
individual—who was the corporation's sole shareholder
and president—and the individual's wife was a partici-

89

pant in the plan, which contained an anti-alienation provision that, except for loans to participants, no benefit or interest available under the plan would be subject to assignment or alienation. The president borrowed money from another of his corporation's pension plans (which later merged into the plan in question), but failed for several years to make any of the required monthly payments, until he repaid the loan in full with the proceeds of the sale of his house. Three weeks after the loan repayment, the president's creditors filed an involuntary petition against him under Chapter 7 of the Bankruptcy Code (11 USCS §§ 701 et seq.).

A Bankruptcy Court, determining that the repayment qualified as a preferential transfer under 11 USCS § 547(b), granted the bankruptcy trustee's request to avoid the loan repayment. The United States District Court for the Eastern District of Tennessee affirmed.

The United States Court of Appeals for the Sixth Circuit, in affirming on the basis of the view that the president was not a "participant" in the plan for ERISA purposes, obviated the question whether, had the president qualified as such a participant, his loan repayment would have been shielded from the trustee's reach (287 F3d 521).

On certiorari, the United States Supreme Court reversed and remanded. In an opinion by GINSBURG, J., joined by REHNQUIST, Ch. J., and STEVENS, O'CONNOR, KENNEDY, SOUTER, and BREYER, JJ., it was held that under an ERISA-covered pension plan, the working owner of business might rank as an "employee" as well as an "employer," and thus qualified as a "participant" who might participate on equal terms with other plan participants, if the plan covered one or more employees other than the owner or the owner's spouse, as:

(1) ERISA's text contained multiple indications that

90

Congress intended working owners to qualify as plan participants.

(2) Congress' aim of the creation of plans that would benefit employers and nonowner employees alike was advanced by this reading of ERISA's text.

(3) Excepting working owners from the ERISA's coverage would have generated administrative difficulties and was hardly consistent with a national uniformity goal.

(4) A 1999 United States Department of Labor advisory opinion had concluded that working owners might qualify as participants in ERISA-covered plans.

SCALIA, J., concurring in the judgment, expressed the view that (1) in the case at hand, the Solicitor General of the United States, in a brief signed by the Acting Solicitor of Labor, had put forward the Department of Labor's official view that working owners (including sole owners, such as the president in the case at hand) could be plan participants under ERISA; but (2) the court's approach deprived administrative agencies of the power (a) to resolve statutory questions promptly and with nationwide effect, and (2) within the reasonable bounds of the text, to change the application of ambiguous laws as time and experience dictated.

THOMAS, J., concurring in the judgment, (1) agreed that the judgment of the Court of Appeals should have been reversed; but (2) expressed the view that (a) ERISA's text was inconclusive, (b) the Supreme Court should have turned to the common-law understanding of the term "employee," and (c) on remand, the Court of Appeals should have been directed to address whether the common-law understanding of the term "employee," as used in ERISA, included the president.

91

COUNSEL

James A. Holifield, Jr. argued the cause for petitioners.

Matthew D. Roberts argued the cause for the United States, as amicus curiae, by special leave of court.

C. Mark Troutman argued the cause for respondent.

_____

GEORGE H. BALDWIN, Petitioner

v

MICHAEL REESE

541 US —, 158 L Ed 2d 64, 124 S Ct 1347

[No. 02-964]

Argued December 8, 2003.
Decided March 2, 2004.

Decision: For purposes of federal habeas corpus requirement of exhausting state remedies, state prisoner held, ordinarily, not to have fairly presented
federal-law claim to state court if it had to read
beyond uninformative petition, brief, or similar
document.

SUMMARY

For purposes of the requirement, under 28 USCS
§ 2254(b)(1), that a state prisoner must exhaust available state remedies before seeking federal habeas corpus relief, the United States Supreme Court has held
that such a prisoner must fairly present a federal-law
claim in each appropriate state court (including a state
supreme court with powers of discretionary review),
thereby alerting that court to the federal nature of the
claim.

An accused was convicted, in an Oregon state court,
on charges of kidnapping and attempted sodomy. After
the accused was unsuccessful on direct appeal, lower
state courts denied him collateral relief. The accused
then petitioned for discretionary review in the Oregon
Supreme Court. This petition asserted, among other
matters, that the accused had received "ineffective

93

assistance of both trial court and appellate court counsel." While the petition alleged that trial counsel's conduct had violated several provisions of the Federal Constitution, the petition did not explicitly say that its appellate-assistance words referred to a federal-law claim. The Oregon Supreme Court denied review.

Subsequently, the accused (1) sought habeas corpus relief in the United States District Court for the District of Oregon, and (2) included a federal-law claim of ineffective assistance of appellate counsel. However, the District Court, in denying the accused relief, ruled that the accused had not fairly presented his appellate-assistance claim to the higher state courts.

The United States Court of Appeals for the Ninth Circuit, in reversing and in ordering a remand, expressed the view that the accused had satisfied the "fair presentation" requirement, on the basis that (1) the justices of the Oregon Supreme Court had had the opportunity to read the lower-state-court decision claimed to be in error; and (2) if the justices had done so, then they would, or should, have realized that the accused's appellate-assistance claim rested upon federal law (282 F3d 1184).

On certiorari, the United States Supreme Court reversed. In an opinion by BREYER, J., joined by REHNQUIST, Ch. J., and O'CONNOR, SCALIA, KENNEDY, SOUTER, THOMAS, and BREYER, JJ., it was held that for the federal habeas corpus purposes of § 2254(b)(1)'s exhaustion requirement:

(1) Ordinarily, a state prisoner does not fairly present a federal-law claim to a state court if the court must read beyond a petition, brief, or similar document which does not alert the court to the presence of the federal-law claim, in order to find material (such as a lower-state-court opinion in the case) that would provide such an alert.

(2) In the case at hand, the accused had failed to meet the "fair presentation" standard with respect to his federal-law claim of ineffective assistance of appellate counsel, for it was appropriate to assume that the accused's petition for discretionary review, had not, by the petition itself, properly alerted the Oregon Supreme Court to the federal nature of this claim.

STEVENS, J., dissenting, expressed the view that (1) in the case at hand, the accused had satisfactorily demonstrated that there was no significant difference between (a) an ineffective-assistance-of-appellate-counsel claim predicated on the Oregon constitution, and (b) one based on federal law; and (2) therefore, the state's courts had had a fair opportunity to assess the accused's federal-law claim.

COUNSEL

Hardy Myers argued the cause for petitioner.
Dennis Balske argued the cause for respondent.

MICHAEL D. CRAWFORD, Petitioner

v

WASHINGTON

541 US —, 158 L Ed 2d 177, 124 S Ct 1354

[No. 02-9410]

Argued November 10, 2003.
Decided March 8, 2004.

Decision: Playing, at accused's trial, of tape-recorded statement in which accused's wife—who did not testify at trial—had described accused's stabbing of victim to police, held to violate confrontation clause of Federal Constitution's Sixth Amendment.

SUMMARY

In Ohio v Roberts (1980) 448 US 56, 65 L Ed 2d 597, 100 S Ct 2531, the United States Supreme Court held that (1) a defendant's right, under the Federal Constitution's Sixth Amendment, to be confronted by the witnesses against the defendant did not bar admission, at a criminal trial, of an unavailable witness' statement against the defendant if the statement bore adequate indicia of reliability; and (2) to meet this test, evidence had to (a) fall within a firmly rooted hearsay exception, or (b) bear particularized guarantees of trustworthiness.

At a trial, in a Washington state court, for assault and attempted murder, the court allowed the state to play for the jury a tape-recorded statement in which the accused's wife—who, because of the state marital privilege that generally barred one spouse from testifying against the other without the other's consent, did not testify at trial—during police interrogation, had described the accused's stabbing of the victim. The trial court concluded that the accused's Sixth Amendment right to be confronted with the witnesses against him did not bar admission of the statement, because the statement bore particularized guarantees of trustworthiness.

The jury convicted the accused of assault. The Washington Court of Appeals, determining that the wife's statement did not bear particularized guarantees of trustworthiness, reversed (107 Wash App 1025). However, the Washington Supreme Court (1) concluded that the statement was reliable because it was nearly identical to—that is, interlocked with—the accused's own statement to the police; and (2) reinstated the conviction (147 Wash 2d 424, 54 P3d 656).

On certiorari, the United States Supreme Court reversed and remanded. In an opinion by SCALIA, J., joined by STEVENS, KENNEDY, SOUTER, THOMAS, GINSBURG, and BREYER, JJ., overruling Ohio v Roberts, supra, it was held that the playing, at the accused's trial, of the wife's tape-recorded statement violated the accused's Sixth Amendment right to be confronted by the witnesses against him, as (1) where testimonial evidence was at issue, the Sixth Amendment demanded unavailability and a prior opportunity for cross-examination; and (2) the state's admission of the wife's testimonial statement against the accused, despite the fact that he had had no opportunity to cross-examine her, alone was sufficient to make out a violation of the Sixth Amendment.

REHNQUIST, Ch. J., joined by O'CONNOR, J., concurring in the judgment, expressed the view that in the case at hand (1) the judgment followed inexorably from Ohio v Roberts and its progeny without any need for overruling that line of cases; and (2) Ohio v Roberts should not be overruled.

COUNSEL

Jeffrey L. Fisher argued the cause for petitioner.

Michael R. Dreeben argued the cause for the United States, as amicus curiae, by special leave of court.

Steven C. Sherman argued the cause for respondent.

IOWA, Petitioner

v

FELIPE EDGARDO TOVAR

541 US —, 158 L Ed 2d 209, 124 S Ct 1379

[No. 02-1541]

Argued January 21, 2004.
Decided March 8, 2004.

Decision: Trial court held not required by Federal Constitution's Sixth Amendment to warn accused that waiving right to counsel at plea hearing (1) entails risk that viable defense will be overlooked, and (2) deprives accused of independent opinion as to whether to plead guilty.

SUMMARY

At a 1996 arraignment in Iowa's District Court for Story County, an accused affirmed that he wanted to represent himself and to plead guilty to a charge of operating a motor vehicle while intoxicated (OWI). The District Court, in conducting a guilty-plea colloquy required by the Iowa rules of criminal procedure, (1) cautioned the accused that by pleading guilty, the accused would give up his right to a trial and his right to be represented by counsel at that trial; and (2) informed the accused of (a) the maximum and minimum penalties for an OWI conviction, and (b) the elements of an OWI charge. The District Court accepted the accused's guilty plea and subsequently imposed the minimum sentence of 2 days in jail and a fine.

In 1998, the accused pleaded guilty to a charge of second-offense OWI. In 2000, when the accused was charged with third-offense OWI in Iowa's District Court for Johnson County, the accused pleaded not guilty and sought to preclude the use of the 1996 OWI conviction to enhance his 2000 offense from an aggravated misdemeanor to a felony. The accused alleged that his 1996 waiver of counsel had not been fully knowing, intelligent, and voluntary—and had thus been invalid under the Federal Constitution's Sixth Amendment—because he had not been made aware of the dangers and disadvantages of self-representation. However, the accused was found guilty and was sentenced on the OWI third-offense charge. The Court of Appeals of Iowa affirmed (2002 Iowa App LEXIS 644).

The Supreme Court of Iowa—in vacating the Court of Appeals' decision, reversing the judgment of the District Court for Johnson County, and ordering a remand—concluded that the accused's 1996 guilty-plea colloquy had been inadequate for Sixth Amendment purposes, as the accused had not been given specific admonitions to the effect that waiving counsel's assistance in deciding whether to plead guilty (1) entailed the risk that a viable defense would be overlooked; and (2) deprived the accused of the opportunity to obtain an independent opinion on whether, under the facts and applicable law, it was wise to plead guilty (656 NW2d 112).

On certiorari, the United States Supreme Court reversed and remanded. In an opinion by GINSBURG, J., expressing the unanimous view of the court, it was held that:

(1) With respect to an accused who does not have the assistance of counsel at a plea hearing, the Sixth Amendment is satisfied when the trial court, before accepting a guilty plea, informs the accused of (a) the

100

nature of the charges against the accused, (b) the accused's right to be counseled regarding the plea, and (c) the range of allowable punishments attendant upon the entry of a guilty plea.

(2) The Sixth Amendment does not require the trial court to give the two specific admonitions at issue.

COUNSEL

Thomas J. Miller argued the cause for petitioner.

Malcolm L. Stewart argued the cause for the United States, as amicus curiae, by special leave of court.

Theresa R. Wilson argued the cause for respondent.

SOUTH FLORIDA WATER MANAGEMENT DIS-
TRICT, Petitioner

v

MICCOSUKEE TRIBE OF INDIANS et al.

541 US —, 158 L Ed 2d 264, 124 S Ct 1537, reh den
(US) 158 L Ed 2d 758, 124 S Ct 2198

[No. 02-626]

Argued January 14, 2004.
Decided March 23, 2004.

Decision: For purposes of Clean Water Act requirement
of permit for discharge of pollutant into nation's
waters, such discharges held to include point
sources that did not themselves generate pollutants.

SUMMARY

The Clean Water Act (33 USCS §§ 1251 et seq.) (1)
in 33 USCS § 1311(a), prohibited "the discharge of any
pollutant by any person" unless done in compliance
with some provision of the Act; (2) in 33 USCS § 1342,
established the National Pollutant Discharge Elimination System (NPDES), which generally required dis-
chargers to obtain permits that limited the type and
quantity of pollutants that could be released into the
nation's waters; (3) in 33 USCS § 1362(12), defined
"discharge of a pollutant" to mean "any addition of
any pollutant to navigable waters from any point
source;" and (4) in 33 USCS § 1362(14), defined
"point source" as "any discernible, confined and dis-

crete conveyance," such as a pipe, ditch, channel, or tunnel, "from which pollutants are or may be discharged."

An Indian tribe and an environmental organization brought, against a Florida water-management agency under the Act, a citizen suit contending that the agency was required to obtain a discharge permit under the NPDES for the agency's pumping of already polluted water—to which the pumping added no pollutants—from a canal into a reservoir.

The United States District Court for the Southern District of Florida granted the tribe's summary-judgment motion. The United States Court of Appeals for the Eleventh Circuit affirmed (280 F3d 1364).

On certiorari, the United States Supreme Court vacated and remanded. In an opinion by O'CONNOR, J., expressing the unanimous view of the court as to holding 1 below, and joined by REHNQUIST, Ch. J., and STEVENS, KENNEDY, SOUTER, THOMAS, GINSBURG, and BREYER, JJ., as to holdings 2 and 3 below, it was held that for purposes of determining whether the pumping of the already polluted water constituted the discharge of a pollutant, so as to be prohibited without a discharge permit under the NPDES:

(1) The § 1362(12) definition of "discharge of a pollutant," by including "any addition of any pollutant to navigable waters from any point source," included point sources that did not themselves generate pollutants.

(2) The case would be remanded for further proceedings regarding factual questions as to whether the source and destination waters for the pumping were distinct water bodies, rather than two hydrologically indistinguishable parts of a single water body.

(3) Left open on remand would be a "unitary waters" argument, according to which permits were not re-

quired when water from one navigable water body was discharged unaltered into another navigable water body.

SCALIA, J., concurring in part and dissenting in part, (1) agreed that a point source was not exempt from NPDES permit requirements merely because the source did not itself add pollutants to the water that it pumped; but (2) expressed the view that the Court of Appeals' disposition of this issue—which addressed the question presented to the Supreme Court on certiorari—ought to be affirmed without reaching other issues.

COUNSEL

Timothy S. Bishop argued the cause for petitioner.

Jeffrey P. Minear argued the cause for the United States, as amicus curiae, by special leave of court.

Dexter W. Lehtinen argued the cause for respondents.

UNITED STATES, Petitioner

v

ABEL COSMO GALLETTI et al.

541 US —, 158 L Ed 2d 279, 124 S Ct 1548

[No. 02-1389]

Argued January 12, 2004.
Decided March 23, 2004.

Decision: United States held authorized to collect partnership's unpaid federal employment taxes, from individuals who had been general partners, in individuals' bankruptcy proceedings, where those taxes had been timely assessed against partnership.

SUMMARY

Generally, with respect to the assessment and collection of federal taxes, it is provided (1) in § 6501(a) of the Internal Revenue Code (26 USCS § 6501(a)), that "the amount of any tax imposed [by the Code] shall be assessed within 3 years after the return was filed"; (2) in § 6203 of the Code (26 USCS § 6203), that "[t]he assessment shall be made by recording the liability of the taxpayer in the office of the Secretary [of the Treasury] in accordance with rules or regulations prescribed by the Secretary"; and (3) in § 6502(a) of the Code (26 USCS § 6502(a)), that if the tax is properly assessed within 3 years, then the limitations period for collection of the tax is extended by 10 years from the date of the assessment.

In addition, § 3402(a)(1) of Code (26 USCS § 3402(a)(1)) requires "every employer making pay-

105

ment of wages" to deduct and withhold employment taxes. Also, § 3403 of the Code (26 USCS § 3403) provides that "[t]he employer shall be liable for the payment of the tax required to be deducted and withheld."

A particular partnership failed to pay significant federal employment-tax liabilities from 1992 to 1995. Under the law of the pertinent state—California—(1) the partnership maintained a separate identity from its general partners; and (2) with some conditions, the general partners were liable for any debt of the partnership. Several individuals, who had been general partners in the partnership, filed petitions for relief, under Chapter 13 of the Bankruptcy Code (11 USCS §§ 1301 et seq.), in 1999 and 2000. The Internal Revenue Service (IRS) filed proofs of claim in these proceedings, for some amounts based on the partnerships' unpaid employment taxes for the years in question. It was not disputed that the IRS had timely assessed those taxes against the partnership. However, the individuals argued that (1) the timely assessment of the partnership had extended the limitations period only against the partnership; and (2) in order to extend the limitations period against the individuals as general partners, the IRS would have had to have separately assessed the general partners within the 3-year limitations period, which the IRS had not done. A Bankruptcy Court and a Federal District Court agreed and sustained the individuals' objections to the IRS' claims.

The United States Court of Appeals for the Ninth Circuit consolidated the resulting appeals and affirmed on basically the same grounds (as amended with rehearing denied, 314 F3d 336).

On certiorari, the United States Supreme Court reversed and remanded. In an opinion by THOMAS, J., expressing the unanimous view of the court, it was held that:

(1) Under § 6501(a), the United States could properly collect the partnership's unpaid employment taxes from the individuals in judicial proceedings—such as the individuals' Chapter 13 proceedings—where the proceedings occurred within § 6502(a)'s 10-year extension that had attached when the employment taxes had been timely assessed against the partnership.

(2) In such circumstances, the United States, in order to obtain § 6502(a)'s extension, had not been required to assess these employment taxes, in addition, separately against each such individual, as among other factors:

(a) For purposes of applying § 6203 with reference to the underlying employment-taxes liability, the liable taxpayer had been the partnership as the employer.

(b) The Federal Government was not required to make separate assessments of a single tax debt against persons or entities secondarily liable for that debt, in order for § 6502(a)'s extended limitations period to apply to those persons or entities.

COUNSEL

Kent L. Jones argued the cause for petitioner.

David R. Haberbush argued the cause for respondents.

JEREMIAH W. (JAY) NIXON, ATTORNEY GENERAL
OF MISSOURI, Petitioner

v

MISSOURI MUNICIPAL LEAGUE et al. (No. 02-
1238)

FEDERAL COMMUNICATIONS COMMISSION and
UNITED STATES, Petitioners

v

MISSOURI MUNICIPAL LEAGUE et al. (No. 02-
1386)

SOUTHWESTERN BELL TELEPHONE, L. P., fka
SOUTHWESTERN BELL TELEPHONE COMPANY,
Petitioner

v

MISSOURI MUNICIPAL LEAGUE et al. (No. 02-
1405)

541 US —, 158 L Ed 2d 291, 124 S Ct 1555

Argued January 12, 2004.
Decided March 24, 2004.

Decision: Authorization, in 47 USCS § 253, of federal
pre-emption of state and local laws prohibiting
ability of "any entity" to provide telecommunications services held not to include entities that were
state subdivisions.

SUMMARY

The Telecommunications Act of 1996 (1) in 47 USCS
§ 253(a), provided that no state or local law could
"prohibit or have the effect of prohibiting the ability of

any entity to provide any interstate or intrastate telecommunications service," and (2) in 47 USCS
§ 253(d), generally authorized the Federal Communications Commission (FCC) to pre-empt enforcement of
any law that violated § 253(a).

After Missouri enacted a statute forbidding the state's
political subdivisions to provide a telecommunications
service or facility, some entities including municipally
owned utilities sought from the FCC an order declaring
the state statute unlawful under 47 USCS § 253. The
FCC, in refusing to declare the state statute pre-
empted, (1) adverted to the principle of Gregory v
Ashcroft (1991) 501 US 452, 115 L Ed 2d 410, 111 S Ct
2395, that Congress needed to be clear before it
constrained traditional state authority to order the
state's government; and (2) concluded that, in
§ 253(a), "any entity" (a) applied to only independent
entities that were subject to state regulation, and (b)
thus, did not include state political subdivisions.

The United States Court of Appeals for the Eighth
Circuit (1) reversed, and (2) said that the word "entity," especially when modified by "any" in § 253(a),
manifested sufficiently clear congressional attention to
governmental entities to satisfy Gregory v Ashcroft (299
F3d 949).

On certiorari, the United States Supreme Court
reversed. In an opinion by SOUTER, J., joined by REH-
NQUIST, Ch. J., and O'CONNOR, KENNEDY, GINSBURG,
and BREYER, JJ., it was held that § 253 did not include,
in "any entity," a state's own subdivisions—and, therefore, § 253 did not affect the power of states and
localities to restrict their own (or their political inferi-
ors') delivery of such services, as:

(1) When a government regulated itself (or a subdivision through which it acted) there was no clear distinction between the regulator and the entity regulated.

(2) Section 253 would not work like a normal pre-emptive statute if § 253 applied to a governmental unit. (3) Section 253(a) was hardly forthright enough to satisfy the principle of Gregory v Ashcrof that Congress needed to be clear before it constrained traditional state authority to order the state's government.

SCALIA, J., joined by THOMAS, J., concurring in the judgment, expressed the view that the Court of Appeals' judgment ought to be reversed on the ground that § 253(a) did not provide the clear statement that would have been required by Gregory v Ashcroft for a federal statute to limit the power of states to restrict the delivery of telecommunications services by their political subdivisions.

STEVENS, J., dissenting, expressed the view that (1) it was manifestly implausible that, when drafting § 253, Congress (a) was unaware that municipally-owned utilities existed, or (b) had deliberately ignored their existence; and (2) there was every reason to believe that, in referring to "any entity" in § 253, Congress meant precisely what it said.

COUNSEL

James A. Feldman argued the cause for federal petitioners in No. 02-1386, and for petitioner in No. 02-1405.

Ronald Molteni argued the cause for state petitioner in No. 02-1238.

David A. Strauss argued the cause for respondents.

UNITED STATES, Petitioner

v

MANUEL FLORES-MONTANO

541 US —, 158 L Ed 2d 311, 124 S Ct 1582

[No. 02-1794]

Argued February 25, 2004.
Decided March 30, 2004.

Decision: Federal Government's authority, under Federal Constitution's Fourth Amendment, to conduct suspicionless inspections at international border held to include authority to remove, disassemble, and reassemble motor vehicle's fuel tank.

SUMMARY

An individual, while driving a station wagon, attempted to enter the United States at an international-border port of entry in southern California. A United States customs inspector conducted an inspection of the station wagon and requested the individual to leave the vehicle.

The station wagon was then taken to a secondary inspection station, where another inspector and a mechanic (1) disassembled the gas tank; (2) found inside a substantial amount of marijuana, which was seized; and (3) reassembled the gas tank. The entire process, including some time to wait for the mechanic to arrive, reportedly took about an hour.

A federal grand jury indicted the individual on some federal drug charges. The individual—relying on a United States Court of Appeals for the Ninth Circuit precedent to the effect that the removal of a gas tank required reasonable suspicion, in order to be consistent with the Federal Constitution's Fourth Amendment—filed a motion to suppress the marijuana recovered from the station wagon's gas tank. When the Federal Government advised the United States District Court for the Southern District of California that the government was not relying on reasonable suspicion as a basis for opposing the motion—as the government believed that the Court of Appeals precedent had been wrongly decided—the District Court relied on this precedent and granted the suppression motion. In turn, the Court of Appeals, citing the same precedent, summarily affirmed the District Court's judgment.

On certiorari, the United States Supreme Court reversed and remanded. In an opinion by REHNQUIST, Ch. J., expressing the unanimous view of the court, it was held that:

(1) In view of the Federal Government's "paramount" interest in protecting the nation's borders, the Federal Government's authority, under the Fourth Amendment, to conduct suspicionless inspections at the international border included the authority to remove, disassemble, and reassemble a motor vehicle's fuel tank.

(2) While some searches of property might be so destructive as to require a different result, the search in question was not one of them.

BREYER, J., concurring, expressed the view that an existing administrative process—which kept track of border searches, including the reasons for the searches—ought to help minimize concerns that gas-tank searches might be undertaken in an abusive manner.

112

COUNSEL

Lisa S. Blatt argued the cause for petitioner.

Steven F. Hubachek argued the cause for respondent.

NATIONAL ARCHIVES AND RECORDS ADMINIS-
TRATION, Petitioner

v

ALLAN J. FAVISH et al.

541 US —, 158 L Ed 2d 319, 124 S Ct 1570, reh den
(US) 158 L Ed 2d 759, 124 S Ct 2198

[No. 02-954]

Argued December 3, 2003.
Decided March 30, 2004.

Decision: Four official-investigation photographs showing person's death scene held exempted from
public disclosure by Freedom of Information Act
provision (5 USCS § 552(b)(7)(C)) exempting
law-enforcement records if production could reasonably be expected to constitute unwarranted
invasion of personal privacy.

SUMMARY

The Freedom of Information Act, as amended
(FOIA) (5 USCS § 552), generally provides for the
public disclosure of federal agency records upon request. However, such disclosure is subject to some
specific FOIA exemptions, including Exemption 7(C)
(5 USCS § 552(b)(7)(C)), which shields from disclosure "records or information compiled for law enforcement purposes" if production "could reasonably be
expected to constitute an unwarranted invasion of
personal privacy."

After the death of a person who had been deputy
counsel to the then President of the United States, five
114

different government investigations, by agencies or officials including two independent counsels, reached the same conclusion, that the person's death had been a suicide. An individual who remained skeptical about this conclusion filed a FOIA request with the Office of Independent Counsel (OIC), which refused the request. The individual then filed a suit, in the United States District Court for the Southern District of California, that sought to compel the production of, among other items, 10 photographs showing the person's death scene, including the person's body or part of it. However, some members of the deceased person's family objected to the photographs' disclosure. Initially, the District Court upheld the OIC's claim of FOIA exemption with respect to these photographs, as the court expressed the view that the privacy interests of the family members outweighed the public interest in the photographs' disclosure.

On appeal, the United States Court of Appeals for the Ninth Circuit, in reversing and remanding, (1) agreed that Exemption 7(C) recognized the family members' right to personal privacy; but (2) expressed the view that (a) FOIA did not condition disclosure on a requesting party's showing that the party had knowledge of misfeasance by an investigating agency, and (b) in the case at hand, the individual had tendered evidence and argument which, if believed, would justify his doubts; and (3) ordered the District Court (a) to examine the photographs in chambers, and (b) consistent with the Court of Appeals' opinion, to balance (i) the effect of the photographs' release on the family members' privacy, against (ii) the public benefit to be obtained by release (217 F3d 1168).

On remand, the District Court ordered the release of five photographs. On a second appeal, the Court of Appeals affirmed in part, as the Court of Appeals, without providing an explanation, effectively upheld the release of four of these five photographs (37 Fed Appx 863).

After the United States Supreme Court granted certiorari (538 US 1012, 155 L Ed 2d 847, 123 S Ct 1928), OIC terminated its operations and transferred its records—including the photographs in dispute—to the National Archives and Records Administration (NARA).

The Supreme Court—substituting NARA as the certiorari petitioner in the case's caption—then reversed and remanded, with instructions effectively to grant summary judgment against the requesting individual with respect to these four photographs. In an opinion by KENNEDY, J., expressing the unanimous view of the court, it was held that Exemption 7(C) exempted the four photographs from disclosure under FOIA, as:

(1) The members of the deceased person's family, in objecting to the photographs' disclosure, had a personal privacy interest, recognized by FOIA under Exemption 7(C), with respect to these death-scene images of the members' close relative.

(2) This privacy interest outweighed the public interest in the photographs' disclosure, so that such disclosure could reasonably be expected to constitute an unwarranted invasion of personal privacy, where—after the five different government inquiries had reached the same conclusion of suicide—the individual requesting disclosure had not produced any evidence that would warrant a belief by a reasonable person that an alleged government impropriety in investigating the death might have occurred.

116

COUNSEL

Patricia A. Millett argued the cause for petitioner.

James Hamilton argued the cause for respondents Shelia Foster Anthony and Lisa Foster Moody in support of petitioner.

Allan J. Favish argued the cause for respondent Allan J. Favish.

———————————

BEDROC LIMITED, LLC, and WESTERN ELITE,
INC., Petitioners

v

UNITED STATES et al.

541 US —, 158 L Ed 2d 338, 124 S Ct 1587

[No. 02-1593]

Argued January 20, 2004.
Decided March 31, 2004.

Decision: Sand and gravel held not to be "valuable
minerals" for purposes of Pittman Act (43 USCS
§§ 351 et seq., later repealed), which required
some land patents to reserve to United States all
coal and other valuable minerals in land in question.

SUMMARY

The Pittman Underground Water Act of 1919 (Pittman Act) (former 43 USCS §§ 351 et seq.) made some
persons eligible to be granted land patents in Nevada.
Under a Pittman Act provision, each such patent was
required to contain a reservation to the United States
of "all the coal and other valuable minerals" in the
land in question. Although the Pittman Act was repealed in 1964, the rights of existing patentees were
reserved.

In 1993, an individual acquired some land in Nevada
that had been granted to the individual's predecessors
in interest under the Pittman Act. After the individual
began extracting sand and gravel from the land, the
United States Department of the Interior's Bureau of
Land Management (1) served him with trespass no-

tices, and (2) ultimately ruled that the individual had trespassed against the Federal Government's reserved interest in the land's "valuable minerals." The Interior Board of Land Appeals affirmed (140 IBLA 295).

A corporation which acquired the land in question in 1995 filed an action, in the United States District Court for the District of Nevada, that sought to quiet title to the land's sand and gravel. However, the District Court, in granting summary judgment to the United States, concluded that the sand and gravel were "valuable minerals" for purposes of the Pittman Act (50 F Supp 2d 1001). The United States Court of Appeals for the Ninth Circuit affirmed (314 F3d 1080).

On certiorari, the United States Supreme Court reversed and remanded. Although unable to agree on an opinion, six members of the court agreed that the sand and gravel had not been reserved to the United States under the Pittman Act.

REHNQUIST, Ch. J., announced the judgment of the court and, in an opinion joined by O'CONNOR, SCALIA, and KENNEDY, J., expressed the view that (1) the word "valuable" in the Pittman Act made clear that Congress did not intend to include sand and gravel in the mineral reservation, for when the Pittman Act became law in 1919, sand and gravel (a) were commercially worthless in Nevada, and (b) could not have constituted a "valuable mineral deposit" within the meaning of the General Mining Act (30 USCS § 22); and (2) the Pittman Act's statutory structure reinforced the unambiguous meaning of the term "valuable minerals."

THOMAS, J., joined by BREYER, J., concurring in the judgment, expressed the view that (1) the Pittman Act's mineral reservation could not be meaningfully distinguished from a provision of the Stock-Raising Homestead Act of 1916 (SRHA) (43 USCS § 291, later repealed), which reserved to the United States "all the coal and other minerals" in some public lands; and (2) the mineral reservations of the Pittman Act and the SRHA did not include sand and gravel.

STEVENS, J., joined by SOUTER and GINSBURG, JJ., dissenting, expressed the view that (1) the Supreme Court ought to have followed Watt v Western Nuclear, Inc. (1983) 462 US 36, 76 L Ed 2d 400, 103 S Ct 2218, which held that gravel found on lands patented under the SRHA was a mineral reserved to the United States; and (2) the Pittman Act's text and legislative history indicated that Congress intended the scope of the mineral reservations in the Pittman Act and the SRHA to be identical.

COUNSEL

R. Timothy McCrum argued the cause for petitioners.

Thomas L. Sansonetti argued the cause for respondents.

UNITED STATES, Petitioner

v

BILLY JO LARA

541 US —, 158 L Ed 2d 420, 124 S Ct 1628

[No. 03-107]

Argued January 21, 2004.
Decided April 19, 2004.

Decision: Congress held authorized to permit Indian tribes, as exercise of inherent authority, to prosecute nonmember Indians; nonmember's subsequent federal prosecution held not barred by double jeopardy clause of Federal Constitution's Fifth Amendment.

SUMMARY

In 1990, the United States Supreme Court held that an Indian tribe lacked sovereign authority to prosecute Indians who were not members of that tribe. However, Congress subsequently amended a provision of the Indian Civil Rights Act of 1968 (25 USCS § 1301(2)) so as to recognize the "inherent power" of Indian tribes to exercise criminal jurisdiction over "all Indians."

A member of the Turtle Mountain Band of Chippewa Indians was married to a member of the Spirit Lake Tribe and lived on the Spirit Lake Reservation in North Dakota. When federal police officers came to the reservation to arrest the Band member for alleged public intoxication, the Band member struck one of the officers. The Band member pleaded guilty in the Spirit Lake Tribal Court to a charge of "violence to a

121

policeman"—a violation of the Spirit Lake tribal code—and served 90 days in jail for that crime.

In the United States District Court for the District of North Dakota, the Federal Government subsequently charged the Band member with the crime of assaulting a federal officer in alleged violation of 18 USCS § 111(a)(1). The Band member moved to dismiss the indictment as assertedly violative of the double jeopardy clause of the Federal Constitution's Fifth Amendment, but the District Court denied the motion (2001 US Dist LEXIS 20182).

A panel of the United States Court of Appeals for the Eighth Circuit affirmed (294 F3d 1004). However, on rehearing in banc, the Court of Appeals reversed and ordered a remand, on the grounds that (1) the Tribal Court, in prosecuting the Band member, had exercised a federal prosecutorial power pursuant to § 1301(2), rather than the Tribal Court's own inherent tribal authority; (2) the "dual sovereignty" doctrine—to the effect that the double jeopardy clause did not bar successive prosecutions brought by separate sovereigns—did not apply to the case at hand; and (3) the second prosecution therefore violated the double jeopardy clause (324 F3d 635).

On certiorari, the United States Supreme Court reversed. In an opinion by BREYER, J., joined by REHNQUIST, Ch. J., and STEVENS, O'CONNOR, and GINSBURG, JJ., it was held that:

(1) The Constitution authorized Congress to permit Indian tribes, as an exercise of inherent tribal authority, to prosecute nonmember Indians.

(2) Congress had exercised such authority in amending § 1301(2).

(3) The Spirit Lake Tribe's prosecution of the Band member thus did not amount to an exercise of federal

power; rather, the Tribe had acted in the capacity of a separate sovereign.

(4) Consequently, the double jeopardy clause did not prohibit the Federal Government from proceeding with the prosecution for a discrete federal offense.

STEVENS, J., concurring, expressed the view that there was nothing exceptional in the conclusion that Congress was permitted to relax restrictions on an ancient inherent Indian tribal power, given the fact that Congress was also permitted to authorize the states to exercise—as their own—inherent powers that the Constitution had otherwise placed off limits.

KENNEDY, J., concurring in the judgment, expressed the view that (1) the Band member's first prosecution was not a delegated federal prosecution, and thus his double-jeopardy argument had to fail; but (2) it was doubtful that the Constitution authorized Congress to permit tribes, as an exercise of inherent tribal authority, to prosecute nonmember Indians.

THOMAS, J., concurring in the judgment, expressed the view that (1) the Tribe had acted as a separate sovereign in prosecuting the Band member; and (2) accordingly, the double jeopardy clause did not bar the subsequent federal prosecution; but (3) the outcome of the case at hand was dictated by two largely incompatible and doubtful assumptions—which had to be accepted as the case came to the Supreme Court—namely, that (a) Congress could regulate virtually every aspect of the tribes without rendering tribal sovereignty a nullity, and (b) the Indian tribes retained inherent sovereignty to enforce their criminal laws against their own members.

SOUTER, J., joined by SCALIA, J., dissenting, expressed the view that (1) Congress could not reinvest tribal

123

courts with inherent criminal jurisdiction over non-member Indians; (2) any tribal exercise of criminal jurisdiction over nonmembers necessarily rested on a delegation of federal power; and (3) a tribe's exercise of this delegated power barred subsequent federal prosecution for the same offense.

COUNSEL

Edwin S. Kneedler argued the cause for petitioner.

Alexander F. Reichert argued the cause for respondent.

HOUSEHOLD CREDIT SERVICES, INC. and MBNA
AMERICA BANK, N. A., Petitioners

v

SHARON R. PFENNIG

541 US —, 158 L Ed 2d 450, 124 S Ct 1741

[No. 02-857]

Argued February 23, 2004.
Decided April 21, 2004.

Decision: Federal Reserve Board's Regulation Z—in specifically excluding (in 12 CFR § 226.4(c)(2)) fees imposed for exceeding credit limit from definition of disclosure term "finance charge"—held to provide binding interpretation of Truth in Lending Act (15 USCS §§ 1601 et seq.).

SUMMARY

The Truth in Lending Act (TILA) (15 USCS §§ 1601 et seq.), among other matters, (1) in 15 USCS § 1637(a), regulated the substance and form of disclosures that creditors offering "open end consumer credit plans" (a term that included credit-card accounts) had to make to consumers; (2) in 15 USCS § 1637(b), required a creditor, with respect to such an open-end plan, to provide a periodic billing statement which included the "amount of any finance charge added to the account during the period"; (3) in 15 USCS § 1605(a), defined a "finance charge" as an amount "payable directly or indirectly by the person to whom the credit is extended, and imposed directly or indirectly by the creditor as an incident to the extension of credit"; and (4) in 15 USCS § 1640, provided a civil remedy for consumers who suffered damages as a result of a creditor's failure to comply with TILA's provisions.

In addition, in 15 USCS § 1604(a), TILA gave the Federal Reserve Board regulatory authority "to effectuate the purposes of [TILA], to prevent circumvention or evasion thereof, or to facilitate compliance therewith." Among other provisions, the Board's Regulation Z, in 12 CFR § 226.4(c)(2), specifically excluded fees imposed for exceeding a credit limit ("over-limit fees") from the definition of the disclosure term "finance charge."

A credit-card holder (1) filed, in the United District Court for the Southern District of Ohio, a purported class action; and (2) claimed that the defendants—the initial issuer of her card and another company which had later acquired an interest—had violated TILA by failing properly to disclose over-limit fees as alleged "finance charges." However, the District Court, on the basis of the Regulation Z exclusion, granted the defendants' motion to dismiss.

On appeal, the United States Court of Appeals for the Sixth Circuit, in reversing in part and in ordering a remand, expressed the view that Regulation Z's exclusion of over-limit fees from the definition of "finance charge" was invalid, as conflicting with § 1605(a)'s "plain" language (as amended, 295 F3d 522, 2002 FED App 219A). The Court of Appeals also denied rehearing (2002 US App LEXIS 18716).

On certiorari, the United States Supreme Court reversed. In an opinion by THOMAS, J., expressing the unanimous view of the court, it was held that Regulation Z—in specifically excluding over-limit fees from the definition of "finance charge"—provided a reasonable interpretation of § 1605(a)'s definition of "finance charge" that was binding on the courts, for:

(1) Section 1605(a) was ambiguous as to whether the term "finance charge" included such over-limit fees, where neither § 1605(a) nor its surrounding provisions provided a clear answer.

(2) The Board had accomplished all of the objectives which Congress had established—in delegating, in § 1604(a), regulatory authority to the Board—by setting forth a clear, easy-to-apply, and easy-to-enforce rule that highlighted the charges which the Board had determined to be most relevant to a consumer's credit decisions.

COUNSEL

Seth P. Waxman argued the cause for petitioners.

Barbara B. McDowell argued the cause for the United States, as amicus curiae, by special leave of court.

Sylvia A. Goldsmith argued the cause for respondent.

ENGINE MANUFACTURERS ASSOCIATION and
WESTERN STATES PETROLEUM ASSOCIATION,
Petitioners

v

SOUTH COAST AIR QUALITY MANAGEMENT DIS-
TRICT et al.

541 US —, 158 L Ed 2d 529, 124 S Ct 1756

[No. 02-1343]

Argued January 14, 2004.
Decided April 28, 2004.

Decision: California subdivision's rules, imposing emission requirements on motor vehicles purchased or
leased by public and private fleet operators, held
not to escape pre-emption under § 209(a) of Clean
Air Act (42 USCS § 7543(a)).

SUMMARY

An air-quality management district—a political subdivision of California that was responsible for air pollution control in counties that included the Los Angeles
metropolitan area—enacted six rules that generally
prohibited various public and private fleet operators
from purchasing or leasing motor vehicles that did not
comply with emission requirements described in the
rules. An engine manufacturers association brought,
against the management district and its officials, a suit
alleging that the fleet rules were pre-empted by § 209 of
the Clean Air Act (42 USCS § 7543), which, in § 209(a)
(42 USCS § 7543(a)), generally prohibited states and
their political subdivision from adopting or attempting

to enforce "any standard" relating to the control of emissions from new motor vehicles or new motor vehicle engines.

However, the United States District Court for the Central District of California (1) concluded that the fleet rules were not "standard[s]" under § 209(a), because the rules regulated only the purchase of vehicles that were otherwise certified for sale in California; and (2) granted summary judgment to the management district and its employees (158 F Supp 2d 1107). The United States Court of Appeals for the Ninth Circuit affirmed on the basis of the District Court's reasoning (309 F3d 550).

On certiorari, the United States Supreme Court vacated and remanded. In an opinion by SCALIA, J., joined by REHNQUIST, Ch. J., and STEVENS, O'CONNOR, KENNEDY, THOMAS, GINSBURG, and BREYER, JJ., it was held that the fleet rules did not, because they addressed the purchase rather than manufacture or sale of vehicles, escape pre-emption under § 209(a), as, among other matters:

(1) Currently, as in 1967 when § 209(a) became law, "standard" was defined in a dictionary as that which was "established by authority, custom, or general consent, as a model or example; criterion; test."

(2) To define "standard" as limited to a production mandate that required manufacturers to ensure that the vehicles they produced had particular emissions characteristics would confuse standards with the means of enforcing standards.

(3) Treating sales restrictions and purchase restrictions differently for pre-emption purposes would make no sense.

(4) It was impossible to find in the language of § 209(a) an exception for standards imposed through purchase restrictions.

SOUTER, J., dissenting, expressed the view that § 209(a) had no pre-emptive application to the fleet rules, as (1) in all pre-emption cases, and particularly in those where Congress had legislated in a field that the states had traditionally occupied, analysis was to start with the assumption that the historic police powers of the states were not to be superseded by the federal statute in question unless that was the clear and manifest purpose of Congress; and (2) legislative history showed that Congress' purpose in passing § 209(a) was to stop states from imposing regulatory requirements that directly limited what manufacturers could sell.

COUNSEL

Carter G. Phillips argued the cause for petitioners.

Theodore B. Olson argued the cause for the United States, as amicus curiae, by special leave of court.

Seth P. Waxman argued the cause for respondents.

RICHARD VIETH, NORMA JEAN VIETH, and SU-
SAN FUREY, APPELLANTS

v

ROBERT C. JUBELIRER, PRESIDENT OF THE
PENNSYLVANIA SENATE, et al.

541 US —, 158 L Ed 2d 546, 124 S Ct 1769

[No. 02-1580]

Argued December 10, 2003.
Decided April 28, 2004.

Decision: With respect to some voters' claims that
Pennsylvania's reapportionment plan for congressional election districts was unconstitutional political gerrymander, adjudication of these claims held
inappropriate.

SUMMARY

In Davis v Bandemer (1986) 478 US 109, 92 L Ed 2d
85, 106 S Ct 2797, which involved Indiana's state
legislative districts, the United States Supreme Court
held that "political gerrymandering" claims were justiciable, but could not agree upon a standard to adjudi-
cate such claims.

Following the 2000 census, the Pennsylvania state
legislature had to redraw the state's congressional
election districts. At the time in question, the Republican Party controlled a majority of both houses of
Pennsylvania's legislature and held the governor's office. Prominent national figures in the Republican
Party allegedly pressured the legislature to adopt a
redistricting plan that would favor that party. The
legislature's plan was signed into law in 2002.

Some registered Pennsylvania voters who were members of the Democratic Party, seeking to enjoin implementation of the plan, brought suit under 42 USCS § 1983 in the United States District Court for the Middle District of Pennsylvania against the state and various state officers. The complaint alleged, among other things, that the plan (1) created malapportioned districts in violation of the one-person, one-vote requirement of Article I, § 2, of the Federal Constitution; and (2) constituted a political gerrymander in violation of Article I and the equal protection clause of the Constitution's Fourteenth Amendment.

A three-judge panel of the District Court dismissed the political-gerrymandering claim (188 F Supp 2d 532), but decided in favor of the plaintiffs on the apportionment claim (195 F Supp 2d 672). Subsequently, the legislature enacted a revised redistricting plan, but the plaintiffs challenged this plan as well. The District Court—in denying the plaintiffs' motion to impose remedial districts—(1) concluded that the revised plan's districts were not malapportioned; and (2) rejected the political-gerrymandering claim, on the grounds that the plaintiffs (a) had not alleged facts indicating that they had been shut out of the political process, and (b) thus could not establish an actual discriminatory effect on themselves (241 F Supp 2d 478). The plaintiffs appealed with respect to the political-gerrymandering claim.

On appeal, the Supreme Court affirmed. Although unable to agree on an opinion, five members of the court agreed that the political-gerrymandering claim ought not to be adjudicated.

SCALIA, J., announced the judgment of the court and, in an opinion joined by REHNQUIST, Ch. J., and O'CONNOR and THOMAS, JJ., expressed the view that (1) political-gerrymandering claims under Article I,

132

§§ 2 and 4, and the equal protection clause were nonjusticiable, as no judicially discernible and manageable standards for adjudicating such claims existed; (2) in particular, the Davis v Bandemer plurality's standard—under which a political-gerrymandering claim could succeed only where plaintiffs showed both intentional discrimination against an identifiable political group and an actual discriminatory effect on that group—had proved unmanageable in application; and (3) Davis v Bandemer ought to be overruled.

KENNEDY, J., concurring in the judgment, expressed the view that (1) the plaintiffs' political-gerrymandering complaint had to be dismissed, as two obstacles to the adjudication of political-gerrymandering claims—(a) a lack of comprehensive and neutral principles for drawing electoral boundaries, and (b) the absence of rules to limit and confine judicial intervention—had not been overcome; but (2) not all possibility of judicial relief ought to be foreclosed in political-gerrymandering cases, as a limited and precise rationale might yet be found to correct an established constitutional violation in some such cases.

STEVENS, J., dissenting, expressed the view that the allegations of one of the plaintiffs were sufficient to establish that (1) the plaintiff had standing to challenge the constitutionality of the plaintiff's particular district; (2) such a district-specific claim was not foreclosed by the Davis v Bandemer plurality's rejection of a statewide claim of political gerrymandering; and (3) the plaintiff—in alleging that a purpose to discriminate against a political minority was (a) the predominant motive of the legislators who designed the plaintiff's district, and (b) the sole justification for that district's bizarre shape—had stated a claim that, at least with respect to the plaintiff's district, Pennsylvania's redistricting plan violated equal-protection principles.

SOUTER, J., joined by GINSBURG, J., dissenting, expressed the view that (1) political gerrymandering was a justiciable issue; (2) in order to challenge a particular district, a plaintiff initially would have to show that (a) the plaintiff was a member of a cohesive political group, (b) the plaintiff's district paid little or no heed to traditional districting principles, (c) there were specific correlations between the district's deviations from traditional districting principles and the distribution of the population of the plaintiff's group, (d) there was a hypothetical district, including the plaintiff's residence, that would remedy the "packing" or "cracking" of the plaintiff's group and would deviate less from traditional districting principles, and (e) the defendants acted intentionally to manipulate the district's shape in order to pack or crack the plaintiff's group; and (3) when such showings were made, the burden would shift to the defendants to justify the district by reference to objectives other than naked partisan advantage.

BREYER, J., dissenting, expressed the view that (1) a legislature's use of political boundary-drawing considerations ordinarily would not violate the equal protection clause; but (2) the risk of harm to "basic democratic principle" would be extreme enough to be unconstitutional, where (a) there was a demonstrated risk of entrenchment in power of a political party that the voters had rejected, (b) partisan considerations rendered traditional district-drawing compromises irrelevant, and (c) no justification other than party advantage could be found; and (3) in the case at hand, there was a strong likelihood that the complaint could have been amended to assert circumstances consistent with those appropriate for judicial intervention.

134

COUNSEL

Paul M. Smith argued the cause for appellants.

John P. Krill, Jr. argued the cause for appellee Jubelirer.

J. Bart DeLone argued the cause for appellees Cortes and Accurti.

EDITH JONES et al., on behalf of herself and a class
of others similarly situated, Petitioners

v

R. R. DONNELLEY & SONS COMPANY

541 US —, 158 L Ed 2d 645, 124 S Ct 1836

[No. 02-1205]

Argued February 24, 2004.
Decided May 3, 2004.

Decision: Former employees' claims, arising under
1991 amendment to 42 USCS § 1981, for hostile
work environment, wrongful termination, and failure to transfer held governed by 28 USCS
§ 1658(a)'s 4-year statute of limitations.

SUMMARY

By enacting 28 USCS § 1658(a), Congress provided a
catchall 4-year statute of limitations for actions arising
under federal statutes enacted after December 1, 1990,
that do not include a limitations provision. Actions
arising under federal statutes enacted on or before
December 1, 1990, that do not include a limitations
provision are governed by the most appropriate or
analogous state statute of limitations.

On November 26, 1994, some former employees
filed a class action in the United States District Court
for the Northern District of Illinois against their former
employer, alleging violations of their rights to make and
enforce contracts under 42 USCS § 1981, as amended
by the Civil Rights Act of 1991 (PL 102-166). Specifically, the employees alleged that they had been subjected to a racially hostile work environment, given an
136

inferior employee status, and wrongfully terminated or denied a transfer in connection with the closing of the employer's Chicago plant. The employer sought summary judgment on the ground that the employees' claims were barred by Illinois' 2-year personal injury statute of limitations.

The employees responded that their claims were governed by the 4-year statute of limitations provided by 28 USCS § 1658(a), since, although 42 USCS § 1981 was enacted before December 1, 1990, their actions could not have been maintained prior to amendment of § 1981 by the Civil Rights Act of 1991. Before the 1991 amendment, the United States Supreme Court had held that § 1981 did not protect against harassing conduct that occurred after the formation of a contract, but the 1991 Act overturned that holding by adding a provision (§ 1981(b)) that defined the term "make and enforce contacts" to include the termination of contracts and the enjoyment of all benefits, privileges, terms, and conditions of the contractual relationship.

The District Court concluded that the employees' claims arose under the 1991 Act, not under § 1981 as originally enacted, and therefore were subject to § 1658(a)'s 4-year statute of limitations (149 F Supp 2d 459).

On appeal, the United States Court of Appeals for the Seventh Circuit reversed, expressing the view that (1) § 1658(a) applies only when an act of Congress creates a wholly new cause of action, one that does not depend on the continued existence of a statutory cause of action previously enacted and kept in force by the amendment; and (2) the 1991 amendment did not satisfy this test, because the text of § 1981(b) could not stand on its own, but merely redefined a term in the original statute without altering the text that provided the basic right of recovery for an individual whose constitutional rights had been violated (305 F3d 717).

On certiorari, the Supreme Court reversed and remanded. In an opinion by STEVENS, J., expressing the unanimous view of the court, it was held that (1) the 1991 Act fully qualified as an act of Congress enacted after December 1, 1990, within the meaning of § 1658(a); and (2) because the employees' hostile work environment, wrongful termination, and failure-to-transfer claims did not allege a violation of the pre-December 1, 1990 version of § 1981 but did allege violations of the amended statute, those claims (a) arose under the amendment to § 1981 contained in the 1991 Act, and (b) were thus governed by § 1658(a)'s 4-year statute of limitations.

COUNSEL

H. Candace Gorman argued the cause for petitioners.

Gregory G. Garre argued the cause for the United States, as amicus curiae, by special leave of court.

Carter G. Phillips argued the cause for respondent.

Kevin C. Newsom argued the cause for Alabama, et al., as amici curiae, by special leave of court.

DOUG DRETKE, DIRECTOR, TEXAS DEPART-
MENT OF CRIMINAL JUSTICE, CORRECTIONAL
INSTITUTIONS DIVISION, Petitioner

v

MICHAEL WAYNE HALEY

541 US —, 158 L Ed 2d 659, 124 S Ct 1847

[No. 02-1824]

Argued March 2, 2004.
Decided May 3, 2004.

Decision: Federal habeas corpus question not decided
as to whether, for purpose of excusing state-court
procedural default, "actual innocence" exception
was applicable to noncapital sentencing; case remanded for consideration of "significant" claim of
ineffective assistance of counsel.

SUMMARY

When a state prisoner's federal constitutional claim
has been procedurally defaulted in state court, a federal
court generally will not entertain the claim in a subsequent habeas corpus petition by the prisoner under 28
USCS § 2254, unless the prisoner can demonstrate
cause and prejudice to excuse the default. However, the
United States Supreme Court has recognized an exception to this cause-and-prejudice requirement, in certain
situations involving "actual innocence" of (1) the
underlying offense, or (2) the aggravating factors used
in capital sentencing.

An accused was found guilty on a Texas charge of
felony theft. While this offense otherwise would have
been punishable by a maximum of 2 years in prison, the

accused also was convicted, in a separate penalty hearing, on a habitual-felony-offender charge. As a result, the accused received an enhanced prison sentence of 16¹/₂ years. This habitual-felony-offender enhancement occurred even though (1) the accused's assertedly "second previous" felony conviction did not qualify, by 3 days, under the state's law; and (2) while one of the pertinent records showed this 3-day discrepancy, neither the prosecutor, nor the defense attorney, nor the witness tendered by the state to authenticate the records, nor the trial judge, nor the jury had noticed the 3-day discrepancy. Subsequently, during the accused's unsuccessful direct appeal, appellate counsel also did not mention the 3-day discrepancy.

The accused thereafter sought state postconviction relief. For the first time, the accused argued that because of the timing discrepancy, he had been ineligible for the habitual-offender enhancement. However, a state habeas corpus court (1) refused to consider the merits of this claim, on the basis that the accused had not raised it, as required by state procedural law, either at trial or on direct appeal; and (2) rejected the accused's related claim that his counsel had provided ineffective assistance by failing to object to, or to appeal, the enhancement. The Texas Court of Criminal Appeals summarily denied the accused's state habeas corpus application.

Subsequently, the accused (1) filed a federal habeas corpus application, under § 2254, in the United States District Court for the Eastern District of Texas; and (2) included (a) a sufficiency-of-the-evidence claim alleging a violation of federal constitutional due process, on the basis of the habitual-offender timing discrepancy, and (b) a related claim of ineffective assistance of counsel. While the state conceded that "the enhancement paragraphs as alleged in the indictment" had not

140

satisfied state law, the state argued that the accused had procedurally defaulted his sufficiency-of-the-evidence claim. The accused's application was referred to a Magistrate Judge, who (1) recommended excusing the procedural default and granting the sufficiency-of-the-evidence claim, on the basis that the accused was "actually innocent" of the sentence; and (2) did not address the ineffective-assistance claim. The District Court adopted the Magistrate Judge's report, granted the application, and ordered the state to resentence the accused "without the improper enhancement."

The United States Court of Appeals for the Fifth Circuit, in affirming, expressed the view that (1) the actual-innocence exception applied to noncapital-sentencing procedures involving a career offender or habitual felony offender; (2) this exception had been satisfied in the case at hand; and (3) the accused was entitled to relief on the merits of his defaulted sufficiency-of-the-evidence claim (306 F3d 257).

On certiorari, the Supreme Court vacated and remanded. In an opinion by O'CONNOR, J., joined by REHNQUIST, Ch. J., and SCALIA, THOMAS, GINSBURG, and BREYER, JJ., it was held that:

(1) With respect to a state prisoner's attempts to excuse a prior state-court procedural default of a federal constitutional claim, when a federal court, in a habeas corpus case, is faced with allegations by the prisoner of "actual innocence," whether of the sentence or of the crime charged, the federal court must first address all nondefaulted claims for comparable relief and other grounds for cause to excuse the procedural default.

(2) Accordingly, in the case at hand, the Supreme Court declined to decide whether the actual-innocence exception was applicable to noncapital sentencing.

(3) Instead, the case would be remanded for consider-

ation of the accused's related ineffective-assistance claim, which a state official had conceded was viable and "significant."

STEVENS, J., joined by KENNEDY and SOUTER, JJ., dissenting, expressed the view that fundamental fairness ought to dictate the outcome of the case at hand, for (1) the accused had been denied due process because, as all parties agreed, there had been no factual basis for the accused's conviction as a habitual offender; (2) the accused had already served a sentence "far in excess" of the 2-year maximum that Texas law had otherwise authorized for the accused's crime; and (3) the Supreme Court's ruling (a) needlessly postponed final adjudication of the accused's claim, and (b) perversely prolonged the very injustice that the cause-and-prejudice standard was designed to prevent.

KENNEDY, J., dissenting, expressed the view that (1) while the case at hand might provide a convenient mechanism to vindicate an important legal principle, the accused had a greater interest in knowing that he would not be reincarcerated for a crime which he did not commit; and (2) it was not clear why the state had not exercised its power and performed its duty to vindicate that interest in the first place.

COUNSEL

R. Ted Cruz argued the cause for petitioner.

Matthew D. Roberts argued the cause for the United States, as amicus curiae, by special leave of court.

Eric M. Albritton argued the cause for respondent.

RANDALL C. SCARBOROUGH, Petitioner

v

ANTHONY J. PRINCIPI, SECRETARY OF VETERANS
AFFAIRS

541 US —, 158 L Ed 2d 674, 124 S Ct 1856

[No. 02-1657]

Argued February 23, 2004.
Decided May 3, 2004.

Decision: Amendment to attorneys'-fees application
under Equal Access to Justice Act provision (28
USCS § 2412(d)(1)(A)) held permissible, after
30-day filing period, to cure failure to allege that
government's position in underlying litigation
lacked substantial justification.

SUMMARY

A provision of the Equal Access to Justice Act (EAJA)
(28 USCS § 2412(d)(1)(A)), in authorizing the payment of attorneys' fees to a prevailing party in an action
against the United States, allows the Federal Government to defeat this entitlement by showing that the
government's position in the underlying litigation was
substantially justified. Another EAJA provision (28
USCS § 2412(d)(1)(B))—prescribing the timing and
content of an application for attorneys' fees—specifies,
among other matters, that the application must (1) be
filed within 30 days of final judgment in the action, and
(2) allege that the government's position was not
substantially justified.

In 1999, a United States Navy veteran prevailed
before the United States Court of Appeals for Veterans

Claims (CAVC) on a claim against the Federal Government's Department of Veterans Affairs for disability benefits. The claimant's counsel filed a timely EAJA application for attorneys' fees, but initially failed to include an allegation that the government's position had not been substantially justified. After the 30-day fee-application filing period had expired, counsel filed an amended application adding the no-substantial-justification allegation. The CAVC, in granting the government's motion to dismiss the application, concluded that the CAVC lacked subject-matter jurisdiction to award attorneys' fees, because of counsel's failure to make the required allegation within the 30-day filing period (13 Vet App 530, 2000 US App Vet Claims LEXIS 515).

The United States Court of Appeals for the Federal Circuit affirmed (273 F3d 1087). However, the United States Supreme Court granted certiorari, vacated, and remanded in light of Edelman v Lynchburg College (2002) 535 US 106, 152 L Ed 2d 188, 122 S Ct 1145, in which the Supreme Court had held that an Equal Employment Opportunity Commission regulation allowed a timely filed employment-discrimination charge to be amended, after the filing deadline had passed, so as to add a required but initially absent verification (536 US 920, 153 L Ed 2d 774, 122 S Ct 2584).

On remand, the Court of Appeals for the Federal Circuit once again affirmed the CAVC's decision, on the ground that the inclusion of a no-substantial-justification allegation in an EAJA attorneys'-fees application was a jurisdictional requirement (319 F3d 1346).

On certiorari, the Supreme Court reversed and remanded. In an opinion by GINBURG, J., joined by REHNQUIST, Ch. J., and STEVENS, O'CONNOR, KENNEDY, SOUTER, and BREYER, JJ., it was held that a prevailing party's timely application for attorneys' fees, pursuant to § 2412(d)(1)(A), could properly be amended, after the 30-day filing period, to cure an initial failure to include a no-substantial-justification allegation, for:

(1) The allegation did not serve an essential notice-giving function.

(2) Allowing the curative amendment would advance Congress's purpose, in enacting EAJA, to reduce the emphasis on the cost of potential litigation in a party's decision whether to challenge unjust governmental action.

(3) The relation-back doctrine, as codified in Rule 15(c) of the Federal Rules of Civil Procedure—permitting relation back of amendments to pleadings when the claim or defense asserted in the amended pleading arose out of the conduct, transaction, or occurrence set forth or attempted to be set forth in the original timely filed pleading—was applicable to an EAJA fee-application amendment.

(4) Section 2412(d)'s waiver of sovereign immunity from liability for fees was not conditioned on a fee applicant's meticulous compliance with each and every requirement of § 2412(d)(1)(B) within 30 days of final judgment.

(5) In the case at hand, it had not been argued that the government would be prejudiced if the prevailing party's allegation were permitted to relate back to the party's timely filed fee application.

(6) EAJA had a built-in check, in that § 2412(d)(1)(A) disallowed fees where special circumstances made an award unjust.

THOMAS, J., joined by SCALIA, J., dissenting, expressed the view that (1) the required no-substantial-justification allegation had to be made within the 30-day deadline; and (2) the relation-back doctrine ought not to apply to an EAJA fee-application amendment, for (a) there was no express allowance for relation back in EAJA, and (b) the sovereign-immunity canon thus ought to apply so as to construe strictly the scope of the government's waiver.

COUNSEL

Brian Wolfman argued the cause for petitioner.
Jeffrey P. Minear argued the cause for respondent.

JAY SHAWN JOHNSON, Petitioner

v

CALIFORNIA

541 US —, 158 L Ed 2d 696, 124 S Ct 1833

[No. 03-6539]

Argued March 30, 2004.
Decided May 3, 2004.

Decision: Case held to lack final state-court judgment required by 28 USCS § 1257 for Supreme Court jurisdiction, where intermediate court, in reversing conviction, had not determined whether accused's evidentiary and prosecutorial-misconduct claims would have independently supported reversal.

SUMMARY

After an accused was convicted, in the Superior Court of Costas County, California, of charges including murder, the Court of Appeal of California, First Appellate District, Division Two, (1) reversed the murder conviction on the basis of the Court of Appeal's view that the accused was entitled to relief under the jury-selection decision in Batson v Kentucky (1986) 476 US 79, 90 L Ed 2d 69, 106 S Ct 1712; and (2) although noting the accused's separate evidentiary and prosecutorial-misconduct claims, did not determine whether those claims would have independently supported reversal of the conviction (88 Cal App 4th 318, 105 Cal Rprt 2d 727). The Supreme Court of California, addressing only the Batson claim, (1) reversed on that ground; and (2) ordered a remand for further proceedings consistent with the court's opinion (30 Cal 4th 1302, 71 P3d 270, 1 Cal Rptr 3d 1).

On certiorari, the United States Supreme Court—after the case had been briefed and argued in the Supreme Court—dismissed for want of jurisdiction. In a per curiam opinion expressing the unanimous view of the court, it was held that the case lacked a final judgment or decree rendered by the highest court of a state in which a decision could have been had, as required by 28 USCS § 1257.

COUNSEL

Stephen B. Bedrick argued the cause for petitioner.
Seth K. Schalit argued the cause for respondent.

RAYMOND L. MIDDLETON, WARDEN, Petitioner

v

SALLY MARIE McNEIL

541 US —, 158 L Ed 2d 701, 124 S Ct 1830

[No. 03-1028]

Decided May 3, 2004.

Decision: California appellate court held not to have unreasonably applied federal law, for purposes of federal habeas corpus provision (28 USCS § 2254(d)(1)), in concluding that jury in murder case had not likely been misled as to "imperfect self-defense" doctrine.

SUMMARY

28 USCS § 2254(d)(1) generally provides that a federal court may grant habeas corpus relief to a state prisoner on a federal constitutional claim, if a state court's prior adjudication of the claim was contrary to, or involved an unreasonable application of, clearly established federal law, as determined by the United States Supreme Court.

The state of California charged an accused with murder, after she had killed her husband. Under the state's "imperfect self-defense" doctrine, a killer's unreasonable, but genuine, fear could reduce a crime from murder to voluntary manslaughter. At trial, the accused asserted—with conflicting prosecution and defense evidence on this issue—that (1) her husband had been abusive, and (2) she had killed him out of fear for her life. The trial judge, when instructing the jury concerning imperfect self-defense, several times used

149

phrases such as an "honest but unreasonable belief." However, the trial judge erred at one point, by adding the words "as a reasonable person" to an instruction on " 'imminent' peril." The accused was convicted of second-degree murder.

On appeal, the California Court of Appeal upheld the accused's conviction, even though the court acknowledged the jury-instruction error, as the court expressed the view that (1) when all of the jury instructions on voluntary manslaughter and imperfect self-defense were considered in their entirety, it was not reasonably likely that the jury would have misunderstood the requirements of the imperfect-self-defense component of voluntary manslaughter; and (2) the prosecutor, in arguing to the jury, had set forth the appropriate standard for imperfect self-defense.

Subsequently, the accused (1) filed a federal habeas corpus petition, and (2) included a claim to the effect that the erroneous jury instruction on imperfect self-defense had violated due process under the Federal Constitution. However, the United States District Court for the Southern District of California denied the petition.

On appeal, the United States Court of Appeals for the Ninth Circuit, in reversing and in ordering a remand, expressed the view that (1) in the context of the overall charge to the jury, the erroneous instruction on imperfect self-defense had deprived the accused of her federal constitutional right to an instruction on one of her defense theories; and (2) for purposes of § 2254(d)(1), the California Court of Appeal, in violation of clearly established Supreme Court law, had improperly (a) assumed that the jury had ignored this clear (but erroneous) instruction, and (b) relied upon the prosecutor's argument (344 F3d 988).

Granting certiorari—and granting a motion by the respondent accused for leave to proceed in forma pauperis—the Supreme Court reversed and remanded. In a per curiam opinion expressing the unanimous view of the Supreme Court, it was held that the Court of Appeals for the Ninth Circuit had failed to give appropriate deference, under § 2254(d)(1), to the California Court of Appeal's denial of relief to the accused on the jury-instruction claim, for:

(1) Given the multiple other instances (at least three) where the jury instructions had correctly said that the accused's belief could have been unreasonable, the state appellate court had not unreasonably applied federal law, when the state appellate court had found that there was no reasonable likelihood that the jury had been misled.

(2) The state appellate court's assumption that the prosecutor's argument to the jury had clarified the ambiguous jury instruction was particularly apt, where the prosecutor's argument had resolved an ambiguity in favor of the accused.

TENNESSEE STUDENT ASSISTANCE CORPORA-
TION, Petitioner

v

PAMELA L. HOOD

541 US —, 158 L Ed 2d 764, 124 S Ct 1905

[No. 02-1606]

Argued March 1, 2004.
Decided May 17, 2004.

Decision: Proceeding instituted by individual, in federal bankruptcy court, to determine dischargeability of her student-loan debt (pursuant to 11 USCS § 523(a)(8)) held not to be suit against state within meaning of Federal Constitution's Eleventh Amendment.

SUMMARY

With respect to bankruptcy proceedings, 11 USCS § 523(a)(8) provides that student-loan debts guaranteed by governmental units are not included in a federal bankruptcy court's general discharge order unless excepting the debt from the order would impose an "undue hardship" on the debtor. Also, in order to discharge such a student-loan debt, Rules 7001(6), 7003, and 7004 of the Federal Rules of Bankruptcy Procedure generally require (1) the filing by a debtor of an "adversary proceeding" against such a governmental unit; and (2) the service of a summons and a complaint.

An individual who had a student-loan debt filed a petition under Chapter 7 of the Bankruptcy Code (11 USCS §§ 701 et seq.) in the United States Bankruptcy

Court for the Western District of Tennessee. Although the individual received a general discharge, the individual had not listed her student loans in the bankruptcy proceeding, and the general discharge did not cover them. In September 1999, the individual reopened her bankruptcy petition for the limited purpose of seeking a determination by the Bankruptcy Court that her student loans were dischargeable. As prescribed by the Bankruptcy Rules, the individual filed a complaint against various defendants. Later, the individual filed an amended complaint in which she included, as an additional defendant, a Tennessee governmental corporation that was an assignee holder of the individual's student-loan debt. The complaint and the amended complaint were served, along with a summons, on each of the named parties.

The state governmental corporation filed a motion to dismiss the complaint for lack of jurisdiction, on the asserted basis of immunity under the Federal Constitution's Eleventh Amendment, which generally prohibited private federal-court suits against states. However, the Bankruptcy Court, in denying the motion, expressed the view that 11 USCS § 106(a) validly abrogated the state governmental corporation's sovereign immunity.

The Bankruptcy Appellate Panel of the United States Court of Appeals for the Sixth Circuit affirmed (262 BR 412).

On appeal, the Court of Appeals for the Sixth Circuit, in affirming, expressed the view that the Federal Constitution's Art I, § 8, cl 4—in providing that Congress would have the power to establish "uniform Laws on the subject of Bankruptcies throughout the United States"—gave Congress the necessary authority to abrogate state sovereign immunity in § 106(a) (319 F3d 755, 2003 FED App 38P).

On certiorari, the United States Supreme Court affirmed and remanded. In an opinion by REHNQUIST, Ch. J., joined by STEVENS, O'CONNOR, KENNEDY, and BREYER, JJ., and joined in pertinent part by SOUTER and GINSBURG, JJ., it was held—without reaching the question of Congress' bankruptcy power under Art I, § 8, cl 4—that the proceeding instituted by the individual in the case at hand to determine, pursuant to § 523(a)(8), the dischargeability of her student-loan debt was not a suit against a state within the meaning of Eleventh Amendment, as:

(1) The Supreme Court had held that the Eleventh Amendment did not bar federal-court jurisdiction over in rem admiralty actions when a state was not in possession of the property.

(2) The discharge of a debt by a bankruptcy court was similarly an in rem proceeding.

(3) There was no reason why the exercise of the federal courts' in rem bankruptcy jurisdiction was more threatening to state sovereignty than the exercise of the federal courts' in rem admiralty jurisdiction.

(4) The particular undue-hardship process by which student-loan debts were discharged did not unconstitutionally infringe a state's sovereignty.

(5) The particular adversary-proceeding method used in the case at hand did not change the result.

SOUTER, J., joined by GINSBURG, J., concurred, except for any implicit approval of the holding in one prior Supreme Court decision.

THOMAS, J., joined by SCALIA, J., dissented, expressing the view that (1) the Supreme Court—which had granted certiorari to decide the Art I, § 8, cl 4 question—should have declined to address the complex and more difficult question regarding the extent to which a bankruptcy court's exercise of its in rem

154

jurisdiction could offend the sovereignty of a creditor state; and (2) while Congress, in § 106(a), had made clear Congress' intent to abrogate state sovereign immunity under the bankruptcy provision in Art I, § 8, cl 4, this provision did not grant Congress the power to do so.

COUNSEL

Daryl J. Brand argued the cause for petitioner.

Leonard H. Gerson argued the cause for respondent.

LEE M. TILL, et ux., Petitioners

v

SCS CREDIT CORPORATION

541 US —, 158 L Ed 2d 787, 124 S Ct 1951

[No. 02-1016]

Argued December 2, 2003.
Decided May 17, 2004.

Decision: With respect to appropriate interest rate to be paid to creditor, under "cram down" bankruptcy provision (11 USCS § 1325(a)(5)(B)(ii)), on allowed secured claim when debt-adjustment plan provided for installment payments, Federal Court of Appeals' judgment reversed, and case remanded for further proceedings.

SUMMARY

For purposes of debt-adjustment plans under Chapter 13 of the Bankruptcy Code (11 USCS §§ 1301 et seq.), 11 USCS § 1325(a)(5) includes a "cram down" option, which authorizes a federal bankruptcy court to approve, despite a secured creditor's objection, a plan providing the creditor both (1) a lien securing an allowed claim, and (2) a promise of future property distributions (such as deferred cash payments). If the cram-down option is used, then 11 USCS § 1325(a)(5)(B)(ii) requires that "the value, as of the effective date of the plan, of property to be distributed under the plan on account of such claim [must be] not less than the allowed amount of such claim." Where a Chapter 13 plan includes a cram-down provision for

156

installment payments of money, the appropriate rate of interest under § 1325(a)(5)(B)(ii) has been disputed.

In the case at hand, an Indiana couple filed a joint Chapter 13 petition for relief. One creditor had a $4,000 allowed secured claim, based on the agreed value of a truck purchased by the couple, prior to filing, under a retail installment contract with a "subprime" interest rate of 21 percent. Pursuant to the cram-down option, the United States Bankruptcy Court for the Southern District of Indiana, over the creditor's objection and after a hearing, confirmed the couple's proposed debt-adjustment plan, which—in providing for installment payments of money to the creditor on this claim—included an interest rate of 9.5 percent, supposedly representing (1) the then national prime rate of 8 percent, plus (2) a "risk adjustment" of 1.5 percent.

On appeal, the United States District Court for the Southern District of Indiana, in reversing, expressed the view that (1) such cram-down interest rates ought to be set, under a "coerced loan" approach, at the level which a creditor could have obtained if the creditor had foreclosed on the loan in question, sold the collateral, and reinvested the proceeds in loans of equivalent duration and risk; and (2) in the case at hand, 21 percent was the appropriate rate, in view of some testimony on behalf of the creditor about the market for subprime loans.

On appeal, the United States Court of Appeals for the Seventh Circuit, in vacating the District Court's judgment and in ordering a remand, expressed the view that the original 21-percent contract rate of interest ought to serve as the "presumptive" cram-down rate, which either the creditor or the couple could challenge with evidence that a higher or lower rate ought to apply (301 F3d 583). The Court of Appeals then denied rehearing en banc (2002 US App LEXIS 21282).

On certiorari, the United States Supreme Court reversed the Court of Appeals' judgment and remanded the case with instructions to remand the case to the Bankruptcy Court for further proceedings. Although unable to agree on an opinion, five Justices agreed that the Court of Appeals had erred in calculating the appropriate interest rate.

STEVENS, J., announced the judgment of the court and, in an opinion joined by SOUTER, GINSBURG, and BREYER, JJ., expressed the view that (1) under § 1325(a)(5)(B)(ii), in such cram-down circumstances, the appropriate interest rate ought to be calculated under a "formula" approach, which (a) did not have the defects of some other proposed approaches, (b) would begin by looking to the national prime rate, reported daily in the press, of interest charged to creditworthy commercial borrowers, and (c) would require a bankruptcy court to adjust the prime rate due to the typically greater risk of nonpayment by bankrupt debtors, after the court held a hearing at which the debtor and any creditors might present evidence about the appropriate risk adjustment, with the evidentiary burden on the creditors; and (2) while, in the case at hand, the issue as to the proper scale for the risk adjustment was not before the Supreme Court, if a bankruptcy court determined that the likelihood of default was so high as to necessitate an "eye-popping" interest rate, then a proposed plan probably ought not to be confirmed.

THOMAS, J., concurring in the judgment, expressed the view that (1) § 1325(a)(5)(B)(ii) did not require the proper interest rate to reflect the risk of nonpayment; (2) in order for a plan to satisfy § 1325(a)(5)(B)(ii), the plan needed only to propose an interest rate that would compensate a creditor for the fact that if the creditor had received the property immediately rather than at a future date, the creditor could have immediately made use of the property; (3) in most, if not all, cases where such a plan proposed a stream of cash payments, the appropriate risk-free rate ought to suffice; and (4) in the case at hand, where the plan's 9.5 percent interest rate was higher than the risk-free rate, the 9.5 percent rate sufficiently compensated the creditor for the fact that instead of receiving $4,000 immediately, the creditor was to receive $4,000 plus 9.5 percent interest.

SCALIA, J., joined by REHNQUIST, Ch. J., and O'CONNOR and KENNEDY, JJ., dissenting, expressed the view that (1) the formula approach for determining Chapter 13 cram-down interest rates would systematically undercompensate secured creditors for the true risks of default, where, for example, the 1.5 per cent risk premium which had been adopted in the case at hand was "far below" anything approaching fair compensation; (2) the risk-free approach (a) was not supported by (i) the statutory context, or (ii) prior case law, and (b) would lead to anomalous results; (3) instead, in such cram-down situations, the contract rate—the interest rate at which a creditor had actually loaned funds to a debtor—ought to be adopted as a presumption that a bankruptcy judge could revise on motion of either party; and (4) if adequate compensation to a creditor would require an "eye-popping" interest rate too high for such a plan to succeed, then the appropriate course would be to refuse to confirm the plan, rather than to reduce the rate to a more palatable level.

COUNSEL

Rebecca J. Harper argued the cause for petitioners.

David B. Salmons, pro hac vice, argued the cause for the United States, as amicus curiae, by special leave of court.

G. Eric Brunstad, Jr. argued the cause for respondent.

TENNESSEE, Petitioner

v

GEORGE LANE et al.

541 US —, 158 L Ed 2d 820, 124 S Ct 1978

[No. 02-1667]

Argued January 13, 2004.
Decided May 17, 2004.

Decision: Title II of Americans with Disabilities Act (42 USCS §§ 12131 et seq.), as applied to cases implementing right of access to courts, held to be valid exercise of Congress' authority under Fourteenth Amendment's § 5 to enforce amendment.

SUMMARY

Two paraplegics who used wheelchairs for mobility—a criminal defendant and a certified court reporter—filed, in a Federal District Court, an action for damages and equitable relief, alleging that Tennessee and a number of its counties had denied them physical access to the state court system in violation of Title II of the Americans with Disabilities Act of 1990 (ADA) (42 USCS §§ 12131 et seq.), which, in 42 USCS § 12132, prohibited any qualified individual with a disability from, by reason of such disability, being excluded from participation in, or denied the benefits of the services, programs, or activities of, a public entity, or being subjected to discrimination by any such entity.

After the District Court denied the state's motion to dismiss on the asserted ground that the state was immune from the suit under the Federal Constitution's Eleventh Amendment, the United States Court of Appeals for the Sixth Circuit eventually (1) affirmed the dismissal denial; and (2) expressed the view that that ADA claims were not barred because they were based on due process principles (40 Fed Appx 911).

On rehearing, the Court of Appeals (1) filed an amended opinion, expressing the view that (a) the due process clause of the Constitution's Fourteenth Amendment protected the right of access to the courts, and (b) the evidence before Congress when it had enacted Title II had established that physical barriers in courthouses and courtrooms had had the effect of denying people with disabilities the opportunity for such access; and (2) ordered a remand of the case for further proceedings (315 F3d 680).

On certiorari, the United States Supreme Court affirmed. In an opinion by STEVENS, J., joined by O'CONNOR, SOUTER, GINSBURG, and BREYER, JJ., it was held that, as applied to the class of cases implicating the fundamental right of access to the courts, Title II constituted a valid exercise of Congress' authority, under § 5 of the Fourteenth Amendment, to enforce the guarantees of the Fourteenth Amendment, as:

(1) The ADA (42 USCS §§ 12101 et seq.) specifically provided, in 42 USCS § 12202, that a state would not be immune, under the Eleventh Amendment, from an action "in federal or state court of competent jurisdiction for a violation of this chapter."

(2) No party disputed the adequacy of that expression of Congress' intent to abrogate the states' Eleventh Amendment immunity.

(3) A finding set forth in 42 USCS § 12101(a)(3), together with the extensive record of the underlying disability discrimination, made clear that inadequate provision of public services and access to public facilities was an appropriate subject for prophylactic legislation.

162

(4) Congress' chosen remedy for this pattern of exclusion and discrimination (Title II's requirement of program accessibility) was congruent and proportional to its object of enforcing the right of access to the courts.

(5) The remedy that Congress had chosen was limited.

(6) Title II's affirmative obligation to accommodate persons with disabilities in the administration of justice was a reasonable prophylactic measure.

SOUTER, J., joined by GINSBURG, J., concurring, expressed the view that if the Supreme Court had engaged in a more expansive inquiry in the instant case, the evidence to be considered would have underscored the appropriateness of action under § 5 to address the situation of individuals with disabilities before the courts, for that evidence would have shown that the judiciary itself had endorsed the basis for some of the discrimination that was subject to congressional remedy under § 5.

GINSBURG, J., joined by SOUTER and BREYER, JJ., concurring, expressed the view that (1) legislation calling upon all government actors to respect the dignity of individuals with disabilities was entirely compatible with the Constitution's commitment to federalism, properly conceived; and (2) the record of discrimination against persons with disabilities considered by Congress in enacting the ADA, at least as the record bore on access to courts, sufficed to warrant the barrier-lowering, dignity-respecting national solution that the people's representatives in Congress had elected to order.

REHNQUIST, Ch. J., joined by KENNEDY and THOMAS, JJ., dissenting, expressed the view that the Supreme Court's decision in the instant case was irreconcilable with (1) the earlier decision in Board of Trustees v

Garrett (2001) 531 US 356, 148 L Ed 2d 866, 121 S Ct 955 (in which the court had held that Congress had not validly abrogated the states' Eleventh Amendment immunity when Congress had enacted Title I of the ADA (42 USCS §§ 12111 et seq.)); and (2) the well-established principles embodied by that decision.

SCALIA, J., dissenting, expressed the view that (1) the "congruence and proportionality" test for determining the validity of § 5 legislation should be replaced with a test that would provide a clear and enforceable limitation supported by the text of § 5; and (2) requiring access for persons with disabilities to all public buildings could not remotely be considered a means of "enforcing" the Fourteenth Amendment.

THOMAS, J., dissenting, expressed the view that Title II could not be a congruent and proportional remedy to the states' alleged practice of denying persons with disabilities access to the courts, as (1) Congress had failed to identify any evidence of such a practice when Congress had enacted the ADA; and (2) Title II regulated far more than the provision of access to the courts.

COUNSEL

Michael E. Moore argued the cause for petitioner.

William J. Brown argued the cause for private respondents.

Paul D. Clement argued the cause for federal respondent.

GRUPO DATAFLUX, Petitioner

v

ATLAS GLOBAL GROUP, L. P., et al.

541 US —, 158 L Ed 2d 866, 124 S Ct 1920

[No. 02-1689]

Argued March 3, 2004.
Decided May 17, 2004.

Decision: Party's postfiling change in citizenship held unable to cure lack of subject-matter jurisdiction that existed at time of filing in federal-court diversity action.

SUMMARY

A limited partnership created under Texas law filed a state-law suit in the United States District Court for the Southern District of Texas against a Mexican corporation. The partnership, asserting Texas citizenship, alleged that the court had diversity-of-citizenship jurisdiction pursuant to 28 USCS § 1332(a). At the time of the filing, the partnership had two partners who were Mexican citizens, but these partners left the partnership before trial began. After trial—resulting in a jury verdict in the partnership's favor—but before the entry of judgment, the corporation filed a motion to dismiss for lack of subject-matter jurisdiction, on the ground that the parties had not been diverse at the time that the complaint was filed. A Magistrate Judge, in granting the motion, reasoned that (1) the partnership was a citizen of each state or foreign country of which any of its partners was a citizen; and (2) because the partnership had had Mexican partners at the time of filing, the partnership was a Mexican citizen.

The United States Court of Appeals for the Fifth Circuit, in reversing and ordering a remand, (1) acknowledged a general rule that, for purposes of determining the existence of diversity jurisdiction, the citizenship of the parties was to be determined with reference to the facts as they existed at the time of filing; but (2) concluded that such a time-of-filing rule was subject to exception where, as in the case at hand, (a) the jurisdictional error was not identified until after the jury's verdict, and (b) the postfiling change in the composition of the partnership assertedly cured the jurisdictional defect (312 F3d 168).

On certiorari, the United States Supreme Court reversed. In an opinion by SCALIA, J., joined by REHNQUIST, Ch. J., and O'CONNOR, KENNEDY, and THOMAS, JJ., it was held that:

(1) In a federal-court action premised upon diversity of citizenship pursuant to § 1332(a), a party's postfiling change in citizenship cannot cure a lack of subject-matter jurisdiction that existed at the time of filing, for—among other reasons—holding that finality, efficiency, and judicial economy could justify suspension of the time-of-filing rule would create an exception of indeterminate scope.

(2) The District Court's lack of diversity-of-citizenship jurisdiction was not cured when the Mexican partners left the partnership, for, among other reasons, (a) a limited partnership, for purposes of federal diversity jurisdiction, was an entity comprising its members, rather than an aggregation composed of its members; (b) to treat a change in the composition of a partnership as a change in the parties to the action—by equating a dropped partner with a dropped party—would be inconsistent with this rule; and (c)

166

creating an exception to the time-of-filing rule in cases involving a postfiling change in the composition of a partnership would waste judicial resources.

GINSBURG, J., joined by STEVENS, SOUTER, and BREYER, JJ., dissenting, expressed the view that (1) although the time-of-filing rule was generally sound, the rule ought not to be applied rigidly in cases involving a postfiling change in the composition of a multimember association such as a partnership; (2) in the case at hand, the initial absence of complete diversity was not fatal to the ensuing adjudication, for the case was indistinguishable from one in which there was a change in the parties to the action; and (3) a departure from the time-of-filing rule in such a case was supported by considerations of finality, efficiency, and economy.

COUNSEL

William J. Boyce argued the cause for petitioner.

Roger B. Greenberg argued the cause for respondents.

BASIM OMAR SABRI, Petitioner

v

UNITED STATES

541 US —, 158 L Ed 2d 891, 124 S Ct 1941

[No. 03-44]

Argued March 3, 2004.
Decided May 17, 2004.

Decision: Federal statutory provision proscribing bribery of state, local, and tribal officials of entities that receive at least $10,000 in federal funds (18 USCS § 666(a)(2)) held to be valid exercise of congressional authority under Federal Constitution's Article I.

SUMMARY

A real estate developer who proposed to build a hotel and retail structure in the city of Minneapolis was indicted for offering, between July 2, 2001, and July 17, 2001, three separate bribes totaling approximately $95,000 to a city councilman, who was also a member of the Board of Commissioners of the Minneapolis Community Development Agency (MCDA). The charges were brought under 18 USCS § 666(a)(2), which imposes federal criminal penalties on anyone who corruptly gives, offers, or agrees to give anything of value to any person, with intent to influence or reward an agent of an organization or of a state, local or Indian tribal government, or any agency thereof, in connection with any business, transaction, or series of transactions of such organization, government, or agency involving anything of value of $5,000 or more. For criminal liability, the statute requires that the organization, government, or agency receive, in any one year period, benefits in excess of $10,000 under a federal program involving a grant, contract, subsidy, loan, guarantee, insurance, or other form of federal assistance (18 USCS § 666(b)). In 2001, the City Council of Minneapolis administered about $29 million in federal funds paid to the city, and in the same period, the MCDA received some $23 million of federal money.

Before trial, the developer moved to dismiss the indictment on the ground that § 666(a)(2) was unconstitutional on its face for failure to require proof of a connection between the federal funds and the alleged bribe as an element of liability. The government responded that even if an additional nexus between the bribery conduct and the federal funds were required, the evidence would easily meet such a standard, because the developer's alleged actions related to federal dollars. Although the developer did not contradict this factual claim, the United States District Court for the District of Minnesota (1) agreed that the law was facially invalid as outside Congress's power to legislate, and (2) dismissed the indictment (183 F Supp 2d 1145). The United States Court of Appeals for the Eighth Circuit, in reversing, concluded that § 666 was a necessary and proper exercise of congressional power (326 F3d 937).

On certiorari, the Supreme Court affirmed and remanded. In an opinion by SOUTER, J., joined by REHNQUIST, Ch. J., and STEVENS, O'CONNOR, GINSBURG, and BREYER, JJ., it was held that § 666(a)(2) was a valid exercise of congressional authority under Article I of the Federal Constitution, notwithstanding that the statute did not require proof of a connection between the federal funds and the alleged bribe as an element of liability, for, among other reasons:

(1) Congress had authority under the Constitution's

spending clause (Art I, § 8, cl 1) to appropriate federal monies to promote the general welfare, and it had corresponding authority under the Constitution's necessary and proper clause (Art I, § 8, cl 18) to see to it that taxpayer dollars appropriated under that power were in fact spent for the general welfare.

(2) While it was true that not every bribe or kickback offered or paid to agents of covered entities would be traceably skimmed from specific federal payments, or show up in the guise of a quid pro quo for some dereliction in spending a federal grant, this possibility portended no enforcement beyond the scope of federal interest.

KENNEDY, J., joined by SCALIA, J., concurring in part, joined in the court's opinion, except for a part in which the court expressed the view that facial challenges to statutes on the basis of overbreadth were to be discouraged.

THOMAS, J., concurring in the judgment, expressed the view that (1) the constitutionality of § 666(a)(2) should have been decided on the court's jurisprudence under the Constitution's commerce clause (Art I, § 8, cl 3), and (2) the court's approach seemed to greatly and improperly expand the reach of Congress' power under the necessary and proper clause.

COUNSEL

Andrew S. Birrell argued the cause for petitioner.

Michael R. Dreeben argued the cause for respondent.

MARCUS THORNTON, Petitioner

v

UNITED STATES

541 US —, 158 L Ed 2d 905, 124 S Ct 2127

[No. 03-5165]

Argued March 31, 2004.

Decided May 24, 2004.

Decision: Police officer who had made lawful custodial arrest of automobile occupant held to be allowed to contemporaneously search automobile's passenger compartment even when officer first made contact with arrestee after arrestee left automobile.

SUMMARY

In New York v Belton (1981) 453 US 454, 69 L Ed 2d 768, 101 S Ct 2680, the United States Supreme Court held that when a police officer made a lawful custodial arrest of an occupant of an automobile, the Federal Constitution's Fourth Amendment allowed the officer to search the vehicle's passenger compartment as a contemporaneous incident of arrest.

Before a city police officer had an opportunity to pull over an automobile that had license tags that had been issued for another vehicle, the driver drove into a parking lot, parked, and left the automobile. The officer then accosted the driver, and, after finding marijuana and cocaine in the driver's pocket, arrested him. Incident to the arrest, the officer searched the automobile and found a handgun under the driver's seat.

The driver was charged with federal drug and firearms crimes. In denying the driver's motion to suppress the handgun as the fruit of an unconstitutional search, a Federal District Court concluded that the automobile search had been valid under Belton.

After the driver was convicted on all counts, he appealed, arguing that Belton was limited to situations where the officer initiated contact with an arrestee while the arrestee was still in the automobile. The United States Court of Appeals for the Fourth Circuit (1) concluded that the search of the driver's automobile had been reasonable under Belton, and (2) affirmed the convictions (325 F3d 189).

On certiorari, the Supreme Court affirmed. In an opinion by REHNQUIST, Ch. J., joined by KENNEDY, THOMAS, and BREYER, JJ., and joined in pertinent part by O'CONNOR, J., it was held that the Belton rule applied even when the officer first made contact with the arrestee after the arrestee had left the vehicle. So long as an arrestee was the sort of "recent occupant" of a vehicle such as the arrestee in the instant case, officers could search the vehicle incident to the arrest, as:

(1) In Belton, the court had placed no reliance on the fact that the officer in that case had ordered the occupants out of the vehicle or initiated contact with them while they remained within the vehicle.

(2) There was no basis to conclude that the span of the area generally within the arrestee's immediate control was to be determined by whether (a) the arrestee exited the vehicle at the officer's direction; or (b) the officer initiated contact with the arrestee while the arrestee remained in the vehicle.

(3) In all relevant aspects, the arrest of a suspect who was next to a vehicle presented identical concerns regarding officer safety and the destruction of evidence as did the arrest of a suspect who was inside the vehicle.

172

(4) In some circumstances it might be safer and more effective for officers to conceal their presence from a suspect until the suspect had left the vehicle.

(5) A rule applying Belton only when an officer initiated contact with a suspect would obfuscate the constitutional limits of a Belton search.

O'CONNOR, J., concurring in part, although stating that the Supreme Court's opinion was a logical extension of the Belton holding, expressed the view that, as a direct consequence of Belton's shaky foundation, lower-court decisions seemed to treat the ability to search a vehicle incident to the arrest of a recent occupant as a police entitlement, rather than as an exception justified by the twin rationales of Chimel v California (1969) 395 US 752, 23 L Ed 2d 685, 89 S Ct 2034.

SCALIA, J., joined by GINSBURG, J., concurring in the judgment, said that (1) the Supreme Court's effort to apply its current doctrine to the search involved in the instant case search stretched the doctrine beyond its breaking point; and (2) the decision below should have been affirmed on the ground that it was reasonable for the officer to have believed that further contraband or similar evidence relevant to the drug offenses for which the driver had been arrested might have been found in the vehicle from which he had just alighted, and which was still within his vicinity at the time of arrest.

STEVENS, J., joined by SOUTER, J., dissenting, said that a fair reading of the Belton opinion, and of the conflicting cases that had given rise to the grant of certiorari in the Belton case, made clear that, in the Belton case, the court had not been concerned with the situation presented in the instant case, as (1) Belton had been demonstrably concerned with only the narrow but common circumstance of a search occasioned by the arrest of a suspect who was seated in or driving an automobile at the time a law-enforcement official approached; and (2) the bright-line rule crafted in Belton was not needed for cases in which the arrestee was first accosted when the arrestee was a pedestrian.

COUNSEL

Frank W. Dunham, Jr. argued the cause for petitioner.

Gregory G. Garre argued the cause for respondent.

―――――――――――

DAVID L. NELSON, Petitioner

v

DONAL CAMPBELL, COMMISSIONER, ALABAMA
DEPARTMENT OF CORRECTIONS, et al.

541 US —, 158 L Ed 2d 924, 124 S Ct 2117

[No. 03-6821]

Argued March 29, 2004.
Decided May 24, 2004.

Decision: Action under 42 USCS § 1983 held to be
appropriate vehicle for Alabama prisoner's Eighth
Amendment claim seeking (1) temporary stay of
execution; and (2) permanent injunction against
"cut down" to assess veins for lethal injection.

SUMMARY

Three days before his scheduled execution by lethal
injection, a state prisoner in Alabama filed, in the
United States District Court for the Middle District of
Alabama, an action under 42 USCS § 1983 against state
prison officials, alleging that the state's intended use of
a "cut-down" procedure, assertedly requiring an inci-
sion into the prisoner's arm or leg to access his severely
compromised veins, would constitute cruel and unusual punishment and deliberate indifference to his
medical needs in violation of the Federal Constitution's
Eighth Amendment. The prisoner, who already had
filed an unsuccessful federal habeas corpus application,
sought (1) a permanent injunction against use of the
cut-down; (2) a temporary stay of execution so that the
District Court could consider the merits of the prisoner's claim; and (3) orders (a) requiring the state

officials to furnish a copy of the protocol on the medical procedures for venous access, and (b) directing the state officials to promulgate a venous-access protocol that comported with contemporary standards.

However, the District Court dismissed the prisoner's complaint, on the ground that the § 1983 claim and stay request were the equivalent of a second or successive habeas corpus application for which the prisoner had not obtained the authorization required under 28 USCS § 2244(b) (286 F Supp 2d 1321).

In affirming, the United States Court of Appeals for the Eleventh Circuit concluded that (1) method-of-execution challenges necessarily sounded in habeas corpus; and (2) the Court of Appeals would have denied a habeas corpus authorization request from the prisoner (347 F3d 910).

On certiorari, the United States Supreme Court reversed and remanded. In an opinion by O'CONNOR, J., expressing the unanimous view of the court, it was held that § 1983 was an appropriate vehicle for the prisoner's Eighth Amendment claim seeking a temporary stay and permanent injunctive relief, as:

(1) The prison officials had conceded that § 1983 would have been an appropriate vehicle for an inmate who was not facing execution to bring a "deliberate indifference" challenge to use of a cut-down to provide medical treatment.

(2) The court saw no reason to treat the prisoner's claim differently solely because he had been condemned to die.

(3) The fact that venous access was a necessary prerequisite to lethal injection did not imply that a particular means of gaining such access was likewise necessary.

(4) The prisoner had alleged alternatives that, if they had been used, would have allowed the state to proceed with the execution as scheduled.

176

(5) The court's holding was consistent with the court's approach to civil rights damages actions, which, like method-of-execution challenges, fell at the margins of habeas corpus.

(6) The ability to bring a § 1983 claim did not entirely free inmates from substantive or procedural limitations.

COUNSEL

Bryan Stevenson argued the cause for petitioner.

Kevin C. Newsom argued the cause for respondents.

MICHAEL YARBOROUGH, WARDEN, Petitioner

v

MICHAEL ALVARADO

541 US —, 158 L Ed 2d 938, 124 S Ct 2140

[No. 02-1684]

Argued March 1, 2004.

Decided June 1, 2004.

Decision: For purposes of determining whether suspect was entitled to federal habeas corpus relief under 28 USCS § 2254(d)(1), California court held to have reasonably applied federal law in holding that suspect had not been in custody during interrogation.

SUMMARY

A 17-year-old suspect, who had allegedly participated in a shooting and an attempted robbery, was called in to a California county sheriff's station for an interview. The suspect's parents brought him to the station and waited in the station's lobby during the 2-hour interview, at which the parents were not present. The interview was conducted by a sheriff's detective, who (1) did not give the suspect the warnings required by Miranda v Arizona (1966) 384 US 436, 16 L Ed 2d 694, 86 S Ct 1602; (2) focused not on the suspect's alleged crimes, but rather on those of another person who had allegedly done the shooting; (3) appealed to the suspect's interest in telling the truth and being helpful to a police officer; and (4) twice asked the suspect if he wanted to take a break. Although the suspect at first denied being present at the shooting, he ultimately admitted that he had helped the other person try to steal the shooting victim's truck and to hide the person's gun after the shooting. At the end of the interview, the suspect went home.

The suspect was subsequently charged with first-degree murder and attempted robbery. A California trial court, concluding that the suspect's interview had been noncustodial for purposes of Miranda, denied the suspect's motion to suppress the statements that he had made at the interview. Ultimately, the suspect was convicted of second-degree murder and sentenced to prison.

The Court of Appeal of California, Second Appellate District, in affirming, (1) considered the circumstances surrounding the interrogation; (2) noted that (a) there had been no intense or aggressive tactics, and (b) the suspect had not been told that he could not leave; and (3) concluded that the suspect had not been in custody (74 Cal App 4th 1099, 88 Cal Rptr 2d 688). The Supreme Court of California denied discretionary review (1999 Cal LEXIS 8696).

The United States District Court for the Central District of California denied the suspect's subsequent petition for a federal writ of habeas corpus, as the District Court concluded that such relief was foreclosed by a provision of the Antiterrorism and Effective Death Penalty Act of 1996 (28 USCS § 2254(d)(1)), under which a federal court may grant a habeas corpus application on behalf of a person held pursuant to a state-court judgment if the state-court adjudication resulted in a decision that was contrary to, or involved an unreasonable application of, clearly established federal law, as determined by the United States Supreme Court.

However, the United States Court of Appeals for the Ninth Circuit, in reversing and ordering a remand, reasoned that (1) the suspect's youth and inexperience had to be factors in the Miranda custody inquiry; (2) the effect of these factors was so substantial as to turn the interview into a custodial interrogation; and (3) § 2254(d)(1) did not bar habeas corpus relief, for in light of the clearly established law considering juvenile status, it was unreasonable to conclude that a reasonable 17-year-old in the suspect's position would have felt that he was at liberty to terminate the interrogation and leave (316 F3d 841).

On certiorari, the United States Supreme Court reversed. In an opinion by KENNEDY, J., joined by REHNQUIST, Ch. J., and O'CONNOR, SCALIA, and THOMAS, JJ., it was held that for purposes of § 2254(d)(1), the California Court of Appeal had reasonably applied clearly established law in holding that the suspect had not been in custody during the interrogation, for:

(1) Although some facts weighed in favor of the view that the suspect had been in custody, other facts weighed against such a finding, as those facts were consistent with an interrogation environment in which a reasonable person would have felt free to terminate the interview and leave.

(2) In the circumstances presented, (a) fair-minded jurists could have disagreed as to whether the suspect was in custody under the Supreme Court's general standard for determining custody, and (b) the California Court of Appeal's application of the Supreme Court's law was reasonable and fit within the matrix of the Supreme Court's prior decisions.

(3) The California Court of Appeal's failure to consider the suspect's age did not provide a proper basis for finding that the California Court of Appeal's decision was an unreasonable application of clearly established law.

(4) The United States Court of Appeals' reliance on the

suspect's prior inexperience with law enforcement was improper, not only under the deferential review standard of § 2254(d)(1), but also as a de novo matter.

O'CONNOR, J., concurring, (1) agreed that under the circumstances presented, the California Court of Appeal's decision could not be called an unreasonable application of federal law simply because that decision failed explicitly to mention the suspect's age; but (2) expressed the view that there might be cases in which a suspect's age would be relevant to the Miranda "custody" inquiry.

BREYER, J., joined by STEVENS, SOUTER, and GINSBURG, JJ., dissenting, expressed the view that (1) in terms of federal law's well-established legal standards, a court had to answer the question whether a suspect was in custody in light of all of the circumstances surrounding the interrogation; and (2) in the case at hand, the suspect had been in custody, for (a) a reasonable person in the suspect's circumstances would not have felt free to terminate the interrogation and leave, and (b) the suspect's age also was relevant to the inquiry.

COUNSEL

Deborah J. Chuang argued the cause for petitioner.

John P. Elwood argued the cause for the United States, as amicus curiae, by special leave of court.

Tara K. Allen argued the cause for respondent.

REPUBLIC OF AUSTRIA et al., Petitioners

v

MARIA V. ALTMANN

541 US —, 159 L Ed 2d 1, 124 S Ct 2240

[No. 03-13]

Argued February 25, 2004.
Decided June 7, 2004.

Decision: Foreign Sovereign Immunities Act of 1976—including 28 USCS § 1605(a)(3), providing that foreign states are not immune from jurisdiction in United States in cases of illegal expropriation—held applicable to pre-1976 conduct.

SUMMARY

The Foreign Sovereign Immunities Act of 1976 (FSIA) (28 USCS §§ 1330, 1602 et seq.) grants foreign states immunity from the jurisdiction of federal and state courts, but expressly exempts certain cases. Thus, for example, the expropriation exception (§ 1605(a)(3)) provides that foreign states are not immune in cases in which rights in property taken in violation of international law are in issue.

In 2000, an Austrian-born United States citizen, who was the niece and heir of an art collector in Austria, filed an action in the United States District Court for the Central District of California against the Republic of Austria and an art gallery that was an instrumentality of the Republic. The action alleged that the gallery had obtained possession of some of the art collector's paintings through wrongful conduct from 1941 to

1948. The niece asserted jurisdiction under the FSIA and claimed that the defendants' alleged actions fell within § 1605(a)(3)'s expropriation exception. The District Court, in denying the defendants' motion to dismiss, concluded that the FSIA applied retroactively to pre-1976 conduct and that the expropriation exception extended to the niece's claims (142 F Supp 2d 1187).

The United States Court of Appeals for the Ninth Circuit, in affirming and ordering a remand, reasoned that applying the FSIA to Austria's alleged wrongdoing was not impermissibly retroactive, as Austria could not legitimately have expected to receive immunity for that wrongdoing even in 1948 (317 F3d 954, amended 327 F3d 1246).

On certiorari, the United States Supreme Court affirmed. In an opinion by STEVENS, J., joined by O'CONNOR, SCALIA, SOUTER, GINSBURG, and BREYER, JJ., it was held that the FSIA applied to claims that were based on conduct that occurred before the FSIA's enactment—and even before the United States adopted, in 1952, a so-called "restrictive theory" of sovereign immunity, under which immunity was recognized with regard to a foreign state's sovereign or public acts, but not private acts—for:

(1) It was appropriate, absent contraindications, for courts to defer to the FSIA as the most recent decision of the political branches on whether the courts ought to take jurisdiction over such claims.

(2) Nothing in the FSIA or the circumstances surrounding its enactment suggested that the FSIA should not apply to pre-enactment conduct.

(3) In this context, it would have been anomalous to presume that an isolated FSIA provision, such as § 1605(a)(3)'s expropriation exception, was of purely

184

prospective application absent any statutory language to that effect.

(4) Applying the FSIA to all pending cases regardless of when the underlying conduct occurred was most consistent with two of the FSIA's principal purposes: (a) clarifying the rules that judges should apply in resolving sovereign immunity claims, and (b) eliminating political participation in the resolution of such claims.

SCALIA, J., concurring, expressed the view that (1) application of a new jurisdictional statute to cases filed after the statute's enactment was not "retroactive" even if the conduct sued upon predated the statute; and (2) it would have been inappropriate for the Supreme Court to undertake a case-specific inquiry into whether United States courts would have asserted jurisdiction at the time of the underlying conduct in question.

BREYER, J., joined by SOUTER, J., concurring, expressed the view that Congress intended § 1605(a)(3)'s expropriation exception to apply retroactively, because (1) the literal language of the FSIA supported such a reading; (2) the legal concept of sovereign immunity, as traditionally applied, was about a defendant's status at the time of suit, not about a defendant's conduct before the suit; (3) the historical practice of the State Department and the courts reflected this classic view; (4) neither reliance nor expectation could justify non-retroactivity in the case at hand; (5) an attempt to read into § 1605(a)(3) a qualification related to the time of conduct, on the basis of reliance or expectation, would have created complications and anomalies; and (6) other legal principles were available to protect a defendant's reasonable reliance on the law at the time that the conduct took place.

KENNEDY, J., joined by REHNQUIST, Ch. J., and THOMAS, J., dissenting, expressed the view that (1) the

Supreme Court was (a) weakening the reasoning and diminishing the force of the rule against the retroactivity of statutes, and (b) telling foreign nations that this rule was unavailable to them in United States courts, despite the fact that treaties and agreements on the subject of expropriation had been reached against a background of the immunity principles that the Supreme Court was now rejecting; (2) the Supreme Court's statement that the executive branch had inherent power to intervene in cases such as the one at hand was inconsistent with the congressional purpose and design of the FSIA; (3) the Supreme Court's reasoning implied a problematic answer to a separation-of-powers question that the case did not present; and (4) the ultimate effect of the Supreme Court's inviting foreign nations to pressure the executive branch was to (a) risk inconsistent results for private citizens, and (b) add prospective instability to foreign relations.

COUNSEL

Scott P. Cooper argued the cause for petitioners.

Thomas G. Hungar argued the cause for the United States, as amicus curiae, by special leave of court.

E. Randol Schoenberg argued the cause for respondent.

CENTRAL LABORERS' PENSION FUND, Petitioner

v

THOMAS E. HEINZ et al.

541 US —, 159 L Ed 2d 46, 124 S Ct 2230

[No. 02-891]

Argued April 19, 2004.
Decided June 7, 2004.

Decision: ERISA's "anti-cutback" provision (29 USCS § 1054(g)), prohibiting pension-plan amendment that would reduce participant's "accrued benefit," held to prohibit amendment expanding types of postretirement employment that would trigger suspension of early-retirement benefits already accrued.

SUMMARY

Two participants in a multiemployer pension plan administered by a labor union retired from the construction industry after accruing enough credits to qualify for early retirement payments under the plan's defined-benefit "service only" pension, that paid the same monthly benefits that the participants would have received had they retired at the usual age. The plan had a rule under which monthly payments to a beneficiary of service-only pensions were suspended while the beneficiary engaged in "disqualifying employment," which, when the two participants retired, was defined by the plan to include a job as a construction worker but not as a construction supervisor.

Subsequently, after the participants had taken jobs as construction supervisors, the plan (1) expanded its

187

"disqualifying employment" definition to include any construction-industry job, and (2) stopped the participants' monthly payments when they continued their supervisor jobs.

The participants sued the plan to recover the suspended benefits on the alleged basis that the suspensions violated the "anti-cutback" rule of § 204(g) of the Employee Retirement Income Security Act of 1974 (ERISA) (29 USCS § 1054(g)), which prohibited any pension-plan amendment that would reduce a participant's "accrued benefit." The United States District Court for the Central District of Illinois granted the plan judgment on the pleadings.

However, the United States Court of Appeals for the Seventh Circuit (1) reversed, and (2) held that imposing new conditions on rights to benefits already accrued violated the anti-cutback rule (303 F3d 802).

On certiorari, the United States Supreme Court affirmed. In an opinion by SOUTER, J., expressing the unanimous view of the court, it was held that the "anti-cutback" rule of § 204(g) prohibited a plan amendment expanding the types of postretirement employment that would trigger a mandatory suspension of early-retirement benefits already accrued, as:

(1) As a matter of common sense, a participant's benefits could not be understood without reference to the conditions imposed on receiving the benefits.

(2) An amendment placing materially greater restrictions on the receipt of benefit reduced the benefit just as surely as did a decrease in the size of the monthly payment.

(3) The court did not see how, in any practical sense, the change of terms in the case at hand could not be viewed as shrinking the value of the participants' pension rights and reducing their promised benefits.

(4) With respect to the anti-cutback rule of § 204(g)

showing up in substantially identical form as
§ 411(d)(6) of the Internal Revenue Code (26 USCS
§ 411(d)(6)), the Internal Revenue Service had approved the interpretation of the anti-cutback rule that
the court was adopting in the case at hand.

BREYER, J., joined by REHNQUIST, Ch. J., and by
O'CONNOR and GINSBURG, JJ., concurring, expressed
an assumption that the court's opinion in the instant
case did not foreclose a reading of ERISA that allowed
the Secretary of Labor or the Secretary of the Treasury
to issue regulations explicitly allowing plan amendments to enlarge the scope of disqualifying employment with respect to benefits attributable to already-
performed services.

COUNSEL

Thomas C. Goldstein argued the cause for petitioner.
John P. Elwood argued the cause for the United
States, as amicus curiae, by special leave of court.
David M. Gossett argued the cause for respondents.

DEPARTMENT OF TRANSPORTATION, et al., Petitioners

v

PUBLIC CITIZEN et al.

541 US —, 159 L Ed 2d 60, 124 S Ct 2204

[No. 03-358]

Argued April 21, 2004.

Decided June 7, 2004.

Decision: National Environmental Policy Act of 1969 (42 USCS §§ 4321 et seq.) and Clean Air Act (42 USCS §§ 7401 et seq.) held not to require Federal Motor Carrier Safety Administration to evaluate environmental effects of some cross-border operations by Mexican-domiciled carriers.

SUMMARY

The National Environmental Policy Act of 1969, as amended (NEPA) (42 USCS §§ 4321 et seq.), generally requires a federal agency to prepare an Environmental Impact Statement (EIS) for a proposed "major Federal action." However, implementing regulations by the Council of Environmental Quality allow a federal agency to prepare a more limited Environmental Assessment (EA) in some situations. If, pursuant to an EA, a federal agency determines that an EIS is not required, then the agency must issue a finding of no significant impact (FONSI).

In addition, under the Clean Air Act, as amended (CAA) (42 USCS §§ 7401 et seq.), some safeguards in 42 USCS § 7506(c)(1) are intended to prevent the Federal Government from interfering with the states' abilities to comply with the CAA's requirements. Under implementing regulations by the Environmental Protection Agency, federal agencies (1) must, in many circumstances, undertake a full conformity review with respect to a proposed action; but (2) are exempted if the proposed action would not cause new emissions to exceed certain threshold amounts.

The case at hand involved the promulgation by the Federal Motor Carrier Safety Administration (FMCSA), an agency within the Department of Transportation, of certain application and safety-monitoring regulations that would allow some cross-border operations by Mexican-domiciled motor carriers to occur, where (1) even though 49 USCS § 13902(a)(1) generally mandated that the FMCSA register any qualified motor carrier, a moratorium on new FMCSA grants of operating authority for Mexican-domiciled motor carriers initially had been imposed, and later had been extended, pursuant to 49 USCS § 10922(*l*); (2) subsequently, the President of the United States, in asserted fulfillment of the North American Free Trade Agreement (32 ILM 605), had expressed an intention to lift the moratorium; and (3) in May 2001, the FMCSA had initially published for comment the proposed regulations in question.

Congress then enacted § 350 of the Department of Transportation and Related Agencies Appropriations Act, 2002 (note following 49 USCS § 13902), which provided (in conditions later extended to appropriations for fiscal years 2003 and 2004) that no funds appropriated under the 2002 Act could be obligated or expended to review or to process any application by a Mexican-domiciled motor carrier for authority to operate in the interior of the United States until the FMCSA implemented specific application and safety-monitoring requirements for such carriers.

In January 2002, the FMCSA issued a FONSI, which—on the basis of an Environmental Assessment released the same day—concluded that no EIS was needed concerning the proposed regulations. In March 2002, the FMCSA (1) issued the application and safety-monitoring regulations as interim rules with a delayed effective date; and (2) in some accompanying materials, said that a full CAA conformity review was not required. The FMCSA, in its analysis under both NEPA and the CAA, did not consider any emissions attributable to the increased presence of Mexican-domiciled motor carriers within the United States. In November 2002, the President lifted the moratorium on qualified Mexican-domiciled motor carriers.

Meanwhile, however, various challengers had (1) filed petitions for judicial review of the FMCSA's application and safety-monitoring regulations; and (2) included arguments that these regulations had been promulgated in violation of NEPA and the CAA. In a 2003 decision, the United States Court of Appeals for the Ninth Circuit agreed, granted the petitions, and ordered a remand, as the Court of Appeals expressed the view that (1) the Environmental Assessment was deficient because it failed to give adequate consideration to the overall environmental impact of the moratorium's lifting on the cross-border operations of Mexican-domiciled motor carriers; and (2) the FMCSA's CAA determination was not reliable, for it reflected an "illusory distinction" between (a) the effects of the regulations, and (b) the effects of the President's "rescission" of the moratorium (316 F3d 1002).

On certiorari, the United States Supreme Court reversed and remanded. In an opinion by THOMAS, J., expressing the unanimous view of the court, it was held that—under the circumstances presented with respect to the FMCSA's promulgation of regulations that would allow the cross-border operations by Mexican-domiciled motor carriers to occur—neither NEPA nor the CAA required the FMCSA to evaluate the environmental effects of such cross-border operations, because the FMCSA lacked the discretion to prevent such cross-border operations, in view of (1) the FMCSA's general registration mandate in § 13902(a)(1), which mandate could be satisfied consistently with § 350's conditions; and (2) the President's lifting of the moratorium.

COUNSEL

Edwin S. Kneedler argued the cause for petitioners.

Jonathan Weissglass argued the cause for respondents.

CITY OF LITTLETON, COLORADO, Petitioner

v

Z. J. GIFTS D-4, L. L. C., a limited liability company,
dba CHRISTAL'S

541 US —, 159 L Ed 2d 84, 124 S Ct 2219

[No. 02-1609]

Argued March 24, 2004.
Decided June 7, 2004.

Decision: City's "adult business" licensing ordinance
held to facially meet requirement, under Federal
Constitution's First Amendment, that such licensing scheme assure prompt judicial review of administrative decision denying license.

SUMMARY

A Colorado city enacted an adult business ordinance
that (1) required businesses such as adult bookstores to
(a) have "adult business" licenses, and (b) comply with
local zoning rules; (2) listed specific circumstances
under which the city would deny a license; (3) set forth
time limits (typically amounting to about 40 days)
within which city officials were required to reach a final
licensing decision; and (4) provided that the final
decision could be appealed to a state court pursuant to
the state's civil procedure rules.

In an area of the city that was not zoned for adult
businesses, a company opened a store that sold adult
books. Instead of applying for a license, the company
filed a suit alleging that the ordinance, on its face,
violated the Federal Constitution. A Federal District
Court rejected the company's allegation. However, the

194

United States Court of Appeals for the Tenth Circuit held that state law did not assure the constitutionally-required prompt final judicial decision (311 F3d 1220).

On certiorari, the United States Supreme Court reversed. In an opinion by BREYER, J., joined by REHNQUIST, Ch. J., and O'CONNOR, THOMAS, and GINSBURG, JJ., joined as to point 1 below by SOUTER and KENNEDY, JJ, and joined as to point 2 below by STEVENS, J., it was held that the licensing ordinance facially met the requirement, under the Federal Constitution's First Amendment, that such a licensing scheme assure prompt judicial review of an administrative decision denying a license, as:

(1) The Supreme Court read the reference, in two opinions joined by a total of six Justices in an earlier Supreme Court case involving a state's motion-picture-censorship statute, to "prompt judicial review" as encompassing a prompt judicial decision.

(2) The state's ordinary judicial-review procedures sufficed to assure prompt judicial access and a prompt judicial decision, as long as the state courts remained sensitive to the need to prevent First Amendment harms and administer those procedures accordingly.

STEVENS, J., concurring in part and concurring in the judgment, said that (1) application of neutral licensing criteria was a ministerial action that regulated speech, rather than an exercise of discretionary judgment that prohibited speech; and (2) a decision to deny a license for failure to comply with these neutral criteria was therefore not subject to the presumption of invalidity that attached to the direct censorship of particular expressive material.

SOUTER, J., joined by KENNEDY, J., concurring in part and concurring in the judgment, (1) agreed with the Supreme Court's opinion that the licensing scheme

195

involved in the instant case was unlike full-blown censorship, so that the ordinance did not need a strict timetable for judicial review to survive a facial challenge; but (2) said that (a) the licensing scheme was not as innocuous as common zoning, for the scheme was triggered by the content of expressive materials to be sold, (b) because the sellers might be unpopular with local authorities, there was a risk of delay in the licensing and review process, and (c) if there was evidence of foot-dragging, then immediate judicial intervention would be required, and judicial oversight or review at any stage of the proceedings would have to be expeditious.

SCALIA, J., concurring in the judgment, expressed the view that (1) the bookstore's activity—pandering of sex—was not protected by the First Amendment; and (2) to the extent that the city ordinance, in targeting sex-pandering businesses, could apply to constitutionally protected expression, the ordinance's excess was not so great as to render the ordinance substantially overbroad and thus subject to facial invalidation.

COUNSEL

J. Andrew Nathan argued the cause for petitioner.

Douglas R. Cole argued the cause for Ohio, et al., as amici curiae, by special leave of court.

Michael W. Gross argued the cause for respondent.

ELK GROVE UNIFIED SCHOOL DISTRICT and
DAVID W. GORDON, SUPERINTENDENT, Petitioners

v

MICHAEL A. NEWDOW et al.

542 US —, 159 L Ed 2d 98, 124 S Ct 2301

[No. 02-1624]

Argued March 24, 2004.
Decided June 14, 2004.

Decision: Student's father—who sought to challenge
addition of words "under God" to Pledge of
Allegiance as violating First Amendment's religion
clauses—held to lack prudential standing to bring
suit against school district in federal court.

SUMMARY

A public school district in California required each
elementary school class to recite daily the Pledge of
Allegiance. The father of one of the students who
participated in this daily exercise filed suit in the
United States District Court for the Eastern District of
California against the United States Congress, the
President of the United States, the state of California,
the school district, the district's superintendent, and
other parties. In the suit, the father (1) sought a
declaration that Congress's addition, in 1954, of the
words "under God" to the Pledge (codified at 4 USCS
§ 4) violated the establishment of religion and free
exercise of religion clauses of the Federal Constitution's First Amendment; (2) sought an injunction
against the district's policy requiring the daily recita-

197

tion of the Pledge; and (3) alleged that the father had standing to sue on his own behalf and as the student's next friend.

The District Court, adopting a Magistrate Judge's recommendation, dismissed the complaint. However, the United States Court of Appeals for the Ninth Circuit, in reversing and ordering a remand, concluded that (1) the father had standing as a parent to challenge a practice that allegedly interfered with his right to direct his child's religious education, and (2) the district's policy violated the establishment of religion clause (292 F3d 597).

Subsequently, the student's mother filed a motion for leave to intervene, or alternatively to dismiss the complaint. The mother asserted that (1) pursuant to a California state court's custody order, (a) the father had the right to consult with the mother on issues relating to the student's education, but (b) the mother was to make the final decisions as to the student's education if the father and mother could not agree; (2) the student had no objection either to reciting or hearing others recite the Pledge or to its reference to God; and (3) it was not in the student's interest to be a party to the suit.

The Court of Appeals, in denying the motion, concluded that (1) the custody order did not deprive the father of standing, under the Constitution's Article III, to object to unconstitutional government action affecting the student, and (2) the mother's objections did not defeat the father's right to seek redress for an alleged injury to his own parental interests (313 F3d 500). The Court of Appeals later issued an order amending its first opinion and denying rehearing in banc (328 F3d 466).

On certiorari, the United States Supreme Court reversed. In an opinion by STEVENS, J., joined by

KENNEDY, SOUTER, GINSBURG, and BREYER, JJ., it was
held that the father lacked prudential standing to bring
the suit, for:

(1) Although California law vested in the father a
cognizable right to influence the student's religious
upbringing, nothing that the mother or the district had
done impaired the father's right to instruct the student
in his religious views.

(2) The father did not have the right, under California
law, to (a) forestall the student's exposure to religious
ideas that the mother endorsed, (b) use his parental
status to challenge the influences to which the student
might be exposed in school when the father and
mother disagreed, or (c) litigate as the student's next
friend.

(3) Thus, (a) disputed family-law rights were entwined
inextricably with the threshold standing inquiry; and
(b) the interests of the father and the student were not
parallel and, indeed, were potentially in conflict.

(4) Some additional asserted bases for standing—that
(a) the father at times had himself attended, and would
in the future attend, class with the student; (b) the
father had considered teaching elementary-school students in the district; (c) the father had attended and
would continue to attend school board meetings at
which the Pledge was routinely recited; and (d) the
district had used the father's tax dollars to implement
its Pledge policy—did not respond to prudential concerns, even if these arguments sufficed to establish
Article III standing.

REHNQUIST, Ch. J., joined by O'CONNOR, J., and
joined in part (as to point 1 below) by THOMAS, J.,
concurring in the judgment, expressed the view that
(1) the Supreme Court's criticisms of the Court of
Appeals' Article III standing decision and the prudential prohibition on third-party standing provided no

basis for denying the father's standing; and (2) the school district's Pledge of Allegiance policy did not violate the establishment of religion clause, for reciting the Pledge, or listening to others recite it, was a patriotic exercise, not a religious one.

O'CONNOR, J., concurring in the judgment, expressed the view that (1) the father had standing to bring his constitutional claim before a federal court; (2) the government was permitted, in a discrete category of "ceremonial deism" cases, to acknowledge or refer to the divine without offending the Constitution; and (3) the appearance of the phrase "under God" in the Pledge of Allegiance constituted an instance of such ceremonial deism.

THOMAS, J., concurring in the judgment, expressed the view that (1) the father had standing; (2) the establishment of religion clause was a federalism provision intended to prevent Congress from interfering with state establishments; (3) it made little sense to incorporate the establishment of religion clause into the Constitution's Fourteenth Amendment so as to be applied against the states; (4) in any event, the school district's Pledge of Allegiance policy did not infringe any religious liberty right that would arise from incorporation of the establishment of religion clause; and (5) the Pledge policy did not infringe the free exercise of religion clause.

SCALIA, J., did not participate.

COUNSEL

Terence J. Cassidy argued the cause for petitioners.

Theodore B. Olson argued the cause for the United States, as amicus curiae, by special leave of court.

Michael A. Newdow, pro se, argued the cause for respondent by special leave of Court.

GALE NORTON, SECRETARY OF THE INTERIOR,
et al., Petitioners

v

SOUTHERN UTAH WILDERNESS ALLIANCE et al.

542 US —, 159 L Ed 2d 137, 124 S Ct 2373

[No. 03-101]

Argued March 29, 2004.
Decided June 14, 2004.

Decision: Federal court's authority, under 5 USCS
§ 706(1), to compel federal agency action held not
to extend to remedying some asserted failures by
Bureau of Land Management to act concerning
use of off-road vehicles.

SUMMARY

An Administrative Procedure Act provision (5 USCS
§ 706(1)) generally authorizes a federal court to "compel [federal] agency action unlawfully withheld or
unreasonably delayed."

The case at hand involved some asserted failures, by
the United States Bureau of Land Management (BLM)
in its stewardship of public lands in Utah, to take
certain actions with respect to the use of off-road
vehicles (ORVs). Several challengers filed suit in the
United States District Court for the District of Utah and
alleged that the District Court had the authority, under
§ 706(1), to remedy the BLM's asserted failures. The
challengers included three claims that (1) under the
Federal Land Policy and Management Act of 1976
(FLPMA) (43 USCS §§ 1701 et seq.), the BLM, by
permitting ORV use in certain "wilderness study areas"

(WSAs)—roadless lands that had been recommended as suitable for "wilderness" designation, without Congress' having acted yet on the recommendation—had violated the FLPMA's nonimpairment mandate (in 43 USCS § 1782(c)) to continue to manage WSAs "in a manner so as not to impair the suitability of such areas for preservation as wilderness"; (2) the BLM had contravened the FLPMA's requirement (in 43 USCS § 1732(a)) to manage public lands in accordance with land-use plans when they were available, by failing to comply with three alleged commitments involving (a) a 1991 resource-management plan for the San Rafael area, and (b) a 1990 ORV-implementation plan for the Henry Mountains area; and (3) under the National Environmental Policy Act of 1969 (NEPA) (42 USCS §§ 4321 et seq.), the BLM had improperly failed to take a "hard look" at whether the BLM ought to undertake supplemental environmental analyses for areas in which ORV use allegedly had increased. However, the District Court entered a dismissal with respect to these three claims.

On appeal, the United States Court of Appeals for the Tenth Circuit, in reversing and in ordering a remand, expressed the view that (1) for purposes of § 706(1), the BLM's nonimpairment obligation under § 1782(c) provided a mandatory and nondiscretionary duty for which a federal court could properly compel compliance; and (2) similar reasoning applied with respect to (a) the land-use-plans claim, and (b) the NEPA claim (301 F3d 1217).

On certiorari, the United States Supreme Court reversed and remanded. In an opinion by SCALIA, J., expressing the unanimous view of the court, it was held that a federal court's authority under § 706(1) did not extend to remedying the BLM's asserted failures with respect to ORV use, as:

(1) With respect to nonimpairment, (a) § 1782(c) did not mandate, with the clarity necessary to support judicial action under § 706(1), the total exclusion of ORV use; and (b) a federal court, under § 706(1), could not properly enter a general order that would compel compliance with § 1782(c)'s broad nonimpairment mandate.

(2) With respect to the land-use plans in question, (a) the challengers' specific points were partially moot; and (b) to the extent that the points were not moot, some "will do" statements in the plans did not provide a legally binding commitment enforceable under § 706(1).

(3) With respect to NEPA, there was no ongoing "major Federal action" in the case at hand that could properly require supplementation.

COUNSEL

Edwin S. Kneedler argued the cause for petitioners.
Paul M. Smith argued the cause for respondents.

UNITED STATES, Petitioner

v

CARLOS DOMINGUEZ BENITEZ

542 US —, 159 L Ed 2d 157, 124 S Ct 2333

[No. 03-167]

Argued April 21, 2004.

Decided June 14, 2004.

Decision: Federal criminal defendant held entitled to plain-error relief from guilty plea, on unpreserved claim that court had failed to give him rule-required warning, only if he could show reasonable probability that, but for error, he would not have entered plea.

SUMMARY

Under Rule 52(b) of the Federal Rules of Criminal Procedure, a plain error affecting substantial rights may be considered on appeal even though the error was not brought to the trial court's attention.

A federal criminal defendant and the government entered into a plea agreement including terms that (1) he would plead guilty to a drug charge, and (2) the government would make a nonbinding sentencing recommendation. The agreement warned the defendant that he could not withdraw his plea if the court did not accept the government's recommendation. During an ensuing hearing at which the defendant pled guilty, a Federal District Court (1) gave him almost all the required warnings required by Rule 11 of the Federal Rules of Criminal Procedure; but (2) failed to give him the required warning, then under Rule 11(e)(2) (later under Rule 11(c)(3)(B)), that he could not withdraw his plea if the court did not accept the government's recommendation. Subsequently, the District Court, in sentencing the defendant to a 10-year prison term, effectively did not accept the government's recommendation.

Even though the defendant did not make a timely objection to the District Court's failure to give the Rule 11 warning in question, the defendant claimed on appeal that he had the right to withdraw his guilty plea as a consequence of the District Court's failure to give the warning. The United States Court of Appeals for the Ninth Circuit, in reversing and in ordering a remand, expressed the view that (1) plain-error review was applicable to the defendant's claim; (2) for the plain-error purpose of showing that the defendant's substantial rights had been affected, the defendant had to prove that (a) the District Court's failure-to-warn error was not minor or technical, and (b) the defendant had not understood the rights at issue when he had entered his guilty plea; and (3) the defendant had satisfied both of these elements (310 F3d 1221).

On certiorari, the United States Supreme Court reversed and remanded. In an opinion by SOUTER, J., joined by REHNQUIST, Ch. J., and STEVENS, O'CONNOR, KENNEDY, THOMAS, GINSBURG, and BREYER, JJ., it was held that:

(1) Under the plain-error requirement of Rule 52(b) to prove an effect on substantial rights, in order for the defendant to obtain relief on direct appellate review of his unpreserved Rule 11 failure-to-warn claim, the defendant was obliged to show a reasonable probability that, but for the District Court's error, he would not have entered his guilty plea.

(2) Thus, the Court of Appeals had used an incorrect test for showing that the defendant's substantial rights had been affected.

SCALIA, J., concurring in the judgment, expressed the view that (1) while he agreed with much of the Supreme Court's opinion, the reasonable-probability standard ought not to be extended to the plain-error context; and (2) instead, where a criminal defendant had failed to object at trial—and thus had the burden of proving that a mistake which the defendant had failed to prevent had had an effect on the defendant's substantial rights—the defendant ought to have to show this effect to have been more likely than not.

COUNSEL

Dan Himmelfarb argued the cause for petitioner.

Myra D. Mossman argued the cause for respondent.

J. ELLIOTT HIBBS, DIRECTOR, ARIZONA DEPART-
MENT OF REVENUE, Petitioner

v

KATHLEEN M. WINN et al.

542 US —, 159 L Ed 2d 172, 124 S Ct 2276

[No. 02-1809]

Argued January 20, 2004.
Decided June 14, 2004.

Decision: Tax Injunction Act (28 USCS § 1341) held
not to bar federal-court suit seeking to enjoin
operation of Arizona statute authorizing state income tax credits for payments funding scholarships to private schools.

SUMMARY

Some Arizona state taxpayers filed, against the director of the state's department of revenue in the United
States District Court for the District of Arizona, a suit
seeking to enjoin, as allegedly violating the establishment of religion clause of the Federal Constitution's
First Amendment, operation of a state statute that
provided a state income tax credit for payments to
certain nonprofit organizations that awarded scholarships to private elementary and secondary schools,
where the statute did not prohibit such scholarships
from covering tuition at schools that provided religious
instruction or that gave religion-based admission preference.

The District Court granted the director's motion to
dismiss on the ground that the Tax Injunction Act
(TIA) (28 USCS § 1341)—which prohibited federal

courts from restraining "the assessment, levy or collection" of any tax under state law where a "plain, speedy and efficient remedy" could be had in state court—barred the suit.

The United States Court of Appeals for the Ninth Circuit (1) reversed, and (2) held that the TIA did not bar federal-court actions challenging state tax credits (307 F3d 1011).

On certiorari, the United States Supreme Court affirmed. In an opinion by GINSBURG, J., joined by STEVENS, O'CONNOR, SOUTER, and BREYER, JJ., it was held that the TIA did not bar the taxpayers' suit, for:
(1) In § 1341 and tax law generally, an assessment was closely tied to the collection of a tax.
(2) In an earlier Supreme Court case, the Federal Government, in discussing tax "assessment," had related "assessment" to the term's collection-propelling function.
(3) In enacting the TIA, Congress had trained its attention on taxpayers who sought to avoid paying their tax bill by pursuing a challenge route other than the one specified by the taxing authority.
(4) The Supreme Court had interpreted and applied the TIA in only cases in which state taxpayers had sought federal-court orders enabling them to avoid paying state taxes.
(5) Other federal courts had not read § 1341 to stop third parties from pursuing constitutional challenges to tax benefits in a federal forum.
(6) Numerous federal-court decisions—including Supreme Court decisions reviewing lower-federal-court judgments—had reached the merits of third-party constitutional challenges to tax benefits without mentioning the TIA.

STEVENS, J., concurring, said that (1) prolonged congressional silence in response to a settled interpretation of a federal statute provided powerful support for maintaining the status quo; (2) in statutory matters, judicial restraint strongly counseled waiting for Congress to take the initiative in modifying rules on which judges and litigants had relied; and (3) in a contest between the dictionary and the doctrine of stare decisis, the latter won.

KENNEDY, J., joined by REHNQUIST, Ch. J., and SCALIA and THOMAS, JJ., dissenting, said that in the instant case, (1) the Supreme Court's analysis of the TIA contrasted with a literal reading of the TIA's terms; and (2) an assertion by the Supreme Court—that legislative histories supported the conclusion that third-party suits not seeking to stop the collection, or to contest the validity, of a tax imposed on the taxpayers were outside Congress' purview in enacting the TIA and the anti-injunction statute on which it was modeled—was not borne out by those sources.

COUNSEL

Samuel Goddard argued the cause for petitioner.

Thomas G. Hungar argued the cause for the United States, as amicus curiae, by special leave of court.

Marvin S. Cohen argued the cause for respondents.

PENNSYLVANIA STATE POLICE, Petitioner

v

NANCY DREW SUDERS

542 US —, 159 L Ed 2d 204, 124 S Ct 2342

[No. 03-95]

Argued March 31, 2004.
Decided June 14, 2004.

Decision: In sexual-harassment/constructive-discharge
suits under Title VII of Civil Rights Act of 1964 (42
USCS §§ 2000e et seq.), affirmative defense—that
plaintiff failed to make use of employer's remedial
policy—held available to some employers.

SUMMARY

A female former employee of the Pennsylvania state
police—alleging that some of her supervisors had
subjected her to sexual harassment of such severity that
she had been forced to resign—brought suit in the
United States District Court for the Middle District of
Pennsylvania against the state police under Title VII of
the Civil Rights Act of 1964 (42 USCS §§ 2000e et seq.).
The District Court, in granting the state police's motion
for summary judgment, concluded that (1) the employee's testimony sufficed to permit a trier of fact to
conclude that the supervisors had created a hostile
work environment; but (2) the employer was not
vicariously liable for the supervisors' conduct, as the
employee had unreasonably failed to avail herself of the
state police's internal procedures for reporting any
harassment.

211

The United States Court of Appeals for the Third Circuit, in reversing and ordering a remand, reasoned that (1) even under the assumption that the state police could assert an affirmative defense based on the employee's alleged failure to avail herself of the state police's program to address sexual harassment claims, genuine issues of material fact existed concerning the effectiveness of that program; (2) the employee had stated a claim of constructive discharge due to hostile work environment; and (3) a constructive discharge, if proved, would constitute a tangible employment action that would render an employer strictly liable and preclude recourse to the affirmative defense in question (325 F3d 432).

On certiorari, the United States Supreme Court vacated and remanded. In an opinion by GINSBURG, J., joined by REHNQUIST, Ch. J., and STEVENS, O'CONNOR, SCALIA, KENNEDY, SOUTER, and BREYER, JJ., it was held that:

(1) With respect to a plaintiff-employee's Title VII claim for constructive discharge resulting from sexual harassment by a supervisor, the employer may, in some cases, properly defend against such a claim by showing that (a) the employer had installed a readily accessible and effective policy for reporting and resolving complaints of sexual harassment, and (b) the plaintiff unreasonably failed to make use of such a preventive or remedial apparatus.

(2) This affirmative defense (a) is available to the employer only where a supervisor's official act—or, in other words, a tangible employment action—does not underlie the constructive discharge; and (2) is not available if the plaintiff has quit in reasonable response to an employer-sanctioned adverse action that officially changed the plaintiff's employment status or situation.

(3) Although the Court of Appeals had correctly ruled

212

that the case at hand, in its current posture, presented genuine issues of material fact concerning the hostile-work-environment and constructive-discharge claims, the Court of Appeals had erred in declaring that the affirmative defense in question was never available in constructive-discharge cases.

THOMAS, J., dissenting, expressed the view that (1) where an alleged constructive discharge resulted only from a hostile work environment and not from a supervisor's adverse employment action, an employer ought to be liable under Title VII only if negligent; and (2) the Court of Appeals' judgment ought to have been reversed, because the employee had not (a) adduced sufficient evidence of an adverse employment action taken because of her sex, or (b) proffered any evidence that the state police had known or should have known of the alleged harassment.

COUNSEL

John G. Knorr, III argued the cause for petitioner.

Irving L. Gornstein argued the cause for the United States, as amicus curiae, by special leave of court.

Donald A. Bailey argued the cause for respondent.

F. HOFFMANN-La ROCHE LTD, et al., Petitioners

v

EMPAGRAN S. A. et al.

542 US —, 159 L Ed 2d 226, 124 S Ct 2359

[No. 03-724]

Argued April 26, 2004.

Decided June 14, 2004.

Decision: Alleged price-fixing activity held excluded from reach of Sherman Act (15 USCS §§ 1 et seq.) by Foreign Trade Antitrust Improvements Act of 1982 (15 USCS § 6a) where plaintiff's claim rested solely on independent foreign harm.

SUMMARY

The Foreign Trade Antitrust Improvements Act of 1982 (FTAIA) (15 USCS § 6a) excludes from the reach of the Sherman Act (15 USCS §§ 1 et seq.) much anticompetitive conduct that causes only foreign injury, by (1) setting forth a general exclusionary rule that the Sherman Act "shall not apply to conduct involving trade or commerce (other than import trade or import commerce) with foreign nations"; and (2) creating a domestic-injury exception bringing such conduct back within the Sherman Act's reach, provided that the conduct (a) has a "direct, substantial, and reasonably foreseeable effect" on American domestic, import, or (certain) export commerce, and (b) such effect gives rise to a Sherman Act claim.

In the United States District Court for the District of Columbia, a purported class action was filed on behalf of foreign and domestic purchasers of vitamins under provisions including § 1 of the Sherman Act (15 USCS § 1). The complaint alleged that the defendants, foreign and domestic vitamin manufacturers and distributors, had engaged in a price-fixing conspiracy, raising the price of vitamin products to customers in the United States and to customers in foreign countries. The manufacturers and distributors moved to dismiss the suit as to some foreign-purchaser plaintiffs— vitamin distributors located in Ukraine, Australia, Ecuador, and Panama—each of which allegedly bought vitamins for delivery outside the United States. The District Court applied the FTAIA and dismissed the foreign purchasers' claims.

On appeal, the United States Court of Appeals for the District of Columbia Circuit—in reversing, vacating the judgment against the foreign purchasers, and ordering a remand—expressed the view that (1) the FTAIA's general exclusionary rule applied to the case at hand, but (2) the FTAIA's domestic-injury exception also applied (315 F3d 338).

On certiorari, the United States Supreme Court vacated and remanded. In an opinion by BREYER, J., joined by REHNQUIST, Ch. J., and STEVENS, KENNEDY, SOUTER, and GINSBURG, JJ., it was held that:

(1) On the assumption, for the purposes of decision, that the alleged anticompetitive price-fixing activity was in significant part foreign, caused some domestic antitrust injury, and independently caused separate foreign injury, this alleged price-fixing activity fell within the FTAIA's general exclusionary rule.

(2) Moreover, on this assumption—and on consideration of the FTAIA's basic purposes, international comity, and Sherman Act history—such alleged price-fixing activity did not fall within the FTAIA's domestic-injury exception where a plaintiff's Sherman Act claim rested solely on the independent foreign harm.

215

(3) The foreign-purchaser plaintiffs in the case at hand remained free to ask the Court of Appeals, on remand, to consider the plaintiffs' argument that the foreign injury alleged in the case at hand was not independent.

SCALIA, J., joined by THOMAS, J., concurring in the judgment, expressed the view that (1) the FTAIA's language was readily susceptible of the interpretation which the Supreme Court provided; and (2) only this interpretation was consistent with the principle that federal statutes ought to be read in accord with the customary deference to the application of foreign countries' laws within their own territories.

O'CONNOR, J., did not participate.

COUNSEL

Stephen M. Shapiro argued the cause for petitioners.

R. Hewitt Pate argued the cause for the United States, as amicus curiae, by special leave of court.

Thomas C. Goldstein argued the cause for respondents.

LARRY D. HIIBEL, Petitioner

v

SIXTH JUDICIAL DISTRICT COURT OF NEVADA,
HUMBOLDT COUNTY, et al.

542 US —, 159 L Ed 2d 292, 124 S Ct 2451

[No. 03-5554]

Argued March 22, 2004.
Decided June 21, 2004.

Decision: Suspect's conviction, under Nevada law, for
refusing to disclose his name to law enforcement
officer during valid investigative stop held not to
violate Federal Constitution's Fourth and Fifth
Amendment guarantees.

SUMMARY

Under Terry v Ohio (1968) 392 US 1, 20 L Ed 2d 889,
88 S Ct 1868, a law enforcement officer's reasonable
suspicion that a person may be involved in criminal
activity permits the officer—consistent with the Federal
Constitution's Fourth Amendment—to stop the person
for a brief time and take additional steps to investigate
further. A Nevada statute required any suspects so
detained to identify themselves.

A deputy sheriff in Nevada, investigating a report of
an assault, approached a suspect and asked him if he
had any identification on him. After the suspect repeat-
edly refused to identify himself, he was arrested and
charged with obstructing the discharge of the deputy
sheriff's official duty. The suspect was convicted in a
Nevada trial court, which agreed that the suspect's

refusal to identify himself, as required by Nevada's "stop and identify" statute, had constituted such an obstruction.

The Sixth Judicial District Court of Nevada, in affirming, rejected the suspect's argument that the application of the "stop and identify" statute to his case violated the Constitution's Fourth and Fifth Amendments. The Supreme Court of Nevada, in denying the suspect's certiorari petition, (1) interpreted the statute to require only that suspects disclose their names, and (2) rejected the Fourth Amendment challenge, on the ground that the statute imposed a commonsense requirement to protect both the public and law enforcement officers (118 Nev 868, 59 P3d 1201). Although the suspect petitioned for rehearing in order to seek explicit resolution of his Fifth Amendment challenge, the petition was denied without opinion.

On certiorari, the United States Supreme Court affirmed. In an opinion by KENNEDY, J., joined by REHNQUIST, Ch. J., and O'CONNOR, SCALIA, and THOMAS, JJ., it was held that:

(1) Nevada's "stop and identify" statute—as interpreted to require only that suspects disclose their names—was consistent with Fourth Amendment prohibitions against unreasonable searches and seizures, for (a) obtaining a suspect's name in the course of a Terry stop served important government interests; (b) the request for identity had an immediate relation to the purpose, rationale, and practical demands of a Terry stop; (c) the threat of criminal sanction helped insure that the request for identity would not become a legal nullity; and (d) the statute did not alter the nature of the stop itself.

(2) The Fourth Amendment was not violated by the deputy sheriff's request for identification or by the suspect's conviction for refusing to comply with the

218

request, for (a) the initial stop had been based on
reasonable suspicion and thus satisfied Fourth Amendment requirements; (b) the request was a commonsense inquiry, not merely an effort to obtain an arrest
for failure to identify after a Terry stop yielded insufficient evidence; and (c) the request was thus reasonably
related in scope to the circumstances which justified
the stop.
(3) The suspect's conviction did not violate the Fifth
Amendment's privilege against compelled self-
incrimination, for the disclosure of the suspect's name
would have presented no reasonable danger of incrimination, as the suspect's refusal was not based on any
articulated real and appreciable fear that his name
would (a) be used to incriminate him, or (b) furnish a
link in the chain of evidence needed to prosecute him.

STEVENS, J., dissenting, expressed the view that the
constitutional right to remain silent, derived from the
Fifth Amendment, did not admit even of the narrow
exception defined by Nevada's "stop and identify"
statute, for (1) a person's identity bore informational
and incriminating worth, even if the name itself was not
inculpatory; and (2) the case at hand thus concerned a
protected testimonial communication for Fifth Amendment purposes.

BREYER, J., joined by SOUTER and GINSBURG, JJ.,
dissenting, expressed the view that (1) under the
Supreme Court's Fourth Amendment precedents, an
officer was permitted to ask a Terry detainee a moder-
ate number of questions to determine identity and to
try to obtain information confirming or dispelling the
officer's suspicions, but the detainee was not obliged to
respond; (2) there were sound reasons, including Fifth
Amendment considerations, for adhering to such a

Fourth Amendment legal condition; and (3) this rule ought not to be eroded with special exceptions.

COUNSEL

Robert E. Dolan argued the cause for petitioner.

Conrad Hafen argued the cause for respondents.

Sri Srinivasan argued the cause for the United States, as amicus curiae, by special leave of court.

AETNA HEALTH INC., fka AETNA U. S. HEALTH-
CARE INC. and AETNA U. S. HEALTHCARE OF
NORTH TEXAS INC., Petitioner

v

JUAN DAVILA (No. 02-1845)

CIGNA HEALTHCARE OF TEXAS, INC., dba CIGNA
CORPORATION, Petitioner

v

RUBY R. CALAD et al. (No. 03-83)

542 US —, 159 L Ed 2d 312, 124 S Ct 2488

Argued March 23, 2004.
Decided June 21, 2004.

Decision: State-court actions alleging that HMOs' failure to cover certain medical services violated state
statute held to be (1) pre-empted by § 502(a)
(1)(B) of ERISA (29 USCS § 1132(a)(1)(B)), and
(2) thus removable to federal court.

SUMMARY

Two beneficiaries of health care plans covered by the
Employee Retirement Income Security Act of 1974
(ERISA) (29 USCS §§ 1001 et seq.) brought separate
Texas state-court suits, alleging that (1) the health
maintenance organizations (HMOs) that administered
the plans had refused to cover certain medical services
in violation of an HMO's duty to exercise ordinary care
under a Texas health care statute; and (2) those refusals
had proximately caused injuries to the beneficiaries.

221

The actions were removed to Federal District Courts on the basis of the HMOs' allegations that the actions fit within the scope of, and were thus completely pre-empted by, § 502(a) of ERISA (29 USCS § 1132(a)), which authorized certain actions by allegedly wronged beneficiaries of employee welfare benefit plans. The District Courts (1) declined to remand the cases to state court, and (2) dismissed the actions with prejudice after the beneficiaries had refused to amend the actions to bring explicit ERISA claims.

After the beneficiaries appealed the refusals to remand to state court, the United States Court of Appeals for the Fifth Circuit consolidated the beneficiaries' cases with several other cases. The Court of Appeals (1) reversed; and (2) found that the beneficiaries' claims did not fall under § 502(a) (307 F3d 298).

On certiorari, the United States Supreme Court reversed and remanded. In an opinion by THOMAS, J., expressing the unanimous view of the court, it was held that the beneficiaries' causes of action fell within the scope of, and were completely pre-empted by, § 502(a)(1)(B), and thus were removable to a District Court, because the duties imposed by the state statute in the context of these beneficiaries' cases did not arise independently of ERISA or the plan terms, as:

(1) A managed-care entity could not be subject to liability under the state statute if the entity denied coverage for any treatment not covered by the health care plan that it was administering.

(2) The beneficiaries' causes of action were not entirely independent of the federally-regulated plan contracts.

(3) The beneficiaries (i) had brought suit only to rectify a wrongful denial of benefits promised under ERISA-regulated plans, and (ii) were not attempting to remedy any violation of a legal duty independent of ERISA.

222

GINSBURG, J., joined by BREYER, J., concurring, expressed the view that Congress and the Supreme Court ought to revisit what was an unjust and increasingly tangled ERISA regime, as the court's coupling of an encompassing interpretation of ERISA's pre-emptive force with a cramped construction of the "equitable relief" allowable under § 502(a)(3) had created a regulatory vacuum in which (1) virtually all state-law remedies were pre-empted, but (2) very few federal substitutes were provided.

COUNSEL

Miguel A. Estrada argued the cause for petitioners.

James A. Feldman argued the cause for the United States, as amicus curiae, by special leave of court.

George P. Young argued the cause for respondents.

David C. Mattax argued the cause for Texas, et al., as amici curiae, by special leave of court.

CHERYL K. PLILER, WARDEN, Petitioner

v

RICHARD HERMAN FORD

542 US —, 159 L Ed 2d 338, 124 S Ct 2441

[No. 03-221]

Argued April 26, 2004.
Decided June 21, 2004.

Decision: Federal District Court's failure to give California prisoner two particular warnings held not to make improper dismissals of two "mixed" habeas corpus petitions—containing both unexhausted and exhausted claims—that prisoner had filed pro se.

SUMMARY

Under Rose v Lundy (1982) 455 US 509, 71 L Ed 2d 379, 102 S Ct 1198, Federal District Courts must dismiss state prisoners' "mixed" habeas corpus petitions—containing both unexhausted and exhausted claims—where "unexhausted" and "exhausted" refer to the prisoners' state-court remedies. Subsequent to the Rose decision, Congress enacted an Antiterrorism and Effective Death Penalty Act of 1996 (AEDPA) provision (28 USCS § 2244(d)(1)) which generally imposed a 1-year limitations period on filing a federal habeas corpus petition. The combined effect of Rose v Lundy and the AEDPA provision was that if a state prisoner filed such a mixed petition toward the end of the limitations period, a Rose-based dismissal could result in the loss of all of the prisoner's claims—including those already exhausted—because

224

the limitations period could expire during the time a petitioner returned to state court to exhaust the unexhausted claims.

In response, the United States Court of Appeals for the Ninth Circuit purported to authorize District Courts to employ a "stay-and-abeyance" procedure with respect to such a mixed petition. This procedure involved (1) the dismissal of any unexhausted claims from the original mixed petition; (2) a stay of the remaining claims, pending exhaustion of the dismissed unexhausted claims in state court; and (3) amendment of the original petition to add the newly exhausted claims, which then were supposed to relate back to the original petition.

In the proceedings in question, shortly before AEDPA's limitations period would have expired, a Califonia prisoner had signed and delivered to prison authorities two pro se federal habeas corpus petitions with respect to two sets of convictions on state homicide charges. A federal Magistrate Judge gave the prisoner three options: (1) the petitions could be dismissed "without prejudice" and the prisoner could refile after exhausting the unexhausted claims; (2) the unexhausted claims could be dismissed and the prisoner could proceed with only the exhausted claims; or (3) the prisoner could contest the Magistrate Judge's finding that some of the claims had not been exhausted. After the prisoner chose the first option for the first petition and failed to respond with respect to the second petition, the United States District Court for the Central District of California dismissed the two petitions "without prejudice."

In both cases, the prisoner then filed habeas corpus petitions in the California Supreme Court, which summarily denied both.

The prisoner subsequently refiled his pro se habeas corpus petitions in the District Court. However, the District Court (1) dismissed both later petitions "with prejudice" as assertedly untimely under AEDPA's limitations period; and (2) denied the prisoner's motions for a certificate of appealability (COA).

The Court of Appeals for Ninth Circuit consolidated the two cases and granted the prisoner's COA motions. Subsequently, the Court of Appeals—in affirming in part, vacating in part, and ordering a remand—expressed the view that (1) with respect to the two earlier petitions of the prisoner in question, if a pro se prisoner filed such a mixed petition, then a District Court had to give two warnings regarding the stay-and-abeyance procedure, to the effect that (a) the District Court would not have the power to consider a motion by the prisoner to stay the mixed petition unless the prisoner opted to amend the petition and to dismiss the then-unexhausted claims, and (b) the prisoner's federal claims would be time-barred, absent cause for equitable tolling, upon the prisoner's return to federal court if the prisoner opted to dismiss the petition "without prejudice" and to return to state court to exhaust all of the prisoner's claims; (2) the prisoner in question also had been misled, at the earlier-petitions stage, by having been told that if he chose the first (dismissal) option, the dismissal would be "without prejudice"; and (3) a pro se habeas corpus petitioner who timely filed a mixed petition that was improperly dismissed by a District Court—and who then returned to state court to exhaust the unexhausted claims and subsequently refiled a second petition "without unreasonable delay"—could have the second petition relate back to the initial timely petition (as amended upon denial of rehearing and rehearing en banc, 330 F3d 1086).

On certiorari, the United States Supreme Court vacated and remanded. In an opinion by THOMAS, J., joined by REHNQUIST, Ch. J., and O'CONNOR, SCALIA, and KENNEDY, JJ., it was held that:

(1) In the case at hand, the District Court's failure to give the California prisoner the two warnings in question did not make improper the District Court's dismissals, pursuant to Rose v Lundy, of the prisoner's two earlier federal habeas corpus petitions, as—without addressing the propriety of the Court of Appeals' stay-and-abeyance procedure—(a) requiring these two warnings would undermine District Court judges' role as impartial decisionmakers; and (b) the two warnings (i) ran the risk of being misleading, and (ii) would not "simply implement" what the Supreme Court had already required under Rose v Lundy.

(2) Because of this no-required-warnings holding, there was no need to reach the second question presented on certiorari, as to whether the prisoner's two later petitions related back to the two "improperly dismissed" earlier petitions.

(3) However, the case at hand was being remanded for further proceedings, given the Court of Appeals' concern that the prisoner had been affirmatively misled "quite apart" from the District Court's failure to give the two warnings in question.

O'CONNOR, J., concurring, expressed the view that (1) the Supreme Court's opinion (a) was limited to the narrow question whether the notifications crafted by the Court of Appeals had to be given, and (b) properly avoided addressing the propriety of the Court of Appeals' stay-and-abeyance procedure generally; (2) equitable tolling might be appropriate if a state prisoner who had filed a mixed federal habeas corpus petition was affirmatively misled, either by the federal court or by the state, concerning the options available; and (3) that was a question for the Court of Appeals to consider on remand.

STEVENS, J., joined by SOUTER, J., concurring in the judgment, (1) agreed with the views expressed below by GINSBURG and BREYER, JJ.; but (2) said that the Supreme Court's judgment, in remanding the case at hand to the Court of Appeals to determine the propriety of equitable tolling, was both consistent with those views and correct.

GINSBURG, J., joined by BREYER, J., dissenting, expressed the view that the Court of Appeals' judgment should have been affirmed to the extent that it had vacated the District Court's dismissal of the prisoner's two later petitions, as (1) regardless of whether particular "advisements" were required, the Supreme Court erred by disposing of the case at hand without addressing the ripe issues concerning (a) the propriety of the stay-and-abeyance procedure, and (b) the highly misleading characterization of the orders dismissing the prisoner's two earlier petitions as "without prejudice"; and (2) the Supreme Court's opinion also postponed the related question whether the dismissal solution of Rose v Lundy bore re-examination in light of AEDPA's subsequently-imposed limitations period.

BREYER, J., dissenting, expressed the view that (1) the Supreme Court should have found the stay-and-abeyance procedure to be legally permissible, and (2) at the earlier-petitions stage, the prisoner should have been informed of this important rights-preserving option.

COUNSEL

Paul M. Roadarmel, Jr. argued the cause for petitioner.

Lisa M. Bassis argued the cause for respondent.

INTEL CORPORATION, Petitioner

v

ADVANCED MICRO DEVICES, INC.

542 US —, 159 L Ed 2d 355, 124 S Ct 2466

[No. 02-572]

Argued April 20, 2004.
Decided June 21, 2004.

Decision: 28 USCS § 1782(a) held to authorize, but not
to require, Federal District Court to order some
discovery requested by private complainant for use
in European Commission antitrust proceeding.

SUMMARY

28 USCS § 1782(a), as amended, authorized a Federal District Court to order some discovery "for use in
a proceeding in a foreign or international tribunal . . .
upon the application of any interested person."

The Commission of the European Communities was
an executive and administrative organ that exercised
responsibility over a wide range of subject areas covered
by the European Union (EU) treaty. The Directorate-
General for Competition ("DG-Competition") of the
Commission (1) operated under the Commission's
aegis, (2) was the EU's primary antitrust law enforcer,
and (3) conducted investigations which ultimately resulted in formal written decisions that, if the DG-
Competition declined to proceed, were subject to EU
judicial review.

A company headquartered in California filed, with
the Commission's DG-Competition, an antitrust complaint against a second company, also headquarted in

230

California. This complaint alleged that the second
company had violated EU competition law with respect
to the European market. While the complaint apparently was still in the investigative stage, the first company requested, from the United States District Court
for the Northern District of California, a discovery
order under § 1782(a), allegedly in connection with
the complaint, to direct the second company to produce some documents that had been produced in
previous antitrust litigation involving the second company. However, the District Court denied the request, as
assertedly unsupported by applicable authority.

On appeal, the United States Court of Appeals for
the Ninth Circuit, in reversing and in ordering a
remand, expressed the view that (1) the Commission
proceeding for which the first company had sought
discovery qualified under § 1782(a); (2) there was no
requirement for the first company to show that what it
sought would also be discoverable in the Commission
proceeding; and (3) the District Court ought to proceed to consider the first company's request on the
merits (292 F3d 664).

On certiorari, the United States Supreme Court
affirmed. In an opinion by GINSBURG, J., joined by
REHNQUIST, Ch. J., and STEVENS, KENNEDY, SOUTER,
and THOMAS, JJ., it was held that:
(1) Under the language of § 1782(a), as confirmed by
its context, § 1782(a) authorized, but did not require, a
District Court to provide assistance to a complainant in
a Commission proceeding that led to a dispositive
ruling—a final administrative action both responsive to
the complaint and reviewable in court—as:
    (a) A complainant before the Commission qualified
as an "interested person."
    (b) The Commission was a "tribunal" when the
Commission acted as a first-instance decisionmaker.

(c) A "proceeding" for which discovery was sought had to be in reasonable contemplation, but did not need to be pending or imminent.

(d) There was no threshold requirement that evidence sought from a District Court had to be discoverable under the law governing the foreign proceeding.

(e) A District Court (i) was not required to grant a discovery application simply because the District Court had the authority to do so, and (ii) had discretion whether to grant such an application, in light of a variety of considerations.

(2) The question whether § 1782(a) assistance was appropriate in the case at hand was not yet resolved.

(3) It would be left to the courts below to assure an airing adequate to determine what, if any, assistance was appropriate.

SCALIA, J., concurring in the judgment, expressed the view that (1) the Supreme Court's disposition of the case at hand was required by § 1782(a)'s text; and (2) thus, it was not only improper, but also unnecessary, for the Supreme Court's opinion to have sought repeated support in the words of a United States Senate committee report.

BREYER, J., dissenting, expressed the view that (1) the Supreme Court had read § 1782(a)'s scope to extend beyond what Congress might reasonably have intended; (2) instead, § 1782(a) ought to be read as subjecting a District Court's broad discovery authority to some categorical limits, including the two limits that (a) when a foreign entity possessed few tribunal-like characteristics, so that the applicability of the word "tribunal" was in serious doubt, then a District Court ought to pay close attention to the foreign entity's own view of the entity's status, and (b) a District Court ought not to permit discovery where both (i) a private person seek-

232

ing discovery would not be entitled to that discovery under foreign law, and (ii) the discovery would not be available under domestic law in analogous circumstances; and (3) a proper application of either of these two limits ought to require the dismissal of the discovery proceeding in the case at hand.

O'CONNOR, J., did not participate.

COUNSEL

Seth P. Waxman argued the cause for petitioner.

Carter G. Phillips argued the cause for Commission of the European Communities, as amicus curiae, by special leave of court.

Patrick Lynch argued the cause for respondent.

Jeffrey P. Minear argued the cause for the United States, as amicus curiae, by special leave of court.

ROBERT JAMES TENNARD, Petitioner

v

DOUG DRETKE, DIRECTOR, TEXAS DEPART-
MENT OF CRIMINAL JUSTICE, CORRECTIONAL
INSTITUTIONS DIVISION

542 US —, 159 L Ed 2d 384, 124 S Ct 2562

[No. 02-10038]

Argued March 22, 2004.

Decided June 24, 2004.

Decision: Texas prisoner seeking federal habeas corpus relief from death sentence held entitled to certificate of appealability under 28 USCS § 2253(c)(2), where reasonable jurists would have found disposition of his low-IQ mitigation claim debatable or wrong.

SUMMARY

In Penry v Lynaugh (1989) 492 US 302, 106 L Ed 2d 256, 109 S Ct 2934, the United States Supreme Court held that in the absence of instructions informing a capital sentencing jury that the jury could consider and give effect to the accused's mitigating evidence of mental retardation or background of childhood abuse, the imposition of a death sentence on the accused violated the Federal Constitution's Eighth Amendment prohibition against cruel and unusual punishments.

In 1986, a defendant was convicted in a Texas trial court on a charge of capital murder. During the trial's penalty phase, the defendant presented evidence that he had low intelligence, in that he had an IQ of 67. The defendant's counsel relied on this evidence in arguing

234

that factors including the defendant's limited mental faculties mitigated his culpability for murder. However, the jury was instructed to consider only two "special issues": whether (1) the defendant's conduct was committed deliberately and with the reasonable expectation of death, and (2) the defendant would probably commit future acts that would constitute a continuing threat to society. The jury answered both of these questions in the affirmative, and the defendant was accordingly sentenced to death. The Court of Criminal Appeals of Texas affirmed the conviction and sentence on direct appeal (802 SW2d 678).

The defendant petitioned for state habeas corpus relief, on the assertion that in light of the instructions given to the jury, his death sentence had been obtained in violation of the Eighth Amendment as interpreted in Penry v Lynaugh. The Court of Criminal Appeals, in denying the petition, reasoned that (1) there was no evidence that the defendant's low IQ had rendered him unable to appreciate the wrongfulness of his conduct, learn from his mistakes, or control his impulses; and (2) there had been no danger that the jury would have given the low-IQ evidence only aggravating effect in answering the future-dangerousness special issue (960 SW2d 57).

The defendant subsequently petitioned for federal habeas corpus relief in the United States District Court for the Southern District of Texas. The District Court—concluding that the jury had had adequate means by which to give effect to the mitigating low-IQ evidence—denied the petition and also denied a certificate of appealability (COA) under 28 USCS § 2253(c)(2).

On appeal, the United States Court of Appeals for the Fifth Circuit denied a COA, on the grounds that (1) the appropriate threshold test for Penry claims was whether there was "constitutionally relevant" mitigating evidence, that is, evidence of a "uniquely severe" permanent handicap that bore a nexus to the crime in question; (2) evidence of low IQ alone did not constitute a uniquely severe condition; (3) no evidence had been introduced that would tie the defendant's IQ score to mental retardation; and (4) even if the defendant's evidence was mental-retardation evidence, his claim would fail, because he had not shown that the crime in question was attributable to his low IQ (284 F3d 591).

The Supreme Court granted certiorari, vacated the Court of Appeals' judgment, and remanded for further consideration in light of Atkins v Virginia (2002) 536 US 304, 153 L Ed 2d 335, 122 S Ct 2242, in which the Supreme Court had held that the execution of criminals who were mentally retarded constituted cruel and unusual punishment in violation of the Eighth Amendment (537 US 802, 154 L Ed 2d 4, 123 S Ct 70). On remand, the Court of Appeals reinstated its prior opinion and affirmed the District Court's judgment, on the ground that the defendant had never argued that the Eighth Amendment prohibited his execution (317 F3d 476).

On certiorari, the Supreme Court reversed and remanded. In an opinion by O'CONNOR, J., joined by STEVENS, KENNEDY, SOUTER, GINSBURG, and BREYER, JJ., it was held that a certificate of appealability ought to have been issued to the defendant, for:

(1) The Court of Appeals, in applying its threshold test, had assessed the defendant's Penry claim under an improper legal standard.

(2) According to the analysis that the Court of Appeals ought to have conducted, reasonable jurists would have found debatable or wrong the District Court's disposition of the defendant's Penry claim, as such jurists

could have concluded that (a) the low-IQ evidence was relevant mitigating evidence, and (b) the jury might have given the low-IQ evidence an aggravating, rather than mitigating, effect in considering the prisoner's future dangerousness.

REHNQUIST, Ch. J., dissenting, expressed the view that (1) the defendant's low intelligence was a relevant mitigating circumstance which the sentencing jury had to be allowed to consider; but (2) reasonable jurists would not have found the District Court's assessment of the constitutional claims debatable or wrong, for the District Court had correctly concluded that the jury instructions had allowed the jury to give some mitigating effect to the evidence of low intelligence.

SCALIA, J., dissenting, expressed the view that there was no basis in the Constitution for a death-penalty requirement that a sentencer had to be allowed to give full consideration and full effect to mitigating circumstances.

THOMAS, J., dissenting, expressed the view that the argument that Texas' special-issues framework had unconstitutionally limited the discretion of the defendant's sentencing jury necessarily relied on Penry v Lynaugh, a decision that had done so much violence to so many settled precedents in an area of fundamental constitutional law that the decision ought not to command the force of stare decisis.

COUNSEL

Robert C. Owen argued the cause for petitioner.
Edward L. Marshall argued the cause for respondent.

RALPH HOWARD BLAKELY, Jr., Petitioner

v

WASHINGTON

542 US —, 159 L Ed 2d 403, 124 S Ct 2531

[No. 02-1632]

Argued March 23, 2004.
Decided June 24, 2004.

Decision: State judge's imposition—on basis of judge's determination that accused, who had pleaded guilty to kidnapping, had acted with deliberate cruelty—of sentence exceeding general statutory maximum held to violate Sixth Amendment right to jury trial.

SUMMARY

The facts admitted by an accused, in pleading guilty to kidnapping his estranged wife, supported, under some statutes of the state of Washington, a maximum prison sentence of 53 months. However, the judge, after hearing the wife's description of the kidnapping, imposed—on the basis of other state statutes allowing in some cases an "exceptional sentence" exceeding the general statutory limit—a 90-month prison sentence on the ground that the accused had acted with "deliberate cruelty," which was a statutorily enumerated ground for an enhanced sentence in a domestic-violence case.

In affirming, the Court of Appeals of Washington, Division 3, rejected the accused's argument that his sentencing procedure had deprived him of his federal constitutional right to have a jury determine beyond a reasonable doubt all facts legally essential to his sen-
238

tence (11 Wash App 851, 47 P3d 149). The Washington Supreme Court denied discretionary review (148 Wash 2d 1010, 62 P3d 889).

On certiorari, the United States Supreme Court reversed and remanded. In an opinion by SCALIA, J., joined by STEVENS, SOUTER, THOMAS, and GINSBURG, JJ., it was held that the judge's imposition of the 90-month sentence violated the accused's right to a jury trial under the Federal Constitution's Sixth Amendment, for:

(1) The purported facts supporting the finding of deliberate cruelty had been neither (a) admitted by the accused, nor (b) found by a jury.

(2) Under state law, the judge could not have imposed the 90-month sentence solely on the basis of the facts admitted in the guilty plea.

(3) The right to a jury trial was no mere procedural formality, but a fundamental reservation to the people of control over the judiciary in the nation's constitutional structure, as the Supreme Court's holding in Apprendi v New Jersey (2000) 530 US 466, 147 L Ed 2d 435, 120 S Ct 2348—that other than the fact of a prior conviction, any fact that increased the penalty for a crime beyond the prescribed statutory maximum had to be submitted to a jury, and proved beyond a reasonable doubt—carried out this design by insuring that a judge's authority to sentence derived wholly from a jury's verdict.

O'CONNOR, J., joined by BREYER, J., and joined in pertinent part by REHNQUIST, Ch. J., and KENNEDY, J., dissenting, said that the legacy of the Supreme Court's opinion in the instant case, whether intended or not, would be the consolidation of sentencing power in the state and federal judiciaries, for (1) Congress and states, faced with the burdens imposed by the extension of Apprendi to the present context, would either trim or eliminate their sentencing guidelines schemes and, with them, 20 years of sentencing reform; and (2) it was thus of little moment that in the instant case, the Supreme Court did not expressly declare guidelines schemes unconstitutional.

KENNEDY, J., joined by BREYER, J., dissenting, said that (1) in the instant case, the Supreme Court disregarded the fundamental principle, under the nation's constitutional system, that different branches of government converse with each other on matters of vital common interest; (2) sentencing guidelines were a prime example of this collaborative process; and (3) the fact that the instant case concerned the work of a state legislature, and not of Congress, if anything, counseled even greater judicial caution.

BREYER, J., joined by O'CONNOR, J., dissenting, said that the decision in the instant case (1) was fraught with consequences that threatened the fairness of the nation's traditional criminal justice system, as the decision (a) distorted historical sentencing or criminal trial practices, and (b) upset settled law on which legislatures had relied in designing punishment systems; and (2) affected tens of thousands of criminal prosecutions, including those in which federal prosecutors would proceed subject to the risk that all defendants in those cases would have to be sentenced, perhaps tried, anew.

COUNSEL

Jeffrey L. Fisher argued the cause for petitioner.

John D. Knodell, Jr. argued the cause for respondent.

Michael R. Dreeben argued the cause for the United States, as amicus curiae, by special leave of court.

DORA B. SCHRIRO, DIRECTOR, ARIZONA DE-
PARTMENT OF CORRECTIONS, Petitioner

v

WARREN WESLEY SUMMERLIN

542 US —, 159 L Ed 2d 442, 124 S Ct 2519

[No. 03-526]

Argued April 19, 2004.
Decided June 24, 2004.

Decision: New rule announced in Ring v Arizona
(2002) 536 US 584, 153 L Ed 2d 556, 122 S Ct
2428—requiring that aggravating factors necessary
for death penalty be found by jury—held not
retroactively applicable to cases already final on
direct review.

SUMMARY

An accused, who had been convicted, in an Arizona
state court, of first-degree murder, was sentenced to
death by the trial judge on the basis of the judge's
finding of aggravating factors, where the state's capital-
sentencing scheme authorized a judge, rather than a
jury, to determine the presence of aggravating factors.
On direct review, the Arizona Supreme Court affirmed
(138 Ariz 426, 675 P2d 686).

While the accused's subsequent federal habeas corpus proceedings were pending in the United States
Court of Appeals for the Ninth Circuit, the United
States Supreme Court, in Ring v Arizona (2002) 536 US
584, 153 L Ed 2d 556, 122 S Ct 2428, announced a new
rule that allowing a sentencing judge, without a jury, to
find an aggravating circumstance necessary for impos-
241

ing the death penalty violated the right to a jury trial
under the Federal Constitution's Sixth Amendment. In
invalidating the accused's death sentence, the Court of
Appeals rejected the argument that Ring did not apply
on the basis that the accused's conviction and sentence
had become final on direct review before Ring was
decided (341 F3d 1082).

On certiorari, the Supreme Court reversed and remanded. In an opinion by SCALIA, J., joined by REH-
NQUIST, Ch. J., and O'CONNOR, KENNEDY, and THOMAS,
JJ., it was held that the new rule announced in Ring did
not apply retroactively to cases already final on direct
review, because:

(1) The Ring rule was properly classified as
procedural—which type of rule generally did not apply
to cases already final on direct review—for the rule
altered the range of permissible methods for determining whether a defendant's conduct was punishable by
death.

(2) The Ring rule did not fall under the retroactivity
exception for watershed rules of criminal procedure
implicating the fundamental fairness and accuracy of
the criminal proceeding, for the Supreme Court could
not confidently say that judicial factfinding seriously
diminished accuracy.

(3) If under DeStefano v Woods (1968) 392 US 631, 20
L Ed 2d 1308, 88 S Ct 2093—in which the Supreme
Court had refused to give retroactive effect to an earlier
Supreme Court decision that applied the Sixth Amendment's jury-trial guarantee to the states—a trial held
entirely without a jury was not impermissibly inaccu-
rate, it was hard to see how a trial in which a judge
found only aggravating factors could be so.

BREYER, J., joined by STEVENS, SOUTER, and GINS-
BURG, JJ., dissenting, said that the new rule announced
in Ring was a watershed procedural ruling that a
242

federal habeas corpus court had to apply when considering a constitutional challenge to a death sentence that was already final on direct review when Ring was decided, as the Ring rule was (1) implicit in the concept of ordered liberty, implicating fundamental fairness; and (2) central to an accurate determination of innocence or guilt, such that failure to apply the rule created an impermissibly large risk that the innocent would be convicted.

COUNSEL

John P. Todd argued the cause for petitioner.

James A. Feldman argued the cause for the United States, as amicus curiae, by special leave of court.

Ken Murray argued the cause for respondent.

RICHARD B. CHENEY, VICE PRESIDENT OF THE
UNITED STATES, et al., Petitioners

v

UNITED STATES DISTRICT COURT FOR THE DIS-
TRICT OF COLUMBIA et al.

542 US —, 159 L Ed 2d 459, 124 S Ct 2576

[No. 03-475]

Argued April 27, 2004.
Decided June 24, 2004.

Decision: Federal Court of Appeals held to have prematurely terminated mandamus inquiry without
reaching separation-of-powers objections raised, by
federal-official defendants including Vice President, to Federal District Court's civil discovery
orders.

SUMMARY

Under the Federal Advisory Committee Act (FACA)
(5 USCS Appx §§ 1 et seq.), 5 USCS Appx § 2 generally
required the public disclosure of specified matters
concerning covered committees. However, 5 USCS
Appx § 3 effectively excluded, from FACA's coverage,
any committee composed wholly of Federal Government officers and employees.

The National Energy Policy Development Group
(NEPDG) was established to give advice and to make
policy recommendations to the President. The NEPDG
was (1) chaired by the then Vice President of the
United States, and (2) formally included only other
federal officers or employees.

Two private organizations filed suits, which were later consolidated in the United States District Court for the District of Columbia, against defendants including the Vice President and other senior officials of the executive branch who had been NEPDG members (the "federal-official defendants"). The organizations (1) included claims to the effect that the NEPDG had violated § 2's public-disclosure requirements, on the basis of a theory (under a United States Court of Appeals for the District of Columbia Circuit precedent) that despite § 3, FACA applied, as various private lobbyists allegedly also had been "de facto" NEPDG members; and (2) sought relief including the production of all materials allegedly subject to FACA's requirements.

All the defendants moved to dismiss. The District Court in pertinent part (1) denied dismissal as to the federal-official defendants; (2) expressed the view that FACA's substantive requirements could be enforced against these defendants under the Mandamus Act (28 USCS § 1361); (3) deferred ruling on the defendants' contention that to apply FACA would violate federal constitutional principles of the separation of powers; (4) declined to decide, at that time, whether mandamus relief actually ought to issue; and (5) allowed the plaintiff organizations to conduct "tightly-reined" discovery, supposedly, as to FACA, (a) to ascertain the NEPDG's structure and membership, and (b) thus, to determine whether the de-facto-membership doctrine applied (219 F Supp 2d 20). Subsequently, the District Court approved the organizations' discovery plan and entered a series of orders allowing discovery to proceed.

The federal-official defendants sought a writ of mandamus (purportedly under 28 USCS § 1651(a)) in the Court of Appeals against the discovery orders. In addition, the Vice President filed a notice of appeal from the same orders. However, the Court of Appeals for the District of Columbia Circuit dismissed both the mandamus petition and the attempted appeal on similar grounds, as the Court of Appeals expressed the view that alternative avenues of relief remained available, where the defendants (1) had not yet asserted executive privilege, and (2) ought to do so "with particularity" (357 US App DC 274, 334 F3d 1096).

After the United States Supreme Court granted certiorari (540 US ——, 157 L Ed 2d 793, 124 S Ct 958), one of the plaintiff organizations filed a motion for the recusal of Justice Scalia, substantially on the basis of the Justice's asserted friendship, or appearance of friendship, with the Vice President. The Supreme Court—saying that it was acting in accordance with its historic practice—referred the recusal motion to Justice Scalia (541 US ——, 158 L Ed 2d 151, 124 S Ct 1532), who denied the motion (541 US ——, 158 L Ed 2d 225, 124 S Ct 1391).

Then, on certiorari, the Supreme Court vacated the Court of Appeals' judgment and remanded the case for further proceedings. In an opinion by KENNEDY, J., joined by REHNQUIST, Ch. J., and STEVENS, O'CONNOR, and BREYER, JJ., and joined in part (as to holding 1 below) by SCALIA and THOMAS, JJ., it was held—without deciding various issues concerning the Vice President's attempted appeal—that:

(1) Under § 1651(a), the Court of Appeals, in dismissing the federal-official defendants' mandamus petition, had prematurely terminated the inquiry without reaching the weighty federal constitutional separation-of-powers objections which the defendants had raised, as the Court of Appeals had mistakenly assumed that a narrow and specific assertion of executive privilege by the defendants was a necessary precondition to consid-

ering these objections, where, among other factors, (a) the need for information was much less weighty than in a criminal case; (b) the District Court had approved overly broad discovery requests which would have provided the organizations with (i) all the disclosure to which they would have been entitled in the event that they prevailed on the merits, and (ii) much more besides; and (c) the defendants had objected, in arguments which had been ignored or rejected, to the scope of discovery and the burden imposed.

(2) An invitation by the defendants, to direct the Court of Appeals to issue the writ of mandamus against the District Court, would be declined.

(3) Instead, it would be left to the Court of Appeals, on remand, to address some arguments by the parties.

STEVENS, J., concurring, expressed the view that (1) contrary to the extraordinary nature of the mandamus remedy under § 1361, the two organizations had sought to obtain, through discovery, information about the NEPDG's work in order to establish the organizations' entitlement under § 1361 to the same information; and (2) the District Court should have required the organizations to demonstrate that particular requests would have tended to establish the organizations' theory of the case.

THOMAS, J., joined by SCALIA, J., concurring in part and dissenting in part, expressed the view that the Court of Appeals' judgment should have been reversed—and the case should have been remanded with an instruction for the Court of Appeals to issue the writ of mandamus in favor of the federal-official defendants—for the District Court had clearly exceeded its authority in issuing the discovery orders, where the mandamus relief which the two organizations had sought in the District Court should have been

247

found to have been unavailable, on the basis that the organizations' right to the FACA materials which they had requested was unclear.

GINSBURG, J., joined by SOUTER, J., dissenting, expressed the view that the Court of Appeals' judgment should have been affirmed, for (1) the Court of Appeals had correctly concluded that it lacked ordinary appellate jurisdiction over the Vice President's appeal; (2) mandamus relief based on the alleged exorbitance of the discovery orders was at least premature, as (a) the Federal Government had decided to resist all discovery, rather than moving for a reduction of the District Court's discovery orders to accommodate separation-of-powers concerns, and (b) nothing in the record intimated a lower-court refusal to reduce discovery; and (3) the District Court should have been allowed, in the first instance, to pursue the District Court's expressed intention tightly to rein in discovery, if the Federal Government so requested.

COUNSEL

Theodore B. Olson argued the cause for petitioners.

Alan B. Morrison argued the cause for respondent Sierra Club.

Paul J. Orfanedes argued the cause for respondent Judicial Watch, Inc.

JEFFREY A. BEARD, SECRETARY, PENNSYLVANIA
DEPARTMENT OF CORRECTIONS, et al., Petitioners

v

GEORGE E. BANKS

542 US —, 159 L Ed 2d 494, 124 S Ct 2504

[No. 02-1603]

Argued February 24, 2004.
Decided June 24, 2004.

Decision: Rule of Mills v Maryland (1988) 486 US 367,
100 L Ed 2d 384, 108 S Ct 1860, pertaining to
mitigating factors in capital sentencing, held to be
new constitutional rule that could not be applied
retroactively on federal habeas corpus review.

SUMMARY

In a Pennsylvania trial court in 1983, a defendant was
convicted of murder and sentenced to death. In 1987,
(1) the Supreme Court of Pennsylvania affirmed the
conviction and death sentence on direct review (513 Pa
318, 521 A2d 1), and (2) the United States Supreme
Court denied certiorari (484 US 873, 98 L Ed 2d 162,
108 S Ct 211).

Subsequently, in Mills v Maryland (1988) 486 US 367,
100 L Ed 2d 384, 108 S Ct 1860, and McKoy v North
Carolina (1990) 494 US 433, 108 L Ed 2d 369, 110 S Ct
1227, the United States Supreme Court announced a
rule that the Federal Constitution's Eighth Amendment forbids states from imposing a requirement that a
jury find a potential mitigating factor unanimously
before that factor may be considered in a capital

sentencing decision. In 1995, the Pennsylvania Supreme Court—in affirming the trial court's denial of postconviction relief—rejected the defendant's claim that the sentencing-phase jury instructions and verdict form in his case had violated the Mills rule (540 Pa 143, 656 A2d 467).

The United States District Court for the Middle District of Pennsylvania denied the defendant's petition for federal habeas corpus relief (63 F Supp 2d 525). However, the United States Court of Appeals for the Third Circuit, in reversing the District Court's judgment, (1) declined to inquire whether the Mills rule applied retroactively in the case at hand, given that the Pennsylvania Supreme Court had applied Mills; and (2) concluded that the Pennsylvania Supreme Court's ruling regarding the application of Mills to the defendant's case had been unreasonable (271 F3d 527).

The United State Supreme Court—in granting certiorari, reversing, and remanding—held that the Court of Appeals had erred in failing to perform a retroactivity analysis pursuant to Teague v Lane (1989) 489 US 288, 103 L Ed 2d 334, 109 S Ct 1060, under which new federal constitutional rules of criminal procedure generally were not to be applied in cases on collateral review (536 US 266, 272, 153 L Ed 2d 301, 122 S Ct 2147). On remand, the Court of Appeals (1) concluded that the Mills rule was retroactively applicable under the test of Teague v Lane, as Mills had not announced a new rule of constitutional law for retroactivity purposes; and (2) reinstated the remainder of the Court of Appeals' previous opinion (316 F3d 228).

On certiorari, the United States Supreme Court reversed and remanded. In an opinion by THOMAS, J., joined by REHNQUIST, Ch. J., and O'CONNOR, SCALIA, and KENNEDY, JJ., it was held that the Mills rule could not be applied to the defendant's case on federal habeas corpus review, for:

(1) The defendant's murder conviction had became final, for purposes of Teague v Lane analysis, at the end of direct review in 1987, not at the time of the Pennsylvania Supreme Court's postconviction proceeding in 1995.

(2) The Mills rule was a new rule for Teague v Lane purposes, as (a) the United States Supreme Court, in reaching its conclusion in Mills and McKoy, had relied on a line of cases that could be thought to support the conclusion in Mills and McKoy, but did not mandate the Mills rule; and (b) reasonable jurists could have differed as to whether this line of cases had compelled the Mills rule.

(3) The Mills rule did not fall within either of two exceptions to the Teague v Lane test, as (a) it had not been argued that the first exception—pertaining to rules (i) forbidding punishment of certain primary conduct, or (ii) prohibiting a certain category of punishment for a class of defendants because of such defendants' status or offense—was applicable in the case at hand; and (b) the Mills rule applied narrowly and worked no fundamental shift in the United States Supreme Court's understanding of the bedrock procedural elements essential to fundamental fairness.

STEVENS, J., joined by SOUTER, GINSBURG, and BREYER, JJ., dissenting, expressed the view that (1) the Mills rule was not new for Teague v Lane purposes, as Mills simply represented a straightforward application of a longstanding view that the Constitution's Eighth and Fourteenth Amendments could not tolerate the infliction of a death sentence under a legal system which permitted that penalty to be wantonly and freakishly imposed; and (2) reasonable jurors could have read Pennsylvania's jury instructions and verdict form to impose a unanimity requirement with respect to mitigating circumstances, in violation of the Mills rule.

SOUTER, J., joined by GINSBURG, J., dissenting, expressed the view that (1) the question presented in the case at hand was ultimately whether the court ought to deem reasonable, and thus immunize from collateral attack—at least at the first stage of the Teague v Lane inquiry—a reading of pre-Mills precedents that accepted the risk of such errors that Pennsylvania's jury instructions and verdict form would have produced; and (2) the majority opinion's reading of Teague v Lane gave too much importance to the finality of capital sentences and not enough to the accuracy of such sentences.

COUNSEL

Ronald Eisenberg argued the cause for petitioners. Albert J. Flora, Jr. argued the cause for respondent.

DONALD H. RUMSFELD, SECRETARY OF DE-
FENSE, Petitioner

v

JOSE PADILLA and DONNA R. NEWMAN, as next
friend of JOSE PADILLA

542 US —, 159 L Ed 2d 513, 124 S Ct 2711

[No. 03-1027]

Argued April 28, 2004.
Decided June 28, 2004.

Decision: Federal habeas corpus petition held improperly filed in Federal District Court in New York,
where petition concerned United States citizen
who was being detained, in Navy brig in South
Carolina, as asserted "enemy combatant."

SUMMARY

Under 28 USCS § 2241(a), writs of habeas corpus
may be granted by various federal courts or judges
"within their respective jurisdictions." Also, (1) 28
USCS § 2242 in effect refers to the respondent to a
§ 2241 petition as "the person who has custody"; and
(2) 28 USCS § 2243 refers to "the person having
custody."

One week after the September 11, 2001, terrorist
attacks in the United States, Congress passed the Authorization for Use of Military Force resolution
(AUMF) (115 Stat 224, note following 50 USCS
§ 1541), which included authorization for the President
to use "all necessary and appropriate force" against
"nations, organizations, or persons" associated with the
September 11 attacks. In May 2002, an individual, who

was a United States citizen, was apprehended within the United States by federal agents supposedly executing a material-witness warrant issued by the United States District Court for the Southern District of New York, in connection with a grand jury investigation into the September 11 attacks. The individual, through his appointed counsel, moved to vacate the warrant. This motion was still pending on June 9, 2002, when the President issued to the Secretary of Defense an order that (1) designated the individual as an "enemy combatant"; (2) directed the Secretary to detain the individual in military custody; (3) invoked the AUMF and the President's authority (under the Federal Constitution's Art II, § 2, cl 1) as "Commander in Chief"; and (4) asserted that the individual was closely associated with an international terrorist organization with which the United States was at war. That same day, the individual was taken into custody by Department of Defense officials and transported to a United States Navy brig in South Carolina, where the individual remained in detention. Meanwhile, the Federal Government (1) notified the District Court ex parte concerning these developments, and (2) asked the court to vacate the material-witness warrant (which the court did).

Also, on June 11, 2002, the individual's counsel filed, in the District Court on the individual's purported behalf, a federal habeas corpus petition under 28 USCS § 2241. The petition, as amended, (1) alleged that the individual was being held "in segregation" at the brig; (2) claimed that the individual's detention violated several provisions of the Constitution; and (3) named as respondents persons including the Secretary of Defense and the brig's commander. The Federal Government moved to dismiss or to transfer the case, arguing in part that (1) the commander, as the individual's immediate custodian, was the only proper respondent to the petition; and (2) the District Court lacked jurisdiction over the commander.

The District Court, in ruling in part for each side, (1) held that the individual's counsel could pursue the petition as "next friend" for the individual; (2) expressed the view that (a) the Secretary's personal involvement in the individual's detention rendered the Secretary a proper respondent, and (b) the court could properly assert jurisdiction over the Secretary under New York's "long-arm" statute; (3) dismissed the commander on the theory that she would be obliged to obey any order which the court directed to the Secretary; (4) on the merits, (a) accepted the Federal Government's contention that the President had authority to detain, as "enemy combatants," citizens captured in the United States during a time of war, but (b) ruled that the individual had the right to controvert alleged facts; (5) granted the individual monitored access to counsel; and (6) indicated that the court would apply a deferential standard to determine whether the record supported the individual's designation as an enemy combatant (233 F Supp 2d 564). Subsequently, the District Court denied a motion for reconsideration (243 F Supp 2d 42), but granted an application to certify some orders for interlocutory appeal (256 F Supp 2d 218).

On appeal, the United States Court of Appeals for the Second Circuit—in ordering a remand with instructions for the District Court to issue a writ of habeas corpus directing the Secretary of Defense to release the individual from military custody within 30 days—expressed the view that (1) the individual's counsel was a proper next friend; (2) on the case's unique facts, the Secretary was a proper respondent, in light of his (a) "legal reality of control" over the individual,

255

and (b) personal involvement in the individual's detention; (3) the District Court had jurisdiction over the
Secretary under New York's long-arm statute; and (4)
on the merits, neither the President's Commander-in-
Chief power nor the AUMF authorized military detentions of American citizens captured in the United States
(as amended, 352 F3d 695).

On certiorari, the United States Supreme Court
reversed the Court of Appeals' judgment and remanded the case for entry of an order of dismissal
without prejudice. In an opinion by REHNQUIST, Ch. J.,
joined by O'CONNOR, SCALIA, KENNEDY, and THOMAS,
JJ., it was held, without reaching the merits concerning
the individual's detention, that the habeas corpus
petition in question had been improperly filed in the
District Court for the Southern District of New
York—and should have been filed in the District Court
for the District of South Carolina—for:

(1) The proper respondent to this petition had been
the brig's commander, rather than the Secretary of
Defense, where (a) as of the time of filing, the commander had been the individual's immediate custodian; and (b) the only reasonable inference from the
record was that the individual's counsel had been aware
of the individual's presence in South Carolina when
counsel had filed the petition.

(2) Within the meaning of § 2241(a), the New York
District Court had not had jurisdiction over the commander, where, at the time of filing, the commander
had been present in South Carolina, the district of
confinement.

(3) The Supreme Court had not made exceptions to
the immediate-custodian and district-of-confinement
rules whenever "exceptional," "special," or "unusual"
cases had arisen.

(4) Even though the merits of the case at hand were of

profound importance, it was just as necessary in important cases, as in unimportant ones, that federal courts took care not to exceed their "respective jurisdictions" established by Congress under § 2241(a).

KENNEDY, J., joined by O'CONNOR, J., concurring, expressed the view that (1) the Supreme Court's analysis relied on the two general rules that a federal habeas corpus action had to be (a) brought against the immediate custodian, and (b) filed in the District Court whose territorial jurisdiction included the place where the custodian was located; and (2) while these two rules could be waived by the Federal Government and were subject to exceptions, (a) even under the most permissive interpretation of the federal habeas corpus statute as a venue provision, the Southern District of New York was not the proper place for the petition in question, and (b) none of the exceptions to the two rules applied in the case at hand.

STEVENS, J., joined by SOUTER, GINSBURG, and BREYER, JJ., dissenting, expressed the view that (1) special circumstances ought to be able to justify exceptions from the general immediate-custodian rule; (2) the case at hand was such an exceptional case, which the Supreme Court had jurisdiction to decide, for (a) the case raised questions of profound importance to the nation, (b) the Federal Government had "shrouded" in secrecy the facts available to the individual's counsel at the time of filing, and (c) in any event, counsel's petition had been properly filed against the Secretary of Defense in the Southern District of New York, where (i) the Secretary had been entrusted with control over the individual, had been personally involved in handling the case, and had had sufficient contacts with the Southern District, and (ii) under traditional venue principles, the Southern Dis-

257

trict of New York, not South Carolina, was the more appropriate place to litigate the petition; and (3) on the merits, the individual was entitled, at least, to a hearing on the justification for his detention by the executive branch.

COUNSEL

Paul D. Clement argued the cause for petitioner.

Jennifer Martinez argued the cause for respondents.

———————

SHAFIQ RASUL, et al., Petitioners

v

GEORGE W. BUSH, PRESIDENT OF THE UNITED
STATES, et al. (No. 03-334)

FAWZI KHALID ABDULLAH FAHAD AL ODAH, et
al., Petitioners

v

UNITED STATES et al. (No. 03-343)

542 US —, 159 L Ed 2d 548, 124 S Ct 2686

Argued April 20, 2004.
Decided June 28, 2004.

Decision: Federal District Court held to have jurisdiction, under federal habeas corpus provision (28 USCS § 2241), to review legality of executive detention of some foreign nationals who were incarcerated at Guantanamo Bay Naval Base in Cuba.

SUMMARY

From 2002 and onward, more than 600 persons who had been captured abroad during hostilities between the United States and the Taliban regime in Afghanistan were held in executive detention at the Guantanamo Bay Naval Base in Cuba. This naval base was occupied by the United States under a lease and treaty recognizing Cuba's ultimate sovereignty, but giving the United States complete jurisdiction and control.

From among these detainees, two Australian citizens and 12 Kuwaiti citizens filed various actions in the United States District Court for the District of Columbia against the United States and some federal and military officials. The plaintiffs (1) denied having engaged in or plotted acts of aggression against the United States; and (2) alleged that they were being held in federal custody in violation of the laws of the United States, in that they had been imprisoned without having been charged with any wrongdoing, permitted to consult counsel, or provided access to courts or other tribunals. The District Court's jurisdiction was invoked under the federal-question statute (28 USCS § 1331), the Alien Tort Statute (28 USCS § 1350), and a federal habeas corpus provision (28 USCS § 2241(c)(3)) that authorized Federal District Courts to entertain habeas corpus applications by persons claiming to be held in custody "in violation of the Constitution or laws or treaties of the United States." The plaintiffs asserted causes of action under statutes such as § 1350 and the general federal habeas corpus statute (28 USCS §§ 2241-2243).

The District Court, construing all of the actions as petitions for writs of habeas corpus, dismissed the actions for want of jurisdiction, on the asserted ground that aliens detained outside the sovereign territory of the United States could not invoke a habeas corpus petition (215 F Supp 2d 55). The United States Court of Appeals for the District of Columbia Circuit, in affirming, concluded that the privilege of litigation in United States courts did not extend to aliens in military custody who had no presence in any territory over which the United States was sovereign (355 US App DC 189, 321 F3d 1134).

On certiorari, the United States Supreme Court reversed and remanded. In an opinion by STEVENS, J., joined by O'CONNOR, SOUTER, GINSBURG, and BREYER, JJ., it was held that the District Court had jurisdiction, under 28 USCS § 2241, to review the legality of the plaintiffs' detention, for:

260

(1) The plaintiffs were not nationals of countries at war with the United States.

(2) A presumption against the extraterritorial application of congressional legislation had no application to the operation of § 2241 with respect to persons detained within the territorial jurisdiction of the United States.

(3) There was little reason to think that Congress intended the geographical coverage of § 2241 to vary depending on the detainee's citizenship, given that § 2241 (a) would have created federal-court jurisdiction over the claims of a United States citizen held at the Guantanamo base, and (b) drew no distinction between United States citizens and aliens held in federal custody.

(4) Application of § 2241 to persons detained at the base was consistent with the historical reach of the writ of habeas corpus.

(5) No party questioned the District Court's jurisdiction over the plaintiffs' custodians.

KENNEDY, J., concurring in the judgment, expressed the view that (1) federal courts had jurisdiction to consider challenges to the legality of the detention of foreign nationals held at the Guantanamo base, in light of (a) the base's status as a United States territory in every practical respect and as a territory far removed from any hostilities, and (b) the indefinite pretrial detention of the detainees; and (2) although there were circumstances in which the courts maintained the power and the responsibility to protect persons from unlawful detention even where military affairs were implicated, there was a realm of political authority over military affairs where the judicial power could not enter.

SCALIA, J., joined by REHNQUIST, Ch. J., and THOMAS, J., dissenting, expressed the view that (1) the majority opinion's holding contradicted a half-century-old Supreme Court precedent on which the military had undoubtedly relied, and (2) the President of the United States—as Commander in Chief—and his subordinates had had every reason to expect that the internment of combatants at the Guantanamo base would not have the consequence of bringing the cumbersome machinery of United States domestic courts into military affairs.

COUNSEL

John J. Gibbons argued the cause for petitioners.

Theodore B. Olson argued the cause for respondents.

YASER ESAM HAMDI and ESAM FOUAD HAMDI as
next friend of YASER ESAM HAMDI, Petitioners

v

DONALD H. RUMSFELD, SECRETARY OF DE-
FENSE, et al.

542 US —, 159 L Ed 2d 578, 124 S Ct 2633

[No. 03-6696]

Argued April 28, 2004.
Decided June 28, 2004.

Decision: 2001 resolution authorizing use of military
force held to provide executive branch with some
authority to detain citizens as "enemy combatants," but individual held to have right to hearing
with, at least, opportunity to present evidence that
he was not enemy combatant.

SUMMARY

The Federal Constitution's suspension clause (Art I,
§ 9, cl 2) provided that the privilege of the writ of
habeas corpus would not be suspended, unless "when
in cases of Rebellion or Invasion" the public safety
might require it. Also, 18 USCS § 4001(a), which was
originally passed in 1971, provided that no United
States citizen would "be imprisoned or otherwise detained by the United States except pursuant to an Act of
Congress."

One week after the September 11, 2001, terrorist
attacks in the United States, Congress passed the Authorization for Use of Military Force resolution
(AUMF) (115 Stat 224, note following 50 USCS
§ 1541), which included authorization for the President

to use "all necessary and appropriate force" against "nations, organizations, or persons" associated with the September 11 attacks. Subsequently, United States and allied armed forces engaged in military operations in Afghanistan, where the Taliban regime was asserted to have supported an organization which had made the September 11 attacks.

An individual who was allegedly a United States citizen (1) was captured or seized in Afghanistan, in circumstances which would be disputed, by forces allied to the United States; and (2) turned over to the United States military. In 2002, the individual was transferred to a United States Navy facility in Virginia. The individual was still being detained there when the individual's father filed, on the individual's purported behalf in the United States District Court for the Eastern District of Virginia, a habeas corpus petition under 28 USCS § 2241. (Later, the individual was transferred to a Navy facility in South Carolina.) The habeas corpus petition (1) named the father and son as petitioners; (2) alleged that the Federal Government had improperly held the individual without access to legal counsel or notice of any charges pending against him; (3) included claims that the detention of the individual—"an American citizen"—(a) had not been legally authorized, and (b) violated provisions including the Federal Constitution's Fifth Amendment; and (4) sought relief including (a) the appointment of counsel, and (b) an order that the individual be released from his "unlawful custody." Although the petition alleged no details in regard to the circumstances surrounding the individual's capture and detention, the father elsewhere claimed that his son (1) had gone to Afghanistan to do relief work, (2) could not have received military training, and (3) had been trapped in Afghanistan once the military operations at issue began.

264

The District Court found that the father was a proper "next friend" of the individual, appointed counsel, and ordered that counsel be given access to the individual. The United States Court of Appeals for the Fourth Circuit, in reversing and remanding, expressed the view that the District Court had failed to extend appropriate deference to the Federal Government's security and intelligence interests (296 F3d 278).

On remand, the Federal Government filed a response and a motion to dismiss the petition. In support, the Federal Government attached a declaration by a Department of Defense official. This declaration (1) said that the individual had been labeled as an "enemy combatant"; and (2) included assertions to the effect that the individual had (a) been affiliated with a Taliban military unit, (b) received weapons training, (c) remained with the unit following the September 11 attacks, and (d) been captured, with a weapon, when the allied forces had been engaged in battle with the Taliban. However, the District Court found that the declaration fell short of supporting the individual's detention. The court ordered the Federal Government to turn over numerous materials for an in-chambers review, supposedly to help determine whether (1) the detention was legally authorized, and (2) the individual had received sufficient process to satisfy provisions including the Fifth Amendment's due process clause.

On appeal, the Court of Appeals, in reversing and in ordering the habeas corpus petition to be dismissed, expressed the view that (1) even though the individual "apparently" was a United States citizen—and even if § 4001(a) required congressional authorization for his detention—the AUMF provided such authorization; (2) no factual inquiry or evidentiary hearing, which would allow the individual to be heard or to rebut the declaration's factual assertions in support of his designation as an "enemy combatant," was necessary or proper, because (a) it was "undisputed" that the individual had been captured in a zone of active combat in a foreign theater of conflict, and (b) any inquiry ought to be circumscribed to avoid judicial intrusion into the military affairs entrusted to the executive branch; and (3) under the most circumscribed definition of conflict, hostilities in Afghanistan had not yet reached their end (316 F3d 450). The Court of Appeals then denied rehearing and rehearing en banc (337 F3d 335).

On certiorari, the United States Supreme Court vacated and remanded. Although the Justices were unable to agree on an opinion, it was held, by two different majorities of Justices, that (1) the AUMF provided the Federal Government's executive branch with some authority to detain United States citizens as enemy combatants; but (2) the detained individual in question had the right to a hearing which would afford him, at least, an opportunity to present evidence that he was not an enemy combatant.

O'CONNOR, J., announced the judgment of the court and, in an opinion joined by REHNQUIST, Ch. J., and KENNEDY and BREYER, JJ., expressed the view that (1) for purposes of the case at hand, an "enemy combatant" was an individual who, according to the executive branch's assertions, (a) had been part of, or supporting forces hostile to, the United States or "coalition partners" in Afghanistan, and (b) had engaged in an armed conflict against the United States there; (2) the AUMF authorized the detention of United States citizens who fell within this definition, for the duration of the particuar conflict in which they had been captured, as (a) such individuals were among those whom Congress whom had sought to target, (b) the detention of such individuals for such a duration was so fundamental and accepted an incident to war as to be an exercise of the "necessary and appropriate force" that the AUMF had authorized, (c) there was no bar to the United States' holding one of its own citizens as an enemy combatant, and (d) active combat operations against Taliban fighters apparently were still ongoing in Afghanistan; (3) however, in the absence of a suspension of the writ of habeas corpus—which suspension was agreed not to have occurred as to the case at hand—and under a balancing of the private and Federal Government concerns, the Fifth Amendment's due process clause demanded that a citizen held in the United States as an asserted "enemy combatant" had to be given a meaningful opportunity to contest the factual basis for that detention before a neutral decisionmaker, including (a) notice of the asserted factual basis, and (b) a fair opportunity to rebut the factual assertions; (4) while the full protections that accompanied challenges to detentions in other settings might prove unworkable and inappropriate in the enemy-combatant setting, the "process" which the individual in question had received so far—supposedly including unspecified screening and military interrogations—was not that to which he was entitled; (5) in the absence of a possibly sufficient, appropriately authorized, and properly constituted military tribunal, a federal court that received a habeas corpus petition from an asserted enemy combatant had to insure that the minimum requirements of due process were achieved; and (6) the individual had the right to access to counsel in connection with the proceedings on remand.

SOUTER, J., joined by GINSBURG, J., concurring in part, dissenting in part, and concurring in the judgment, expressed the view that (1) in light of § 4001(a), which ought to be read broadly, the Federal Government had failed to show that the AUMF authorized the detention of the individual in question, even on the

facts which the Federal Government claimed; (2) even
if there might be a limited emergency power to detain
a citizen, the individual in question had been locked up
for more than 2 years; (3) while, under this finding that
the individual's detention was unauthorized, any questions of what process he might be due would not
normally be reached, the need to give practical effect to
a majority's rejection of the Federal Government's
position called for joining with the plurality (of Justice
O'Connor's opinion) in ordering remand on terms
closest to those which this opinion would have imposed; (4) the terms of the plurality's remand would
allow the individual to offer evidence that he was not an
enemy combatant; (5) he should at the least have the
benefit of that opportunity; and (6) while this opinion
did not mean to imply agreement with some of the
plurality's conclusions, this opinion could not disagree
with (a) the plurality's determinations (given the plurality's view of the AUMF) that someone in the individual's position was entitled, at a minimum, to (i)
notice of the claimed factual basis for holding him, and
(ii) a fair chance of rebuttal before a neutral decisionmaker, or (b) the plurality's affirmation of the individual's right to counsel.

SCALIA, J., joined by STEVENS, J., dissenting, expressed the view that (1) in the absence of a proper
suspension of the writ of habeas corpus, a citizen who
was accused of being an enemy combatant—and who
was being held, within the United States, in the territorial jurisdiction of a federal court that was open—was
entitled, under the Constitution's suspension clause,
either to criminal trial or to a judicial decree requiring
the citizen's release; (2) thus, the individual in question, a "presumed" American citizen, was entitled to a
habeas corpus decree requiring his release unless (a)
criminal proceedings were promptly brought, or (b)

Congress had suspended the writ; (3) the AUMF was not such a suspension; (4) the AUMF did not even authorize the detention of a citizen with the clarity necessary to overcome the prescription of § 4001(a); (5) prescribing procedural protections, through balancing under the due process clause, ought to have no place where, as in the case at hand, the Constitution and the common law already supplied an answer; and (6) the proper role of habeas corpus was to determine the legality of executive-branch detention, not to supply the omitted process necessary to make such detention legal.

THOMAS, J., dissenting, expressed the view that the habeas corpus challenge in the case at hand ought to fail, as (1) even though it was proper for the judicial branch to resolve the issue whether the executive branch's detention of the individual in question was lawful, the issue ought to come to the Supreme Court with (a) the strongest presumptions in favor of the Federal Government, and (b) the President's having the power to make virtually conclusive factual findings; (2) Congress, in the AUMF, had authorized the President to detain those persons that the executive branch determined to be enemy combatants; (3) the President's authority to detain ought not to be limited by requiring that the record establish that United States troops were still involved in active combat in Afghanistan, where the power to detain ought not to end with the cessation of formal hostilities; (4) the President's detention authority, at least while hostilities continued, comported with the due process clause, where (a) the executive branch's decision that a detention was necessary to protect the public did not need to be, and ought not to be, subjected to judicial second-guessing, and (b) even under a balancing approach, the Federal Government's overriding interest in protecting the nation ought to justify depriving the individual in question of his liberty; (5) in such circumstances, the Federal Government ought not to be required to choose between (a) using standard criminal processes, and (b) suspending the writ of habeas corpus; and (6) a detainee's access to counsel would not always be warranted.

COUNSEL

Frank W. Dunham, Jr. argued the cause for petitioners.

Paul D. Clement argued the cause for respondents.

MISSOURI, Petitioner

v

PATRICE SEIBERT

542 US —, 159 L Ed 2d 643, 124 S Ct 2601

[No. 02-1371]

Argued December 9, 2003.

Decided June 28, 2004.

Decision: Accused's incriminating statement made after receiving Miranda warnings, where warnings were not given until interrogation had produced confession, held inadmissible at accused's Missouri trial.

SUMMARY

An accused who had made an incriminating statement to a police officer at a police station—after the accused had (1) been warned, pursuant to Miranda v Arizona (1966) 384 US 436, 16 L Ed 2d 694, 86 S Ct 1602, of her right, under the Federal Constitution's Fifth Amendment, to remain silent, and her federal constitutional right to the assistance of counsel; and (2) signed a waiver of these rights—was charged with murder. Prior to the officer's giving the accused the Miranda warnings, the officer had obtained a confession during 30 to 40 minutes of questioning the accused.

After a state trial court in Missouri had suppressed the accused's prewarning statement but had admitted the postwarning one, the accused was convicted of second-degree murder. The Missouri Court of Appeals affirmed.

The Missouri Supreme Court (1) reversed the accused's conviction; and (2) determined that, because the officer's interrogation of the accused had been nearly continuous, the postwarning statement, which was the product of the inadmissible prewarning statement, should have been suppressed (93 SW3d 700).

On certiorari, the United States Supreme Court affirmed. Although unable to agree on an opinion, five members of the court agreed that the accused's postwarning statement was inadmissible at trial.

SOUTER, J., announced the judgment of the court and, in an opinion joined by STEVENS, GINSBURG, and BREYER, JJ., expressed the view that the accused's postwarning statement was inadmissible at trial, because the officer's midstream recitation of warnings after his initial interrogation and the accused's unwarned confession could not effectively have complied with Miranda's constitutional requirement, as the officer's question-first tactic effectively had threatened to thwart Miranda's purpose of reducing the risk that a coerced confession would be admitted—and the facts in the instant case did not reasonably support a conclusion that the warnings given could have served their purpose—for (1) when, as in the instant case, Miranda warnings were inserted in the midst of coordinated and continuing interrogation, the warnings were likely to (a) mislead, and (b) deprive an accused of knowledge essential to the accused's ability to understand the (i) nature of the accused's rights, and (ii) consequences of abandoning them; and (2) it ordinarily would be unrealistic to treat two spates of integrated and proximately-conducted questioning as independent interrogations subject to independent evaluation simply because Miranda warnings had formally punctuated them in the middle.

272

BREYER, J., concurring, said that with respect to the two-stage interrogation technique of the type in question, there ought to be a rule under which courts excluded the "fruits" of the initial unwarned questioning unless the failure to warn was in good faith, as (1) prosecutors and judges had long understood how to apply the "fruits" approach; and (2) in the workaday world of criminal-law enforcement, the administrative simplicity of the familiar had significant advantages over a more complex exclusionary rule.

KENNEDY, J., concurring in the judgment, said that (1) the technique used by the officer in the instant case had (a) distorted the meaning of Miranda, and (b) furthered no legitimate countervailing interest; and (2) if, as in the instant case, a deliberate two-step strategy had been used, then postwarning statements that were related to the substance of prewarning statements ought to be excluded unless curative measures—such as (a) a substantial break in time and circumstances between the prewarning statement and the Miranda warning, or (b) an additional warning that explained the likely inadmissibility of the prewarning statement—were taken before the postwarning statement was made.

O'CONNOR, joined by REHNQUIST, Ch. J., and by SCALIA and THOMAS, JJ., dissenting, said that (1) the officer's two-step interrogation procedure ought to have been analyzed under the voluntariness standards that were central to the Fifth Amendment and had been reiterated in Oregon v Elstad (1985) 470 US 298, 84 L Ed 2d 222, 105 S Ct 1285; (2) Elstad commanded that if the accused's first statement was shown to have been involuntary, then the court was required to examine whether the taint had dissipated through (a) the passing of time, or (b) a change in circumstance; (3)

the accused's postwarning statement ought to be suppressed if the accused showed that it was involuntary despite the Miranda warnings; and (3) although this analysis ought to be left for the Missouri courts to conduct on remand, (a) unlike the officers in Elstad, the officer in the instant case had referred to the accused's unwarned statement during the second part of the interrogation when the accused had made a statement at odds with her unwarned confession, and (b) such a tactic might bear on the voluntariness inquiry.

COUNSEL

Karen K. Mitchell argued the cause for petitioner.

Irving L. Gornstein argued the cause for the United States, as amicus curiae, by special leave of court.

Amy M. Bartholow argued the cause for respondent.

UNITED STATES, Petitioner

v

SAMUEL FRANCIS PATANE

542 US —, 159 L Ed 2d 667, 124 S Ct 2620

[No. 02-1183]

Argued December 9, 2003.
Decided June 28, 2004.

Decision: Police officers' failure to finish giving accused
Miranda warnings held not to require suppression,
at trial, of pistol found by officer as result of
accused's voluntary statement.

SUMMARY

At an accused's home, a police officer arrested the
accused for allegedly violating a restraining order. A
second police officer, who had been told by a federal
agent that the accused, a convicted felon, illegally
possessed a pistol, (1) attempted to inform the accused
of his rights under Miranda v Arizona (1966) 384 US
436, 16 L Ed 2d 694, 86 S Ct 1602; but (2) got no
further than the right, under the self-incrimination
clause of the Federal Constitution's Fifth Amendment,
to remain silent before being interrupted by the accused, who asserted that he knew his rights. Neither
officer attempted to complete the Miranda warnings,
and, eventually, the accused, in response to questioning
from the second officer, revealed the location of the
pistol.

The accused was indicted for possession of a firearm
by a convicted felon, in violation of federal law. A
Federal District Court granted the accused's motion to

suppress the pistol at trial. The United States Court of Appeals for the Tenth Circuit affirmed the suppression, on the ground that the pistol constituted the fruit of an unwarned statement (304 F3d 1013).

On certiorari, the United States Supreme Court reversed and remanded. Although unable to agree on an opinion, five members of the court agreed that the officers' failure to finish giving the accused Miranda warnings did not require suppression, at trial, of the pistol.

THOMAS, J., announced the judgment of the court and, in an opinion joined by REHNQUIST, Ch. J., and SCALIA, J., said that (1) the Miranda rule (a) protected against violations of the self-incrimination clause, which was not implicated by the introduction at trial of physical evidence resulting from voluntary statements, and (b) was not a code of police conduct; (2) police did not violate the Constitution, or even the Miranda rule, by mere failures to warn; and (3) because police could not violate the self-incrimination clause by taking unwarned though voluntary statements, an exclusionary rule could not be justified by reference to a deterrence effect on law enforcement.

KENNEDY, J., joined by O'CONNOR, J., concurring in the judgment, said that (1) admission of nontestimonial physical fruits did not run the risk of admitting into trial an accused's coerced self-incriminating statements; (2) in light of the important probative value of reliable physical evidence, it was doubtful that exclusion could be justified by a deterrence rationale sensitive to both law enforcement interests and an accused's rights during an in-custody interrogation; and (3) it was unnecessary to decide whether (a) the officer's failure in the instant case to give the accused the full Miranda warnings ought to be characterized as a violation of the

Miranda rule, or (b) there was anything to deter so long as the unwarned statements were not later introduced at trial.

SOUTER, J., joined by STEVENS and GINSBURG, JJ., dissenting, said that in the instant case (1) the issue presented was whether courts should apply the fruit-of-the-poisonous-tree doctrine lest they create an incentive for the police to omit Miranda warnings before custodial interrogation; and (2) the Supreme Court, in closing its eyes to the consequences of giving an evidentiary advantage to those who ignored Miranda, added an important inducement for interrogators to ignore the Miranda rule.

BREYER, J., dissenting, said that (1) the fruit-of-the-poisonous-tree approach ought to be extended to the extent that courts would exclude physical evidence derived from unwarned questioning unless the failure to provide Miranda warnings had been in good faith; and (2) because the courts below had made no explicit finding as to good or bad faith, the case at hand ought to have been remanded for such a determination.

COUNSEL

Michael R. Dreeben argued the cause for petitioner.
Jill M. Wichlens argued the cause for respondent.

FLORA HOLLAND, WARDEN, Petitioner

v

JESSIE L. JACKSON

542 US —, 159 L Ed 2d 683, 124 S Ct 2736

[No. 03-1200]

Decided June 28, 2004.

Decision: Court of Appeals reviewing request for habeas corpus relief under 28 USCS § 2254(d) held to have erred in finding state-court decision concerning ineffective-assistance-of-counsel claim to be unreasonable application of clearly established federal law.

SUMMARY

An accused was convicted of murder and sentenced to life imprisonment by a Tennessee state court at a trial at which the state's principal evidence was eyewitness testimony by a person who claimed to have been with his girlfriend—who did not testify at the trial—at the scene of the victim's shooting when it had occurred.

The accused sought state postconviction relief, alleging that his trial counsel had been ineffective in failing to conduct an adequate investigation. However, the state court denied relief, finding that counsel's performance had not been deficient and that, in any event, the accused had suffered no prejudice from counsel's performance. Eventually, the accused filed a "Motion for Hearing in Nature of Motion for New Trial," alleging for the first time, 7 years after the accused's conviction, that the girlfriend would now testify that she had not been with the witness on the night of the shooting. The state court denied this motion.

The Tennessee Court of Criminal Appeals (1) affirmed the denial of the new-trial motion; and (2) in upholding the denial of postconviction relief, concluded that (a) there had never been any showing on the record of favorable testimony that would have been elicited from the girlfriend had counsel interviewed her, and (b) even if the accused's "unsubstantiated pleading," were accepted as true, it failed to rise to the level of contradicting what the witness had claimed to have seen at the shooting scene.

The accused then sought federal habeas corpus relief. The United States District Court for the Middle District of Tennessee granted the state's motion for summary judgment, as the District Court (1) found that there had been ineffective assistance of counsel and a reasonable probability of prejudice; but (2) observed that it could grant relief only if the state court's adjudication of the accused's claim had been, as required under 28 USCS § 2254(d)(1) "contrary to, or involved an unreasonable application of, clearly established Federal law"; and (3) concluded that the state court's application of the test of the effectiveness of counsel announced by the United States Supreme Court in Strickland v Washington (1984) 466 US 668, 80 L Ed 2d 674, 104 S Ct 2052—that to establish ineffective assistance in violation of the Federal Constitution's Sixth Amendment, an accused had to show (a) lack of reasonably effective assistance, and (b) a reasonable probability that, but for counsel's unprofessional errors, the result at trial would have different—was erroneous but not unreasonable (1995 Tenn Crim App LEXIS 985).

The United States Court of Appeals for the Sixth Circuit, reversing, concluded that the accused was entitled to relief under § 2254(d)(1) on the grounds that (1) the state court had unreasonably applied the Strickland test, given that the girlfriend's statement undermined the credibility of the witness's testimony; and (2) the state court's opinion was contrary to Strickland because the opinion had assessed prejudice under a preponderance-of-the-evidence standard rather than a reasonable-probability standard (80 Fed Appx 392).

Granting certiorari and granting leave to proceed in forma pauperis, the United States Supreme Court reversed. In a per curiam opinion expressing the views of REHNQUIST, Ch. J., and O'CONNOR, SCALIA, KENNEDY, and THOMAS, JJ., it was held that the Court of Appeals had erred in (1) finding the state court's application of Strickland unreasonable on the basis of evidence not properly before the state court; and (2) holding that the state court had acted contrary to federal law by requiring proof of prejudice by a preponderance of the evidence rather than by a reasonable probability.

STEVENS, SOUTER, GINSBURG, and BREYER, JJ., indicated, without a written opinion, that they would deny the state's certiorari petition.

JOHN D. ASHCROFT, ATTORNEY GENERAL, Petitioner

v

AMERICAN CIVIL LIBERTIES UNION et al.

542 US —, 159 L Ed 2d 690, 124 S Ct 2783

[No. 03-218]

Argued March 2, 2004.

Decided June 29, 2004.

Decision: Federal District Court held not to have abused its discretion in granting preliminary injunction against enforcement of Child Online Protection Act (47 USCS § 231).

SUMMARY

The Child Online Protection Act (COPA) (47 USCS § 231) prohibited any person from knowingly, in interstate or foreign commerce by means of the World Wide Web, making any communication for commercial purposes that was available to any minor and that included any material that was harmful to minors. One month before COPA was scheduled to go into effect, a group of organizations filed suit against the United States Attorney General in the United States District Court for the Eastern District of Pennsylvania to challenge COPA's validity under the Federal Constitution's First Amendment.

In 1999, the District Court (1) concluded that the organizations were likely to prevail, as (a) COPA was likely to burden some speech that was protected for adults, and (b) there had been no showing as to the relative effectiveness of COPA and various proposed less restrictive alternatives; and (2) granted the organizations' motion for a preliminary injunction barring the Federal Government from enforcing COPA until the merits of the organizations' claims could be adjudicated (31 F Supp 2d 473).

The United States Court of Appeals for the Third Circuit, in affirming, reasoned that COPA's use of "contemporary community standards" to identify material that was harmful to minors rendered COPA substantially overbroad (217 F3d 162). However, on certiorari, the United States Supreme Court vacated and remanded, on the ground that COPA's reliance on community standards to identify material that was harmful to minors did not, by itself, render COPA facially overbroad for First Amendment purposes (535 US 564, 152 L Ed 2d 771, 122 S Ct 1700).

On remand, the Court of Appeals—again affirming the District Court's judgment—concluded that the District Court had not abused its discretion in granting the preliminary injunction, as COPA was not (1) narrowly tailored to serve a compelling government interest, or (2) the least restrictive means available for the government to serve the interest of preventing minors from using the Internet to gain access to materials that were harmful to them (322 F3d 240).

On certiorari, the Supreme Court affirmed and remanded. In an opinion by KENNEDY, J., joined by STEVENS, SOUTER, THOMAS, and GINSBURG, JJ., it was held that the Court of Appeals was correct to conclude that the District Court had not abused its discretion in granting the preliminary injunction—and substantial practical considerations argued in favor of upholding the injunction and allowing the case at hand to proceed to trial—for:

(1) On the record, there were a number of plausible less restrictive alternatives to COPA, primarily blocking

and filtering software that was (a) likely to be more effective than COPA as a means of restricting children's access to materials harmful to them; and (b) an available alternative, as Congress could enact programs to promote the use of such software.

(2) The potential harms from reversing the injunction outweighed those of leaving the injunction in place by mistake pending a trial on the merits, as (a) there was a potential for extraordinary harm and a serious chill upon protected speech if the injunction were to be reversed; (b) no prosecutions had yet been undertaken under COPA, so none would be disrupted if the injunction stood; and (c) the government, in the interim, could enforce obscenity laws already on the books.

(3) There were substantial disputes remaining in the case as to the effectiveness of less restrictive alternatives.

(4) The record did not reflect (a) current realities as to Internet technology; or (b) other federal statutes, passed after the District Court had made its factfindings, that might qualify as less restrictive alternatives.

STEVENS, J., joined by GINSBURG, J., concurring, expressed the view that (1) a sufficient basis for deciding the case at hand was the principle that the government was not permitted to penalize speakers for making available to the general World Wide Web audience that which the least tolerant communities in America deemed unfit for their children's consumption; and (2) in view of the gravity of the burdens COPA imposed on Web speech, the possibility that Congress might have accomplished the goal of protecting children from harmful materials by other, less drastic means was a matter to be considered with special care.

SCALIA, J., dissenting, expressed the view that (1) COPA was constitutional, (2) nothing in the First

283

Amendment entitled the type of material covered by COPA to a strict-scrutiny standard of review; and (3) because the business of commercial pornography could—consistent with the First Amendment—be banned entirely, COPA's lesser restrictions raised no constitutional concern.

BREYER, J., joined by REHNQUIST, Ch. J., and O'CONNOR, J., dissenting, expressed the view that COPA (1) as a restriction of nonobscene expression, had to be subjected to the most exacting scrutiny; and (2) was constitutional, for (a) COPA imposed a burden on protected speech that was no more than modest, (b) COPA significantly advanced the compelling interest of protecting minors from exposure to commercial pornography on the Internet, and (c) there was no serious and practically available less restrictive way to further this interest.

COUNSEL

Theodore B. Olson argued the cause for petitioner. Ann E. Beeson argued the cause for respondents.

JOSE FRANCISCO SOSA, Petitioner

v

HUMBERTO ALVAREZ-MACHAIN et al. (No. 03-
339)

UNITED STATES, Petitioner

v

HUMBERTO ALVAREZ-MACHAIN et al. (No. 03-
485)

542 US —, 159 L Ed 2d 718, 124 S Ct 2739

Argued March 30, 2004.
Decided June 29, 2004.

Decision: Mexican individual held not entitled to remedy, under either Federal Tort Claims Act (28
USCS §§ 1346(b)(1), 2671 et seq.) or Alien Tort
Statute (28 USCS § 1350), with respect to his
allegation that Drug Enforcement Administration
had instigated his abduction from Mexico for
criminal trial in United States.

SUMMARY

The Federal Tort Claims Act (FTCA) (28 USCS
§§ 1346(b)(1), 2671 et seq.) removes the sovereign
immunity of the United States for certain tort suits, but
is subject to some exceptions, including the FTCA's 28
USCS § 2680(k) exception for "[a]ny claim arising in a
foreign country." Also, the Alien Tort Statute (ATS)
(28 USCS § 1350), which was originally enacted in
1789, provides that Federal District Courts "shall have
original jurisdiction of any civil action by an alien for a
285

tort only, committed in violation of the law of nations or a treaty of the United States."

A Mexican individual (1) filed suit in the United States District Court for the Central District of California; (2) alleged that the Drug Enforcement Administration (DEA) had instigated his abduction from Mexico for criminal trial in the United States (at which he had been granted a judgment of acquittal); and (3) included claims to the effect that (a) the United States was liable under the FTCA, and (b) another Mexican person, who allegedly had been involved in the abduction, was liable under the ATS for an asserted violation of international law. The District Court granted the Federal Government's motion to dismiss the FTCA claim, but awarded summary judgment and $25,000 in damages to the individual on the ATS claim.

On appeal, a panel of the United States Court of Appeals for the Ninth Circuit, in pertinent part, affirmed the ATS judgment, reversed the FTCA dismissal, and ordered a remand (266 F3d 1045). On rehearing en banc, the Court of Appeals reached the same disposition, as the en banc court expressed the view that (1) the ATS not only provided federal courts with subject-matter jurisdiction, but also created a cause of action for an alleged violation of the law of nations; (2) for such purposes, there was a "clear and universally recognized norm" prohibiting arbitrary arrest and detention; (3) the FTCA's foreign-country exception did not bar the suit, for under a "headquarters doctrine," the individual's abduction in Mexico had been the direct result of wrongful acts of planning and direction by DEA agents in the United States; (4) the United States was liable under the FTCA on a false-arrest basis, for the DEA assertedly had lacked the authority to effect the individual's arrest and detention in Mexico (331 F3d 604).

On certiorari, the United States Supreme Court reversed. In an opinion by SOUTER, J., joined in part (as to holding 1 below) by REHNQUIST, Ch. J., and STEVENS, O'CONNOR, SCALIA, KENNEDY, and THOMAS, JJ., expressing the unanimous view of the court in part (as to holdings 2-4 below), and joined in part (as to holding 5 below) by STEVENS, O'CONNOR, KENNEDY, GINSBURG, and BREYER, JJ., it was held that with respect to the individual's allegation that the DEA had instigated his abduction from Mexico for criminal trial in the United States:

(1) The individual was not entitled to a remedy under the FTCA, because § 2680(k) applied, for (a) the alleged actions in Mexico were most naturally understood as the kernel of a barred claim arising in a foreign country; and (b) contrary to the Court of Appeals' headquarters doctrine, § 2680(k) barred all claims based on any injury suffered in a foreign country, regardless of where the tortious act or omission occurred.

(2) The ATS was in terms in terms a jurisdictional statute creating no new causes of action.

(3) This jurisdictional grant was best read as originally having been enacted on the understanding that common law would provide a cause of action for the modest number of international-law violations with a potential for personal liability at the time.

(4) The ATS right of action asserted by the individual did not fall within this modest number.

(5) The individual was not otherwise entitled to a remedy under the ATS, for when his claim was gauged against the existing state of international law, his claim did not meet the requirement that federal courts ought not to recognize private claims, under federal common law, for violations of any international-law norm with

less definite content and acceptance among civilized nations than the historical paradigms familiar when the ATS had been enacted.

SCALIA, J., joined by REHNQUIST, Ch. J., and THOMAS, J., concurring in part and concurring in the judgment, expressed the view that (1) not much ought to be added to the Supreme Court's detailed opinion; and (2) only one thing ought to be subtracted, the Supreme Court's ATS reservation of a discretionary power in the federal judiciary to create causes of action for the enforcement of international-law-based norms, as the lawmaking role invited by this reservation committed the federal judiciary to a task which it was neither authorized nor suited to perform.

GINSBURG, J., joined by BREYER, J., concurring in part and concurring in the judgment, (1) agreed with the Supreme Court's disposition of the individual's ATS claim; and (2) expressed the view that the individual's FTCA claim ought to be rejected on a different basis under § 2680(k)'s foreign-country exception, by instead applying a "last significant act or omission" rule that would work to identify Mexico as the place where the case at hand arose.

BREYER, J., concurring in part and concurring in the judgment, expressed the view that an additional consideration for recognizing, under the ATS, a norm of international law ought to be to ask whether the exercise of jurisdiction would be consistent with those notions of comity that led each nation to respect the sovereign rights of other nations by limiting the reach of the nation's own laws and their enforcement.

COUNSEL

Paul D. Clement argued the cause for petitioner in No. 03-485.

Carter G. Phillips argued the cause for petitioner in No. 03-339.

Paul L. Hoffman argued the cause for respondents.

GLOSSARY OF COMMON LEGAL TERMS

Abatement
The extinguishment of a lawsuit.

Abstention doctrine
The doctrine whereby a federal court may decline to exercise, or may postpone the exercise of, its jurisdiction, where a case involves a controlling question of state law.

Action
A lawsuit.

Administrative determination
A decision by a government board, agency or official, rather than by a court.

Administrator
One appointed by a court to settle the estate of a deceased person. The feminine form is "administratrix."

Admiralty
The body of law governing maritime cases.

Affidavit
A sworn written statement.

Amicus curiae
One who, not being a party to a lawsuit, assists the court in deciding the case.

Antitrust laws
Laws prohibiting restrictions on competition.

Appealable
That which may be taken to a higher court for review.

Appellant
One who appeals to a superior court from the order of an inferior court.

Appellee
A party against whom a case is appealed from an inferior court to a superior court.

Arbitration
The submission of a dispute to a selected person—not a court—for decision.

Arraign
To call a person before a judge or commissioner to answer criminal charges made against him.

Array
The whole body of persons, summoned to attend court, from whom a jury will be selected.

Assignee
One to whom property or a right is transferred.

Assignor
The transferor of property or a right.

Bill of Rights
The first ten amendments to the United States Constitution.

Brief
A written legal argument submitted to the court deciding the case.

Calendar
A list of cases awaiting decision in a court.

Capital crime
An offense punishable by death.

Cause of action
A right to legal redress.

292

Cease-and-desist order
An order to stop doing specified acts.

Certiorari
A superior court's order to a lower court to send up the record of a case for review by the superior court.

Choice of remedies
An election of which form of legal redress to seek.

Civil
Not criminal, as a civil lawsuit.

Class action
A lawsuit on behalf of persons too numerous to participate actively therein.

Commerce clause
The provision of the United States Constitution giving Congress power to regulate commerce with foreign nations, among the states.

Common law
The body of the law apart from constitutions, treaties, statutes, ordinances, and regulations.

Contempt
An exhibition of scorn or disrespect toward a judicial or legislative body.

Continuance
A postponement of proceedings.

Copyright
The exclusive privilege of publishing literary or artistic productions.

Coram nobis
A means of challenging a court's judgment, especially in criminal cases.

Court of Appeals
See United States Court of Appeals.

Cross Appeal
An appeal filed by the person against whom an appeal is taken.

De novo
Anew or over again, such as a trial de novo.

Devise
A will provision making a gift of land.

Disputes clause
A provision in a government contract for the settlement of disputes between the contractor and the government by decision of a government board or official.

District court
See United States District Court.

Diversity case
A case decided by a federal court because the parties are citizens of different states.

Double jeopardy
Placing a person twice in jeopardy of conviction for the same offense.

Due process clause
The provision of the United States Constitution that no person shall be deprived of life, liberty, or property without due process of law.

En banc
With all the judges of the court sitting.

Equal protection
The guaranty of the United States Constitution that no person or class of persons shall be denied the same protection of the laws that is enjoyed by other persons or classes of persons in like circumstances.

Establishment clause
The provision of the United States Constitution that Congress shall make no law respecting an establishment of religion.

Federal District Court
See District court.

Federal question jurisdiction
The jurisdiction of federal courts over cases presenting questions of federal law.

Felony
A crime punishable by death or by imprisonment in a state prison.

Forma pauperis
Without the payment of legal fees in advance.

Full faith and credit clause
The provision of the United States Constitution that full faith and credit shall be given in each state to the public acts, records, and judicial proceedings of every other state.

Habeas corpus
A judicial inquiry into the legality of the restraint of a person.

Indictment
A grand jury's accusation of crime.

Interlocutory
That which settles an intervening matter but does not decide a case.

Intestate
One who dies without leaving a valid will.

Jurisdiction of subject matter
The power to decide a certain type of case.

Just compensation clause
The provision of the United States Constitution that no private property may be taken for public use without just compensation.

Laches
Delay barring the right to special forms of relief.

Legatee
One to whom personal property is given by will.

Lessee
A tenant.

Lessor
A landlord.

Libel
Written defamation; in maritime cases, a suit in court.

Lien
A charge upon property for the payment of a debt.

Local action
A lawsuit, especially one involving rights to land, which can be brought only in the place where the wrong was committed.

Maintenance and cure
The legal duty of a seaman's employer to care for him during his illness.

Mandamus
A judicial command to perform an official duty.

Misdemeanor
Any crime not punishable by death or by imprisonment in a state prison.

Patent
The exclusive right of manufacture, sale, or use secured by statute to one who invents or discovers a new and useful device or process.

Per curiam
By the court as a whole.

Per se
By itself.

Plaintiff
A person who brings a lawsuit.

Plenary
Full or complete.

Police power
The power inherent in the states as sovereigns and not derived under any written constitution.

Prima facie
At first sight; with regard to evidence, that which, if unexplained or uncontradicted, is sufficient to establish a fact.

Privileges and immunities clause
The provision of the United States Constitution that no state shall make or enforce any law which abridges the privileges or immunities of citizens of the United States.

Pro hac vice
For this occasion.

Pro se
For himself; in his own behalf.

Proximate cause
The immediate cause of injury.

Public defender
A lawyer employed by the public to defend persons accused of crime.

Recognizance
A bail bond.

Remand
To order to be sent back.

Res judicata
The doctrine that a final judgment is binding on the parties to the lawsuit and the matter cannot be relitigated.

Respondent
The defendant in an action; with regard to appeals, the party against whom the appeal is taken.

Sanction
The penalty to be incurred by a wrongdoer.

Saving clause
A statutory provision preserving rights which would otherwise be annihilated by the statute.

Seaworthy
The reasonable fitness of a vessel to perform the service which she has undertaken to perform.

Statute of frauds
A statute rendering certain types of contracts unenforceable unless in writing.

Statute of limitations
A statute fixing a period of time within which certain types of lawsuits or criminal prosecutions must be begun.

Subpoena
Legal process to require the attendance of a witness.

Substantial federal question
A question of federal law of sufficient merit to warrant decision of the case by a federal court.

Substantive offense
An offense which is complete in itself and does not depend on the establishment of another offense.

Summary judgment
A judgment without a trial.

Supremacy clause
The provision of the United States Constitution that the Constitution, federal laws enacted pursuant thereto, and federal treaties shall be the supreme law of the land, binding the judges in every state, notwithstanding any state law to the contrary.

Surety
One who binds himself with another, called the principal, for the performance of an obligation with respect to which the principal is already bound and primarily liable.

Surrogate
The judge of a court dealing largely with wills and decedents' estates.

Tort
A wrong independent of contract; a breach of duty which the law, as distinguished from a mere contract, has imposed.

Tortfeasor
One who commits a tort; a wrongdoer.

Transitory action
An action which may be brought wherever the defendant may be served with process.

Trespass
An injury intentionally inflicted on the person or property of another.

Trier of fact
One who decides questions of fact.

United States Code
The official compilation of statutes enacted by Congress.

United States Court of Appeals
The intermediate level of federal courts above the United States District Courts but below the Supreme Court of the United States.

United States District Court
A federal trial court.

Unseaworthy
See Seaworthy.

USC
See United States Code.

USCS
The abbreviation for United States Code Service, Lawyers Edition, which is a publication annotating the federal laws, arranged according to the numbering of the United States Code.

Venue
The place where a case may be tried.

Writ of certiorari
See Certiorari.

Writ of error coram nobis
See Coram nobis.

TABLE OF CASES

PAGE

A

ACLU, Ashcroft v .... 159 L Ed 2d 690
Advanced Micro Devices, Inc., Intel Corp. v . 159 L Ed 2d 355
Aetna Health Inc. v Davila .... 159 L Ed 2d 312
Alaska Dep't of Envtl. Conservation v EPA ... 157 L Ed 2d 967
Altmann, Republic of Aus. v .... 159 L Ed 2d 1
Alvarado, Yarborough v .... 158 L Ed 2d 938
Alvarez-Machain, Sosa v .... 159 L Ed 2d 718
Ashcroft v ACLU .... 159 L Ed 2d 690
Atlas Global Group, L.P., Grupo Dataflux v .. 158 L Ed 2d 866
Aus., Republic of v Altmann .... 159 L Ed 2d 1

B

Baldwin v Reese .... 158 L Ed 2d 64
Banks, Beard v .... 159 L Ed 2d 494
Banks v Dretke .... 157 L Ed 2d 1166
Banks, United States v .... 157 L Ed 2d 343
Barnhart v Thomas .... 157 L Ed 2d 333
Beard v Banks .... 159 L Ed 2d 494
BedRoc Ltd., LLC v United States .... 158 L Ed 2d 338
Blakely v Washington .... 159 L Ed 2d 403
Bush, Rasul v .... 159 L Ed 2d 548

C

California, Johnson v .... 158 L Ed 2d 696
Campbell, Nelson v .... 158 L Ed 2d 924
Castro v United States .... 157 L Ed 2d 778
Cent. Laborers' Pension Fund v Heinz ...... 159 L Ed 2d 46
Chao, Doe v .... 157 L Ed 2d 1122
Cheney v United States Dist. Court .... 159 L Ed 2d 459
Cline, Gen. Dynamics Land Sys. v .... 157 L Ed 2d 1094
Close, Muhammad v .... 158 L Ed 2d 32
Crawford v Washington .... 158 L Ed 2d 177

D

Davey, Locke v .... 158 L Ed 2d 1
Davila, Aetna Health Inc. v .... 159 L Ed 2d 312
Doe v Chao .... 157 L Ed 2d 1122

TABLE OF CASES

	PAGE
Dominguez Benitez, United States v	159 L Ed 2d 157
DOT v Pub. Citizen	159 L Ed 2d 60
Dretke, Banks v	157 L Ed 2d 1166
Dretke v Haley	158 L Ed 2d 659
Dretke, Tennard v	159 L Ed 2d 384

E

Edwards, SEC v	157 L Ed 2d 813
Elk Grove Unified Sch. Dist. v Newdow	159 L Ed 2d 98
Empagran S.A., F. Hoffmann-La Roche Ltd. v	159 L Ed 2d 226
Engine Mfrs. Ass'n v S. Coast Air Quality Mgmt. Dist.	158 L Ed 2d 529
EPA, Alaska Dep't of Envtl. Conservation v	157 L Ed 2d 967
Esparza, Mitchell v	157 L Ed 2d 263

F

Favish, Nat'l Archives & Records Admin. v	158 L Ed 2d 319
FEC, McConnell v	157 L Ed 2d 491
Fellers v United States	157 L Ed 2d 1016
F. Hoffmann-La Roche Ltd. v Empagran S.A.	159 L Ed 2d 226
Fisher, Illinois v	157 L Ed 2d 1060
Flamingo Indus. (USA) Ltd., United States Postal Serv. v	158 L Ed 2d 19
Flores-Montano, United States v	158 L Ed 2d 311
Ford, Pliler v	159 L Ed 2d 338
Frew v Hawkins	157 L Ed 2d 855

G

Galletti, United States v	158 L Ed 2d 279
Gen. Dynamics Land Sys. v Cline	157 L Ed 2d 1094
Gentry, Yarborough v	157 L Ed 2d 1
Groh v Ramirez	157 L Ed 2d 1068
Grupo Dataflux v Atlas Global Group, L.P.	158 L Ed 2d 866

H

Haley, Dretke v	158 L Ed 2d 659
Hamdi v Rumsfeld	159 L Ed 2d 578
Hawkins, Frew v	157 L Ed 2d 855
Heinz, Cent. Laborers' Pension Fund v	159 L Ed 2d 46
Hendon, Raymond B. Yates, M.D., P.C. Profit Sharing Plan v	158 L Ed 2d 40
Hernandez, Raytheon Co. v	157 L Ed 2d 357
Hibbs v Winn	159 L Ed 2d 172
Hiibel v Sixth Judicial Dist. Court	159 L Ed 2d 292
Holland v Jackson	159 L Ed 2d 683

PAGE

Hood, Tenn. Student Assistance Corp. v .... 158 L Ed 2d 764
Household Credit Servs. v Pfennig .... 158 L Ed 2d 450
Husain, Olympic Airways v .... 157 L Ed 2d 1146

I

Illinois v Fisher .... 157 L Ed 2d 1060
Illinois v Lidster .... 157 L Ed 2d 843
Intel Corp. v Advanced Micro Devices, Inc. ... 159 L Ed 2d 355
Iowa v Tovar .... 158 L Ed 2d 209

J

Jackson, Holland v .... 159 L Ed 2d 683
Johnson v California .... 158 L Ed 2d 696
Jones v R. R. Donnelley & Sons Co. .... 158 L Ed 2d 645
Jubelirer, Vieth v .... 158 L Ed 2d 546

K

Kontrick v Ryan .... 157 L Ed 2d 867

L

Lamie v United States Tr. .... 157 L Ed 2d 1024
Lane, Tennessee v .... 158 L Ed 2d 820
Lara, United States v .... 158 L Ed 2d 420
Law Offices of Curtis V. Trinko, LLP, Verizon
    Communs., Inc. v .... 157 L Ed 2d 823
Lidster, Illinois v .... 157 L Ed 2d 843
Littleton, City of v Z. J. Gifts D-4, L.L.C. ..... 159 L Ed 2d 84
Locke v Davey .... 158 L Ed 2d 1

M

Maryland v Pringle .... 157 L Ed 2d 769
Maryland, Virginia v .... 157 L Ed 2d 461
McConnell v FEC .... 157 L Ed 2d 491
McNeil, Middleton v .... 158 L Ed 2d 701
Miccosukee Tribe of Indians, S. Fla. Water
    Mgmt. Dist. v .... 158 L Ed 2d 264
Middleton v McNeil .... 158 L Ed 2d 701
Missouri v Seibert .... 159 L Ed 2d 643
Mitchell v Esparza .... 157 L Ed 2d 263
Mo. Mun. League, Nixon v .... 158 L Ed 2d 291
Muhammad v Close .... 158 L Ed 2d 32

N

Nat'l Archives & Records Admin. v Favish ... 158 L Ed 2d 319
Nelson v Campbell .... 158 L Ed 2d 924
Newdow, Elk Grove Unified Sch. Dist. v ..... 159 L Ed 2d 98

TABLE OF CASES

PAGE

Nixon v Mo. Mun. League .... 158 L Ed 2d 291
Norton v S. Utah Wilderness Alliance .... 159 L Ed 2d 137

O
Olympic Airways v Husain .... 157 L Ed 2d 1146

P
Padilla, Rumsfeld v .... 159 L Ed 2d 513
Pa. State Police v Suders .... 159 L Ed 2d 204
Patane, United States v .... 159 L Ed 2d 667
Pfennig, Household Credit Servs. v .... 158 L Ed 2d 450
Pliler v Ford .... 159 L Ed 2d 338
Principi, Scarborough v .... 158 L Ed 2d 674
Pringle, Maryland v .... 157 L Ed 2d 769
Pub. Citizen, DOT v .... 159 L Ed 2d 60

R
Ramirez, Groh v .... 157 L Ed 2d 1068
Rasul v Bush .... 159 L Ed 2d 548
Raymond B. Yates, M.D., P.C. Profit Sharing
  Plan v Hendon .... 158 L Ed 2d 40
Raytheon Co. v Hernandez .... 157 L Ed 2d 357
Reese, Baldwin v .... 158 L Ed 2d 64
R. R. Donnelley & Sons Co., Jones v .... 158 L Ed 2d 645
Rumsfeld, Hamdi v .... 159 L Ed 2d 578
Rumsfeld v Padilla .... 159 L Ed 2d 513
Ryan, Kontrick v .... 157 L Ed 2d 867

S
Sabri v United States .... 158 L Ed 2d 891
Scarborough v Principi .... 158 L Ed 2d 674
Schriro v Summerlin .... 159 L Ed 2d 442
S. Coast Air Quality Mgmt. Dist., Engine Mfrs.
  Ass'n v .... 158 L Ed 2d 529
SCS Credit Corp., Till v .... 158 L Ed 2d 787
SEC v Edwards .... 157 L Ed 2d 813
Seibert, Missouri v .... 159 L Ed 2d 643
S. Fla. Water Mgmt. Dist. v Miccosukee Tribe of
  Indians .... 158 L Ed 2d 264
Sixth Judicial Dist. Court, Hiibel v .... 159 L Ed 2d 292
Sosa v Alvarez-Machain .... 159 L Ed 2d 718
Suders, Pa. State Police v .... 159 L Ed 2d 204
Summerlin, Schriro v .... 159 L Ed 2d 442
S. Utah Wilderness Alliance, Norton v ...... 159 L Ed 2d 137

TABLE OF CASES

PAGE

T

Tennard v Dretke .... 159 L Ed 2d 384
Tennessee v Lane .... 158 L Ed 2d 820
Tenn. Student Assistance Corp. v Hood ...... 158 L Ed 2d 764
Thomas, Barnhart v .... 157 L Ed 2d 333
Thornton v United States .... 158 L Ed 2d 905
Till v SCS Credit Corp. .... 158 L Ed 2d 787
Tovar, Iowa v .... 158 L Ed 2d 209

U

United States v Banks .... 157 L Ed 2d 343
United States, BedRoc Ltd., LLC v .... 158 L Ed 2d 338
United States, Castro v .... 157 L Ed 2d 778
United States v Dominguez Benitez .... 159 L Ed 2d 157
United States, Fellers v .... 157 L Ed 2d 1016
United States v Flores-Montano .... 158 L Ed 2d 311
United States v Galletti .... 158 L Ed 2d 279
United States v Lara .... 158 L Ed 2d 420
United States v Patane .... 159 L Ed 2d 667
United States, Sabri v .... 158 L Ed 2d 891
United States, Thornton v .... 158 L Ed 2d 905
United States Dist. Court, Cheney v .... 159 L Ed 2d 459
United States Postal Serv. v Flamingo Indus.
  (USA) Ltd. .... 158 L Ed 2d 19
United States Tr., Lamie v .... 157 L Ed 2d 1024

V

Verizon Communs., Inc. v Law Offices of Curtis
  V. Trinko, LLP .... 157 L Ed 2d 823
Vieth v Jubelirer .... 158 L Ed 2d 546
Virginia v Maryland .... 157 L Ed 2d 461

W

Washington, Blakely v .... 159 L Ed 2d 403
Washington, Crawford v .... 158 L Ed 2d 177
Winn, Hibbs v .... 159 L Ed 2d 172

Y

Yarborough v Alvarado .... 158 L Ed 2d 938
Yarborough v Gentry .... 157 L Ed 2d 1

Z

Z. J. Gifts D-4, L.L.C., City of Littleton v ..... 159 L Ed 2d 84

INDEX

A

ABDUCTION AND KIDNAPPING.
Additional sanctions, courts' power to add.
  Judge's imposition of sentence exceeding general statutory
    maximum held to violate defendant's Sixth Amendment right
    to jury trial, 159 L Ed 2d 403.
Jury and jury trial.
  Judge's imposition of sentence exceeding general statutory
    maximum held to violate defendant's Sixth Amendment right
    to jury trial, 159 L Ed 2d 403.

ACCESS TO COURTS.
Americans with Disabilities Act.
  Title II a valid exercise of Congress' authority under Fourteenth
    Amendment, 158 L Ed 2d 820.

ACCIDENTS.
Aviation.
  Warsaw Convention.
    What constitutes an accident.
      Flight attendant's refusal to move asthmatic passenger away
        from smoking section deemed "accident" sufficient to
        impose liability, 157 L Ed 2d 1146.

ACTUAL INNOCENCE EXCEPTION.
Habeas corpus.
  Nondefaulted claims coupled with procedurally defaulted claim
    that would be addressed if actual innocence exception
    applied.
    Consideration of nondefaulted claims rather than considering
      actual innocence issue, 158 L Ed 2d 659.

ADMINISTRATIVE PROCEDURE ACTS.
Bureau of land management.
  Off-road vehicle use in wilderness study areas.
    Federal court's authority to "compel agency action unlawfully
      withheld or unreasonably delayed," 159 L Ed 2d 137.

ADULT OR X-RATED BUSINESSES OR MOVIES.
Licensing provisions.
  Prompt judicial review of administrative decision denying license,
    159 L Ed 2d 84.
Ordinances.
  Licensing ordinance.
    Prompt judicial review of administrative decision denying
      license, 159 L Ed 2d 84.

AGE DISCRIMINATION.
Age discrimination in employment.
Construction and application of act.
Employers may favor older employees over younger ones, 157 L Ed 2d 1094.
Employee benefit plans, generally.
Employers may favor older employees over younger ones, 157 L Ed 2d 1094.
Fringe benefits, generally.
Employers may favor older employees over younger ones, 157 L Ed 2d 1094.

AID OR ASSISTANCE.
Bribery.
State, local, or tribal officials of entities that receive federal funds.
Federal statute proscribing bribery of officials a valid exercise of Congress' authority under Article I of Constitution, 158 L Ed 2d 891.

ALL-TERRAIN VEHICLES.
Bureau of land management.
Wilderness study areas, vehicle use in.
Federal court's authority to "compel agency action unlawfully withheld or unreasonably delayed" under administrative procedure act, 159 L Ed 2d 137.

AMERICANS WITH DISABILITIES ACT.
Access to courts.
Title II a valid exercise of Congress' authority under Fourteenth Amendment, 158 L Ed 2d 820.
Enforcement.
Access to courts.
Title II a valid exercise of Congress' authority under Fourteenth Amendment, 158 L Ed 2d 820.

ARREST.
Search and seizure.
Automobiles, validity of warrantless search of motor vehicle.
Search allowed incident to arrest when police officer first made contact with arrestee after arrestee left automobile, 158 L Ed 2d 905.

ATTORNEYS AT LAW.
Ineffective assistance of counsel.
Habeas corpus, federal relief.
Application of Strickland test.
Unreasonable application of federal law, 159 L Ed 2d 683.

AUTOMOBILES AND HIGHWAY TRAFFIC.
Highway checkpoint program.
Information-seeking highway stop not unreasonable seizure in violation of Fourth Amendment, 157 L Ed 2d 843.

AUTOMOBILES AND HIGHWAY TRAFFIC —Cont'd
Passenger or guest.
Warrantless search, passenger compartment of automobile.
Search allowed incident to arrest when police officer first made
contact with arrestee after arrestee left automobile, 158 L
Ed 2d 905.
Search and seizure.
Arrest, automobile searched incident to, generally.
Warrantless search of automobile allowed when police officer
first made contact with arrestee after arrestee left
automobile, 158 L Ed 2d 905.
Roadblocks.
Information-seeking highway checkpoint not unreasonable
seizure in violation of Fourth Amendment, 157 L Ed 2d
843.
Warrantless search.
Allowed incident to arrest when police officer first made contact
with arrestee after arrestee left automobile, 158 L Ed 2d 905.

AVIATION.
Death.
Limitation of liability, Warsaw Convention.
Flight attendant's refusal to move asthmatic passenger away
from smoking section deemed an "accident" sufficient to
impose liability, 157 L Ed 2d 1146.
Warsaw Convention.
Flight attendant's refusal to move an asthmatic passenger away
from smoking section deemed an "accident" sufficient to
impose liability, 157 L Ed 2d 1146.

B

BANKRUPTCY.
Attorneys' fees.
Chapter 7 cases.
Debtors' attorneys not authorized to receive compensation from
estate funds under 11 USCS § 330(a)(1) unless employed
as authorized under § 327, 157 L Ed 2d 1024.
Cram down option.
Interest, appropriate rate of, 158 L Ed 2d 787.
Discharge of indebtedness.
In rem nature of proceeding, 158 L Ed 2d 764.
States.
Student loan debts guaranteed by governmental units.
Proceeding to determine dischargeability of student loan debt
not a suit against state, 158 L Ed 2d 764.
Time and date.
Forfeiture of right to rely on time constraints, 157 L Ed 2d 867.
Interest on money.
Cram down option.
Appropriate rate of interest, 158 L Ed 2d 787.

BANKRUPTCY —Cont'd
Sovereign immunity of states.
Student loan debts guaranteed by governmental units.
Proceeding to determine dischargeability of student loan debt not a suit against state, 158 L Ed 2d 764.
Student loans.
Sovereign immunity.
Proceeding to determine dischargeability of student loan debt not a suit against state, 158 L Ed 2d 764.
Time and date.
Discharge of indebtedness.
Forfeiture of right to rely on time constraints, 157 L Ed 2d 867.

BORDER PATROLS OR SEARCHES.
Automobiles.
Motor vehicle searches.
Suspicionless search of gas tank, 158 L Ed 2d 311.
Motor vehicle searches.
Suspicionless search of gas tank, 158 L Ed 2d 311.
Suspicionless searches.
Vehicles, 158 L Ed 2d 311.

BORROWED CONSTITUTIONS OR PROVISIONS.
Limitation of actions.
Federal 4 year limitation for claims under enactments made after 1990.
Amendment in 1991 to statute allowing action to be maintained, 158 L Ed 2d 645.

BRADY CLAIM.
Fair trial.
Federal habeas corpus review.
Informers, identity of.
Suppression of evidence that key witness was paid informant entitled petitioner to writ of habeas corpus, 157 L Ed 2d 1166.

BRIBERY.
State, local, and tribal officials of entities that receive federal funds.
Federal statute proscribing bribery of officials a valid exercise of Congress' authority under Article I of Constitution, 158 L Ed 2d 891.

BUREAU OF LAND MANAGEMENT.
Administrative procedure act.
Off-road vehicle use in wilderness study areas.
Federal court's authority to "compel agency action unlawfully withheld or unreasonably delayed," 159 L Ed 2d 137.
Off-road vehicle use in wilderness study areas.
Administrative procedure act.
Federal court's authority to "compel agency action unlawfully withheld or unreasonably delayed," 159 L Ed 2d 137.

C

CAPITAL OFFENSES AND PUNISHMENT.
Aggravating or mitigating circumstances.
Federal question, Federal Constitution held violated by Maryland
capital sentencing instructions which reasonable jurors could
interpret as requiring unanimous finding as to particular
mitigating circumstances.
No retroactive application of rule on federal habeas corpus
review, 159 L Ed 2d 494.
Incompetent or insane persons, mitigation of penalty.
Low I.Q. mitigation claim.
Certificate of appealability ought to have issued when court
of appeals assessed defendant's Penry v. Lynaugh claim
under improper legal standard, 159 L Ed 2d 384.
Jury decision, rather than sentencing judge sitting alone,
required where aggravating circumstance requirement serves
as functional equivalent of element of greater offense.
Not retroactively applicable to cases already final on direct
review, 159 L Ed 2d 442.
Civil rights and discrimination.
Eighth Amendment claim challenging use of cut down procedure
to access veins for lethal injection allowed under 42 USCS
§ 1983, 158 L Ed 2d 924.
Procedures for imposition of death penalty.
Lethal injection.
Cut down procedure, use of to access veins.
Eighth Amendment claim challenging use of procedure
allowed under 42 USCS § 1983, 158 L Ed 2d 924.
Federal question.
Aggravating or mitigating circumstances, Federal Constitution
held violated by Maryland capital sentencing instructions
which reasonable jurors could interpret as requiring
unanimous finding as to particular mitigating circumstances.
No retroactive application of rule on federal habeas corpus
review, 159 L Ed 2d 494.
Habeas corpus.
Cause and prejudice.
Requirement, in federal habeas corpus proceedings, of showing
of cause and prejudice with respect to relief from state
criminal conviction or sentence.
Demonstration of cause and prejudice, 157 L Ed 2d 1166.
Lethal injection.
Cut down procedure, use of to access veins.
Eighth Amendment claim challenging use of procedure
allowed under 42 § 1983 despite prior habeas
applications, 158 L Ed 2d 924.
Mills v Maryland rule.
Held to be new constitutional rule that could not be applied
retroactively on federal habeas corpus review, 159 L Ed 2d
494.

CAPITAL OFFENSES AND PUNISHMENT —Cont'd
Incompetent or insane persons.
Mitigation of penalty.
Low I.Q. mitigation claim.
Certificate of appealability ought to have issued when court
of appeals assessed defendant's Penry v. Lynaugh claim
under improper legal standard, 159 L Ed 2d 384.
Jury and jury trial.
Aggravating circumstances.
Finding of aggravating circumstance only factor which can
result in death sentence.
Jury decision, rather than sentencing judge sitting alone,
required where aggravating circumstance requirement
serves as functional equivalent of element of greater
offense.
Not retroactively applicable to cases already final on direct
review, 159 L Ed 2d 442.
Lethal injection.
Cut down procedure, use of to access vein.
Eighth Amendment claim challenging use of procedure allowed
under 42 USCS § 1983, 158 L Ed 2d 924.
Retroactive effect.
Rule that aggravating factors necessary for death penalty be
found by jury not retroactively applicable to cases already
final on direct review, 159 L Ed 2d 442.

CARRIERS.
Environmental law.
National Environmental Policy Act and Clean Air Act held not to
require federal motor carrier safety administration to
evaluate environmental effects of cross-border operations of
Mexican-domiciled carriers, 159 L Ed 2d 60.

CERTIORARI.
Jurisdiction.
State court decision.
Final judgment of state court, 158 L Ed 2d 696.
States and state courts.
Final judgment of state court.
Jurisdictional requirement, 158 L Ed 2d 696.
Supreme Court appellate jurisdiction.
State courts.
Final judgment of state court, 158 L Ed 2d 696.

CHECKPOINTS.
Seizure of vehicles.
Information-seeking highway stop not unreasonable seizure in
violation of Fourth Amendment, 157 L Ed 2d 843.

CHILD ONLINE PROTECTION ACT.
Discretion in granting preliminary injunction against enforcement
pending constitutionality determination, 159 L Ed 2d 690.

CHILDREN AND MINORS.
Freedom of speech and press.
Child online protection act.
Discretion in granting preliminary injunction against
enforcement pending constitutionality determination, 159 L
Ed 2d 690.
Parties.
Standing.
Non-custodial father lacked prudential standing to bring suit
against daughter's school district to challenge district's
requirement that students recite pledge of allegiance, 159
L Ed 2d 98.

CIVIL RIGHTS AND DISCRIMINATION.
Claim by state prisoner, for damages caused by acts which if proven
would render his conviction invalid.
Favorable-termination requirement not applicable when
prisoner's challenge threatens no consequence for the
conviction or the duration of sentence, 158 L Ed 2d 32.
Sexual harassment.
Vicarious liability of employer.
Affirmative defense.
Employer installed a readily accessible, effective policy for
reporting complaints and plaintiff unreasonably failed to
make use of procedure, 159 L Ed 2d 204.

CLAIMS AGAINST GOVERNMENT.
Alien tort statute.
Abduction from Mexico for criminal trial in United States.
Jurisdiction-only nature of statute, 159 L Ed 2d 718.
Eleventh amendment.
Americans with disabilities act.
Title II a valid exercise of Congress' authority under
Fourteenth Amendment, 158 L Ed 2d 820.
Foreign state or country.
Abduction from Mexico for criminal trial in United States.
Action against DEA under tort claims act, 159 L Ed 2d 718.
Headquarters doctrine.
Abduction from Mexico for criminal trial in United States.
Action against DEA under tort claims act, 159 L Ed 2d 718.
Injunctions.
Public officers and employees, injunctive relief, permissibility of.
Consent decrees.
Enforcement of decree against state officials not barred by
Eleventh Amendment, 157 L Ed 2d 855.
Privacy Act.
Actual damages must be proved in order to qualify for minimum
statutory award under act, 157 L Ed 2d 1122.

CLAIMS AGAINST GOVERNMENT —Cont'd
Public officers and employees.
Injunctive relief, permissibility of.
Consent decrees.
Enforcement of decree against state officials not barred by
Eleventh Amendment, 157 L Ed 2d 855.

CLEAN WATER ACT.
Discharge of pollutant, 158 L Ed 2d 264.
NPDES permits.
Point sources.
Discharge of pollutant.
Conveyance of pollutant without adding to pollution sufficient
to constitute discharge of pollutant into waters, requiring
permit, 158 L Ed 2d 264.
Point sources.
Discharge of pollutant.
Conveyance of pollutant without adding to pollution sufficient
to constitute discharge of pollutant into waters, requiring
permit, 158 L Ed 2d 264.

COLLATERAL ATTACK.
Prisons and prisoners.
Claim by state prisoner for damages caused by acts which if
proven would render his conviction invalid.
Favorable-termination requirement not applicable when
prisoner's challenge threatens no consequence for the
conviction or the duration of sentence, 158 L Ed 2d 32.

COLLEGES AND UNIVERSITIES.
Freedom of speech and press.
State postsecondary scholarship program.
Prohibition against students who receive scholarship funds
from pursuing a theology degree not a viewpoint restriction
on speech, 158 L Ed 2d 1.
Religion and religious matters.
State postsecondary scholarship program.
Prohibition against students who receive scholarship funds
from pursuing a theology degree not a violation of first
amendment, 158 L Ed 2d 1.

CONFESSIONS.
Attorneys at law.
Absence of counsel.
Admissibility of statements made after indictment and in
absence of counsel.
Deliberate elicitation of incriminating information as
violation of defendant's Sixth Amendment rights, 157 L
Ed 2d 1016.
Continuous interrogation of suspect.
Pre-Miranda warning confession inadmissible, 159 L Ed 2d 643.

CONFESSIONS —Cont'd
Interruption of Miranda warnings by suspect giving voluntary confession.
Failure to finish warnings not requiring suppression of physical evidence, 159 L Ed 2d 667.

CONFRONTATION OF WITNESSES.
Cross examination as core of trustworthiness, 158 L Ed 2d 177.
Good or bad faith.
Cross examination as core of trustworthiness, 158 L Ed 2d 177.
Hearsay.
Trustworthiness and reliability of.
Cross examination as core of trustworthiness, 158 L Ed 2d 177.
Husband and wife.
Marital privilege barring spouse's testimony.
Recorded statement of spouse not admissible absent cross examination, 158 L Ed 2d 177.
Marital privilege barring spouse's testimony.
Recorded statement of spouse not admissible absent cross examination, 158 L Ed 2d 177.
Preliminary hearings.
Unavailable witness, admission of testimony of unavailable witness given under direct examination questioning by defense counsel.
Cross examination as core of trustworthiness, 158 L Ed 2d 177.

CONGRESS.
Bribery.
Federal statute proscribing bribery of officials of entities that receive federal funds a valid exercise of authority under Article I of Constitution, 158 L Ed 2d 891.
Fourteenth amendment.
Enforcement by appropriate legislation.
Congress' power to enforce by appropriate legislation.
Americans with Disabilities Act, 158 L Ed 2d 820.
"Necessary and proper clause."
Bribery.
Federal statute proscribing bribery of officials of entities that receive federal funds a valid exercise of authority under Article I of Constitution, 158 L Ed 2d 891.

CONSENT JUDGMENT OR DECREE.
Sovereign immunity.
Enforcement of consent decree against state officials not barred by Eleventh Amendment, 157 L Ed 2d 855.

CONSTRUCTION AND INTERPRETATION.
Age discrimination laws.
Employers may favor older employees over younger ones, 157 L Ed 2d 1094.

CONSTRUCTION AND INTERPRETATION —Cont'd
Identical words in different parts of statute.

Presumption that identical words are intended to have the same meaning yields where context shows that words used in different parts of statute were intended to have different meanings, 157 L Ed 2d 1094.

CONTEMPORANEOUS ACTS OR MATTERS.
Search.

Contemporaneous warrantless search of automobile allowed incident to arrest when police officer first made contact with arrestee after arrestee left automobile, 158 L Ed 2d 905.

CONTROVERSY.
Gerrymandering.

Political gerrymandering claims nonjusticiable, 158 L Ed 2d 546.

CRAM-DOWN PROVISION.
Interest, appropriate rate of, 158 L Ed 2d 787.

CRIMINAL LAW.
Elements of crime.

Sentencing factors, distinguishing from elements of crime.

Capital offenses and punishment.

Jury decision, rather than sentencing judge sitting alone, required where aggravating circumstance requirement serves as functional equivalent of element of greater offense.

Not retroactively applicable to cases already final on direct review, 159 L Ed 2d 442.

CRUEL AND UNUSUAL PUNISHMENT.
Lethal injection as method of execution.

Cut down procedure, use of to access veins.

Eighth Amendment claim challenging use of procedure allowed under 42 USCS § 1983, 158 L Ed 2d 924.

CUSTODY OF CHILDREN.
Parties.

Standing.

Non-custodial father lacked prudential standing to bring suit against daughter's school district to challenge district's requirement that students recite pledge of allegiance, 159 L Ed 2d 98.

D

DAMAGES.
Prisoners.

Claims for damages caused by acts which if proven would render his conviction invalid.

Favorable-termination requirement not applicable when prisoner's challenge threatens no consequence for the conviction or the duration of sentence, 158 L Ed 2d 32.

DAMAGES —Cont'd
Privacy Act.
Actual damages must be proved before recovery allowed, 157 L
Ed 2d 1122.
DEFENSES.
Sexual harassment.
Affirmative defense of employer.
Employer installed a readily accessible, effective policy for
reporting complaints and plaintiff unreasonably failed to
make use of procedure, 159 L Ed 2d 204.
DEFERENCE OF COURT.
Habeas corpus.
State courts.
Jury instruction on imperfect self defense.
Deference to state court decision that jury not likely misled
by single erroneous instruction, 158 L Ed 2d 701.
DEFERENCE TO ADMINISTRATIVE INTERPRETATION.
Age discrimination.
Deference to EEOC's interpretation not required when regular
interpretive method leaves no serious question of intent, 157
L Ed 2d 1094.
DEMONSTRATIVE OR REAL EVIDENCE.
Preservation of evidence.
Failure to preserve potentially useful evidence not a denial of due
process where bad faith on part of police not shown.
Discovery request by defendant.
Effect on subsequent destruction of evidence, 157 L Ed 2d
1060.
DESCRIPTION OR IDENTIFICATION.
Names.
Stop and identify statute requiring Terry stop suspect to disclose
name does not violate Fourth or Fifth Amendments, 159 L Ed
2d 292.
DESTRUCTION OF EVIDENCE.
State's failure to preserve potentially useful evidence not violative
of due process, where bad faith of police not shown.
Discovery request by defendant.
Effect on subsequent destruction of evidence, 157 L Ed 2d 1060.
DISCLOSURE.
Brady rule.
Informer, identity of.
Prosecution's failure to disclose entitled petitioner to writ of
habeas corpus, 157 L Ed 2d 1166.
Due process.
Favorable evidence: disclosure of evidence favorable to accused,
prosecutor's duty.
Informer, identity of.
Prosecutor's failure to disclose entitled petitioner to writ of
habeas corpus, 157 L Ed 2d 1166.

DISCLOSURE —Cont'd
Name.
Stop and identify statute requiring Terry stop suspect to disclose name does not violate Fourth or Fifth Amendments, 159 L Ed 2d 292.

DISCOVERY AND DISCOVERY PROCEEDINGS.
European Communities, commission of.
Antitrust.
Federal district court authorized, under 28 USCS § 1782(a), to order discovery requested by private complainant for use in European Commission antitrust proceeding, 159 L Ed 2d 355.
Federal Advisory Committee Act, 159 L Ed 2d 459.
Mandamus.
Federal Advisory Committee Act.
National energy policy development group, 159 L Ed 2d 459.
Privileged matter.
Federal Advisory Committee Act, 159 L Ed 2d 459.

DISMISSAL, DISCONTINUANCE, AND NONSUIT.
Habeas corpus.
Mixed petitions containing both exhausted and unexhausted claims.
Federal district court's failure to give particular warnings about statute of limitations to prisoner held not to make improper the dismissal of mixed petitions that prisoner had filed pro se, 159 L Ed 2d 338.

DISPARITY IN AGE.
Discrimination: suit under Age Discrimination in Employment Act.
Employers may favor older employees over younger ones, 157 L Ed 2d 1094.

DISTRICT COURTS AND JUDGES.
Administrative procedure act.
Federal court's authority to "compel agency action unlawfully withheld or unreasonably delayed," 159 L Ed 2d 137.
Bureau of land management.
Administrative procedure act.
Federal court's authority to "compel agency action unlawfully withheld or unreasonably delayed," 159 L Ed 2d 137.

DIVERSITY OF CITIZENSHIP.
Change.
Postfiling change in citizenship cannot cure lack of subject matter jurisdiction that existed at time of filing, 158 L Ed 2d 866.
Dismissal, discontinuance, and nonsuit.
Jurisdictional defect.
Postfiling change in citizenship cannot cure lack of subject matter jurisdiction that existed at time of filing, 158 L Ed 2d 866.

DIVERSITY OF CITIZENSHIP —Cont'd
Elimination of parties to complete diversity.
Postfiling change in citizenship cannot cure lack of subject matter
jurisdiction that existed at time of filing, 158 L Ed 2d 866.
Limited partnership.
Postfiling change in citizenship cannot cure lack of subject matter
jurisdiction that existed at time of filing, 158 L Ed 2d 866.
Partnership.
Postfiling change in citizenship cannot cure lack of subject matter
jurisdiction that existed at time of filing, 158 L Ed 2d 866.
Postfiling change in citizenship cannot cure lack of subject matter
jurisdiction that existed at time of filing, 158 L Ed 2d 866.

DOUBLE JEOPARDY.
Dual sovereigns, prosecutions by.
Tribal court prosecution of nonmember Indian.
Subsequent federal court prosecution not barred on strength of
dual sovereign theory, 158 L Ed 2d 420.
Indians.
Tribal court prosecution of nonmember Indian.
Subsequent federal court prosecution not barred.
Dual sovereign theory, 158 L Ed 2d 420.

DOUBLE QUESTIONING.
Miranda v. Arizona.
Continuous interrogation of suspect.
Prewarning confession inadmissible, 159 L Ed 2d 643.

DRIVING WHILE INTOXICATED.
Checkpoints.
Information-seeking highway stops.
Not unreasonable seizure in violation of Fourth Amendment,
157 L Ed 2d 843.
Search and seizure.
Information-seeking highway checkpoint.
Not unreasonable seizure in violation of Fourth Amendment,
157 L Ed 2d 843.

DUAL SOVEREIGNTY.
Double jeopardy.
Indian tribal court prosecution of nonmember Indian.
Subsequent federal court prosecution not barred on strength of
dual sovereign theory, 158 L Ed 2d 420.

DUE PROCESS.
Access to courts.
Americans with disabilities act.
Title II a valid exercise of Congress' authority, 158 L Ed 2d
820.
Americans with Disabilities Act.
Access to courts.
Title II a valid exercise of Congress' authority under
Fourteenth Amendment, 158 L Ed 2d 820.

DUE PROCESS —Cont'd
Brady rule.
Informer, identity of.
Prosecution's failure to disclose identity of informer violated petitioner's due process rights, entitling him to writ of habeas corpus, 157 L Ed 2d 1166.
Enemy combatant.
Right to present evidence as to status as enemy combatant, 159 L Ed 2d 578.

DURESS OR COERCION.
Presumptions and burden of proof.
Failure to finish Miranda warnings, 159 L Ed 2d 667.

E

EARLY RETIREMENT.
Anti-cutback provision of ERISA.
Amendment to pension plan expanding types of post-retirement employment that would trigger suspension of already accrued benefits prohibited, 159 L Ed 2d 46.

ELECTIONS AND VOTING.
Equal protection.
Gerrymander of state legislative districts as diluting votes.
Political gerrymandering claims nonjusticiable, 158 L Ed 2d 546.
Intent or motive.
Partisan gerrymander of districts.
Political gerrymandering claims nonjusticiable, 158 L Ed 2d 546.
Justiciable controversy.
Gerrymandering.
Political gerrymandering claims nonjusticiable, 158 L Ed 2d 546.

ELEVENTH AMENDMENT.
Abrogating state immunity.
Due process.
Legislation to implement.
Congruence and proportionality requirements satisfied, 158 L Ed 2d 820.
Americans with disabilities act.
Title II a valid exercise of Congress' authority under Fourteenth Amendment, 158 L Ed 2d 820.

EMISSIONS.
Automobiles and highway traffic.
Preemption of local emission control rules by § 209(a) of Clean Air Act, 158 L Ed 2d 529.

ENEMY COMBATANT.
Definition, 159 L Ed 2d 578.

ENEMY COMBATANT —Cont'd
Due process.
Right to present evidence as to status as enemy combatant, 159 L
    Ed 2d 578.
Habeas corpus.
Federal court jurisdiction over foreign detainees at Guantanamo
    naval base.
    Plaintiffs not nationals of countries at war with United States,
        159 L Ed 2d 548.
Petition of alleged enemy combatant improperly filed in New York
    district court where petitioner was being detained in South
    Carolina, 159 L Ed 2d 513.
Right to present evidence as to status as enemy combatant, 159 L
    Ed 2d 578.

ENVIRONMENTAL IMPACT STATEMENTS.
Federal motor carrier safety administration.
Evaluation by administration of environmental effects of
    cross-border operations of Mexican-domiciled carriers not
    required under National Environmental Policy Act, 159 L Ed
    2d 60.

ENVIRONMENTAL LAW.
Administrative control.
Bureau of land management.
    Federal court's authority to "compel agency action unlawfully
        withheld or unreasonably delayed" under administrative
        procedure act, 159 L Ed 2d 137.
Off-road vehicles.
Bureau of land management.
    Federal court's authority to "compel agency action unlawfully
        withheld or unreasonably delayed" under administrative
        procedure act, 159 L Ed 2d 137.

ENVIRONMENTAL PROTECTION AGENCY.
Best available control technology (BACT).
Authority of EPA to determine reasonableness of a state
    permitting agency's justification for its BACT decision, 157 L
    Ed 2d 967.
Prevention of significant deterioration program of the Clean Air Act.
Best available control technology (BACT).
    Authority of EPA to determine reasonableness of a state
        permitting agency's justification for its BACT decision, 157
        L Ed 2d 967.
Stop construction orders.
Supervisory authority of EPA to issue if it determined that a
    state agency had not made a reasonable best available
    control technology decision, 157 L Ed 2d 967.

EQUAL ACCESS TO JUSTICE ACT.
Application for fees.
Not substantially justified position of US, allegation required.
Amendment of application after 30 day deadline to include
required allegation.
Relation back of amendment so that timeliness preserved,
158 L Ed 2d 674.
Relation back.
Application for fees.
Not substantially justified position of US, allegation required.
Amendment of application after 30 day deadline to include
required allegation.
Timeliness preserved by relation back of amendment, 158
L Ed 2d 674.

EVIDENCE.
Preservation of evidence.
State's failure to preserve potentially useful evidence not a denial
of due process where criminal defendant did not show bad
faith on part of police.
Discovery request by defendant.
Effect on subsequent destruction of evidence, 157 L Ed 2d
1060.

EXCLUSION OR SUPPRESSION OF EVIDENCE.
Attorneys.
Sixth Amendment right to counsel.
Deliberate elicitation standard.
Self incriminating statements made due to violation of
standard, 157 L Ed 2d 1016.
Habeas corpus.
Evidence favorable to accused.
Informant status of witness suppressed, defendant entitled to
writ of habeas corpus, 157 L Ed 2d 1166.
Informers, identity of.
Habeas corpus.
Petitioner entitled to writ of habeas corpus on basis of claim
that prosecution suppressed evidence concerning
paid-informant status of key witness, 157 L Ed 2d 1166.

EXEMPTIONS AND EXCLUSIONS.
Foreign trade antitrust improvements act.
Anticompetitive conduct that causes only foreign injury, exclusion
from Sherman act, 159 L Ed 2d 226.

EXHAUSTION OF REMEDIES.
Claim by state prisoner, for damages caused by acts which if proven
would render his conviction invalid.
Favorable-termination requirement not applicable when
prisoner's challenge threatens no consequence for the
conviction or the duration of sentence, 158 L Ed 2d 32.

EX PARTE YOUNG DOCTRINE.
Consent decree.
Judicial enforcement of consent decree against state officials not
barred by doctrine, 157 L Ed 2d 855.

EXPERIMENTS OR TESTS.
Preservation of evidence.
State's failure to preserve potentially useful evidence not a due
process violation where criminal defendant did not show bad
faith on part of police.
Discovery request by defendant.
Effect on subsequent destruction of evidence, 157 L Ed 2d
1060.

F

FAIR AND IMPARTIAL PROCEEDING.
Evidence.
Disclosure of evidence favorable to accused, prosecutor's duty
under due process clause.
Informer, identity of.
Prosecution's failure to disclose identity of informer a
violation of due process, 157 L Ed 2d 1166.

FAMILY AND RELATIVES.
Parties.
Standing.
Non-custodial father, who could not sue as next friend of
daughter under state law, lacked prudential standing to
bring suit against daughter's school district in federal
court, 159 L Ed 2d 98.

FEDERAL ADVISORY COMMITTEE ACT.
Public disclosures.
National energy policy development group, 159 L Ed 2d 459.

FEDERAL MOTOR CARRIER SAFETY ADMINISTRATION.
Environmental law.
National environmental policy act and clean air act held not to
require FMCSA to evaluate environmental effects of
cross-border operations of Mexican-domiciled carriers, 159 L
Ed 2d 60.

FLAG.
Pledge of allegiance.
Non-custodial father lacked standing to bring suit against
daughter's school district to challenge district's requirement
that students recite pledge of allegiance, 159 L Ed 2d 98.
Schools and education.
Religious freedom.
Non-custodial father lacked prudential standing to bring suit
against daughter's school district to challenge district's
requirement that students recite pledge of allegiance, 159
L Ed 2d 98.

FOREIGN SOVEREIGN IMMUNITIES ACT.
Austria.
Expropriation exception applicable to pre-enactment conduct, 159
L Ed 2d 1.
Expropriation exception.
Applicable to pre-enactment conduct, 159 L Ed 2d 1.
Pre-enactment conduct.
Applicability of act, 159 L Ed 2d 1.
Retroactive application.
Expropriation exception.
Applicable to pre-enactment conduct, 159 L Ed 2d 1.

FOREIGN STATE OR COUNTRY.
Abduction from Mexico for criminal trial in United States.
Action against DEA under tort claims act.
Claim arising in foreign country exception, 159 L Ed 2d 718.
Expropriation.
Foreign sovereign immunities act.
Expropriation exception.
Retroactive application, 159 L Ed 2d 1.
Jurisdiction.
Abduction from Mexico for criminal trial in United States.
Action against DEA under tort claims act.
Alien tort statute, applicability, 159 L Ed 2d 718.

FOREIGN TRADE ANTITRUST IMPROVEMENTS ACT.
Independent foreign harm.
Alleged price-fixing activity excluded from reach of Sherman act
by FTAIA where plaintiff's claim rested solely on
independent foreign harm, 159 L Ed 2d 226.

FOURTEENTH AMENDMENT.
Enforcement.
Congress' power to enforce by appropriate legislation.
Americans with Disabilities Act, 158 L Ed 2d 820.

FREEDOM OF INFORMATION ACT.
Exemptions and exclusions.
Law enforcement records.
Privacy invasion resulting from release of records, 158 L Ed 2d
319.
Police records.
Privacy invasion resulting from release of records, 158 L Ed 2d
319.
Privacy invasion resulting from release of records.
Law enforcement records, 158 L Ed 2d 319.

FREEDOM OF SPEECH AND PRESS.
Child online protection act.
Discretion in granting preliminary injunction against
enforcement pending constitutionality determination, 159 L
Ed 2d 690.

FREEDOM OF SPEECH AND PRESS —Cont'd
Religious freedom.
State postsecondary scholarship program.
Prohibition against students who receive scholarship funds
from pursuing a theology degree not a viewpoint restriction
on speech, 158 L Ed 2d 1.

FRUIT OF POISONOUS TREE DOCTRINE.
Interruption of Miranda warnings by suspect giving voluntary
confession.
Failure to finish warnings not requiring suppression of physical
evidence, 159 L Ed 2d 667.
Self-incrimination.
Deliberately elicited statements without presence of counsel.
Relationship between 5th and 6th amendment protections, 157
L Ed 2d 1016.

G

GAS TANKS.
Border searches.
Suspicionless search of vehicle at border crossing, 158 L Ed 2d
311.

GERRYMANDERING.
Equal protection.
Political gerrymandering claims nonjusticiable, 158 L Ed 2d 546.

GOOD OR BAD FAITH.
Evidence.
Preservation of potentially useful evidence, due process.
Discovery request.
Effect on subsequent destruction of evidence, 157 L Ed 2d
1060.

GUANTANAMO NAVAL BASE.
Federal court jurisdiction over foreign detainees.
Plaintiffs not nationals of countries at war with United States,
159 L Ed 2d 548.

GUILTY PLEA.
Acceptance.
Rule 11 of federal rules of criminal procedure.
Plain error rule.
Warnings, failure of district court to give required warnings.
Defendant must show reasonable probability that, but for
district court's error, defendant would not have entered
guilty plea, 159 L Ed 2d 157.
Appeal and error.
Plain error review.
Warnings, failure of district court to give required warnings,
159 L Ed 2d 157.

GUILTY PLEA —Cont'd
Attorneys at law.
Right to counsel.
Waiver of right to counsel at plea stage.
Warnings, requirements as to, 158 L Ed 2d 209.
Estoppel and waiver.
Attorneys at law, waiver of right to counsel at plea stage.
Warnings, requirements as to, 158 L Ed 2d 209.
Federal rule of criminal procedure 11.
Acceptance of plea.
Plain error rule.
Warnings, failure of district court to give required warnings.
Defendant must show reasonable probability that, but for
court's error, defendant would not have entered guilty
plea, 159 L Ed 2d 157.
Warnings.
Failure of district court to give warnings required by Rule 11 of
federal rules of criminal procedure.
Plain error review.
Defendant must show reasonable probability that, but for
court's error, defendant would not have entered guilty
plea, 159 L Ed 2d 157.
Withdrawal.
Warnings, failure of district court to give required warnings.
Plain error review.
Defendant must show reasonable probability that, but for
court's error, defendant would not have entered guilty
plea, 159 L Ed 2d 157.

H

HABEAS CORPUS.
Actual innocence exception.
Nondefaulted claims coupled with procedurally defaulted claim
that would be considered if actual innocence exception
applied.
Consideration of nondefaulted claims rather than considering
actual innocence issue, 158 L Ed 2d 659.
Appeal and error.
Certificate of appealability.
Substantial showing of denial of constitutional right to justify
grant.
Debatability of district court's constitutional ruling among
reasonable jurists satisfies substantial showing standard,
157 L Ed 2d 1166.
Brady rule.
Informer, identity of.
Prosecution's failure to disclose identity of informer entitled
petitioner to writ of habeas corpus, 157 L Ed 2d 1166.

HABEAS CORPUS —Cont'd
Cause and prejudice standard.
Demonstration of cause and prejudice, 157 L Ed 2d 1166.
Custody.
Determination of when is person in custody.
Federal law reasonably applied in court's holding that suspect
not in custody during interrogation, 158 L Ed 2d 938.
Enemy combatant.
Foreign detainees at Guantanamo naval base.
Plaintiffs not nationals of countries at war with United
States, 159 L Ed 2d 548.
Right to present evidence as to status as enemy combatant, 159
L Ed 2d 578.
Petition of person detained as asserted enemy combatant
improperly filed in New York district court where petitioner
was being detained in South Carolina, 159 L Ed 2d 513.
State court determination of custody for Miranda purposes.
Federal law reasonably applied in court's holding that suspect
not in custody during interrogation, 158 L Ed 2d 938.
Damages.
State prisoner claim for damages caused by acts which if proven
would render his conviction invalid.
Favorable-termination requirement not applicable when
prisoner's challenge threatens no consequence for the
conviction or the duration of sentence, 158 L Ed 2d 32.
Due process.
Informer, identity of.
Prosecution's failure to disclose identity of informer violated
due process, entitled petitioner to writ of habeas corpus,
157 L Ed 2d 1166.
Exhaustion of remedies.
Federal constitutional claims.
Presentation to state court.
Fair presentation requirement not satisfied if state court
must read beyond petition, brief, or similar papers to
find material alerting it to the presence of a federal
claim, 158 L Ed 2d 64.
Prisoners.
Damages claim based on acts which if proven would render
conviction invalid.
Favorable-termination requirement not applicable when
prisoner's challenge threatens no consequence for the
conviction or the duration of sentence, 158 L Ed 2d 32.
Ineffective assistance of counsel.
Application of Strickland test.
Unreasonable application of federal law, 159 L Ed 2d 683.

HABEAS CORPUS —Cont'd
Jurisdiction.
Enemy combatant.
Foreign detainees at Guantanamo naval base.
Plaintiffs not nationals of countries at war with United
States, 159 L Ed 2d 548.
Petition of person detained as asserted enemy combatant
improperly filed in New York district court where petitioner
was being detained in South Carolina, 159 L Ed 2d 513.
Mixed petitions containing both exhausted and unexhausted claims.
Federal district court's failure to give warnings about statute of
limitations to prisoner held not to make improper the
dismissal of mixed petitions that prisoner had filed pro se,
159 L Ed 2d 338.
Nondefaulted claims coupled with procedurally defaulted claim.
Actual innocence exception to procedural default.
Consideration of nondefaulted claims rather than considering
actual innocence issue, 158 L Ed 2d 659.
Place or location.
Detention: district of detention as place where writ is sought.
Petition improperly filed in New York district court where
petitioner was being detained in South Carolina, 159 L Ed
2d 513.
Pro se representation.
Federal district court's failure to give warnings about statute of
limitations to prisoner held not to make improper the
dismissal of "mixed" petitions that prisoner filed pro se, 159 L
Ed 2d 338.
State courts.
Unreasonable application of federal law or precedent.
Ineffective assistance of counsel, 159 L Ed 2d 683.
Jury instruction as to imperfect self defense, error.
Deference to state court's finding that jury not likely misled
by erroneous instruction, 158 L Ed 2d 701.
Unreasonable application of federal law.
Jury instruction as to imperfect self defense, error.
Deference to state court's finding that jury not likely misled by
erroneous instruction, 158 L Ed 2d 701.
Warnings.
Mixed petitions containing exhausted and unexhausted claims.
Federal district court's failure to warn pro se petitioner about
statute of limitations held not to make improper the
dismissal of mixed petitions, 159 L Ed 2d 338.

HEALTH MAINTENANCE ORGANIZATIONS.
ERISA.
Failure of HMO to cover certain medical services.
State court actions alleging HMO's failure violated state
statute preempted by ERISA, 159 L Ed 2d 312.

HONESTY OR DISHONESTY.
Hearsay.
  Confrontation clause of Sixth Amendment as accepting hearsay so
    reliable and trustworthy that there is no material departure
    from rule that accused have right to confront those against
    him.
    Cross examination as core of trustworthiness, 158 L Ed 2d 177.
HUSBAND AND WIFE.
Confrontation of witnesses.
  Marital privilege barring spouse's testimony.
    Recorded statement of spouse not admissible absent cross
      examination, 158 L Ed 2d 177.

I

INCOME TAXES.
Deductions and credits.
  Schools and education.
    Tax credits for payments funding scholarships to private
      schools.
      Tax injunction act not a bar to federal court suit seeking to
        enjoin operation of state statute authorizing credits, 159
        L Ed 2d 172.
Withholding taxes.
  Partnership failing to withhold.
    Assessment of partnership to extend statute of limitations.
      General partners bound by extension without need of
        separate assessment, 158 L Ed 2d 279.
INCOMPETENT OR INSANE PERSONS.
Mitigation of death penalty, consideration of defendant's
    retardation, family history, and emotional disturbance in.
  Certificate of appealability ought to have issued when court of
    appeals assessed defendant's Penry v. Lynaugh claim under
    improper legal standard, 159 L Ed 2d 384.
INDECENCY, LEWDNESS, AND OBSCENITY.
Child online protection act.
  Discretion in granting preliminary injunction against
    enforcement pending constitutionality determination, 159 L
    Ed 2d 690.
Children and minors.
  Child online protection act.
    Discretion in granting preliminary injunction against
      enforcement pending constitutionality determination, 159 L
      Ed 2d 690.
INDIANS.
Congress.
  Tribal court jurisdiction over nonmember Indians.
    Constitutionality of Congressional expansion of jurisdiction to
      include nonmember Indians as part of inherent power of
      Indian tribes, 158 L Ed 2d 420.

INDIANS —Cont'd
Double jeopardy.
Tribal court prosecution of nonmember Indian.
Subsequent federal court prosecution not barred.
Dual sovereign theory, 158 L Ed 2d 420.
Jurisdiction.
Nonmembers.
Congressional lifting of restriction on jurisdiction over
nonmembers deemed constitutional, 158 L Ed 2d 420.
Tribal courts.
Jurisdiction.
Nonmembers.
Congressional lifting of restriction on jurisdiction over
nonmembers deemed constitutional, 158 L Ed 2d 420.

INFORMERS.
Due process.
Identity of informer.
Prosecution's failure to disclose identity of informer held to
violate due process, entitling petitioner to habeas corpus
relief, 157 L Ed 2d 1166.
Identity of informer.
Disclosure of identity, generally.
Prosecution's failure to disclose identity of informer held
violation of due process, entitling petitioner to writ of
habeas corpus, 157 L Ed 2d 1166.
Withholding disclosure of, generally.
Prosecution's failure to disclose identity of informer held a
violation of due process, entitling petitioner to writ of
habeas corpus, 157 L Ed 2d 1166.

INJUNCTIONS.
Child online protection act.
Discretion in granting preliminary injunction against
enforcement pending constitutionality determination, 159 L
Ed 2d 690.
Eleventh Amendment.
Consent decrees.
Enforcement of decree against state officials not barred by
Eleventh Amendment, 157 L Ed 2d 855.

IN PERSONAM OR IN REM.
Bankruptcy.
Discharge of debt by bankruptcy court an in rem proceeding, 158
L Ed 2d 764.

INTENT OR MOTIVE.
Gerrymander of state legislative districts.
Political gerrymandering claims nonjusticiable, 158 L Ed 2d 546.
Legislative apportionment, partisan gerrymander of state
legislative districts.
Political gerrymandering claims nonjusticiable, 158 L Ed 2d 546.

INTENT OR MOTIVE —Cont'd
Partisan gerrymander of state legislative districts.
Political gerrymandering claims nonjusticiable, 158 L Ed 2d 546.

INTEREST ON MONEY.
Truth in Lending Act.
Over-limit fees excluded from definition of finance charge.
Regulation Z exclusion as reasonable interpretation of act, 158 L Ed 2d 450.

INTERNATIONAL LAW AND MATTERS.
Claims against government.
Abduction from Mexico for criminal trial in United States.
Action against DEA under tort claims act, 159 L Ed 2d 718.
Alien tort statute, applicability.
Abduction from Mexico for criminal trial in United States, 159 L Ed 2d 718.
Sovereign immunity.
Expropriation exception in Foreign Sovereign Immunities Act.
Retroactive application, 159 L Ed 2d 1.

INTERNET.
Child online protection act.
Discretion in granting preliminary injunction against enforcement pending constitutionality determination, 159 L Ed 2d 690.

INTERROGATION.
Continuous interrogation of suspect.
Pre-Miranda warning confession inadmissible, 159 L Ed 2d 643.

INVESTIGATIONS AND INVESTIGATORS.
Preservation of evidence.
State's failure to preserve potentially useful evidence held not to constitute denial of due process.
Discovery request by defendant.
Effect on subsequent destruction of evidence, 157 L Ed 2d 1060.

J

JOB DISCRIMINATION.
Constructive discharge.
Sexual harassment.
Affirmative defense of employer.
Employer installed a readily accessible, effective policy for reporting complaints and plaintiff unreasonably failed to make use of procedure, 159 L Ed 2d 204.
Limitation of actions.
Racial harassment.
Federal 4 year limitation for claims under enactments made after 1990 applied where action not maintainable but for 1991 amendment to statute, 158 L Ed 2d 645.

JOB DISCRIMINATION —Cont'd
Racial harassment.
Limitation of actions.
Federal 4 year limitation for claims under enactments made after 1990 applied where action not maintainable but for 1991 amendment to statute, 158 L Ed 2d 645.
Reverse discrimination.
Age Discrimination in Employment Act.
Employers may favor older employees over younger ones, 157 L Ed 2d 1094.
Sexual harassment.
Constructive discharge.
Affirmative defense of employer.
Employer installed a readily accessible, effective policy for reporting complaints and plaintiff unreasonably failed to make use of procedure, 159 L Ed 2d 204.

JURISDICTION.
Foreign Sovereign Immunities Act.
Expropriation exemption.
Retroactive application to pre-enactment conduct, 159 L Ed 2d 1.

JURY AND JURY TRIAL.
Sentence and punishment.
Length of sentence.
Judge's imposition of sentence exceeding general statutory maximum held to violate defendant's Sixth Amendment right to jury trial, 159 L Ed 2d 403.

L

LABOR AND EMPLOYMENT.
Grievances and grievance procedures.
Sexual harassment.
Affirmative defense of employer.
Employer installed a readily accessible, effective policy for reporting complaints and plaintiff unreasonably failed to make use of procedure, 159 L Ed 2d 204.
Transfer or removal of cases.
ERISA preemption.
State court actions alleging HMO's failure to cover certain medical services, 159 L Ed 2d 312.
Vicarious liability of employer.
Sexual harassment case under Title VII.
Affirmative defense of employer.
Employer installed a readily accessible, effective policy for reporting complaints and plaintiff unreasonably failed to make use of such procedure, 159 L Ed 2d 204.

LAND POLICY AND MANAGEMENT ACT.
Non-impairment mandate.
  Bureau of land management.
    Off-road vehicles, use in wilderness study areas.
      Federal court's authority to "compel agency action unlawfully
        withheld or unreasonably delayed" under administrative
        procedure act, 159 L Ed 2d 137.
LEGISLATIVE HISTORY AND INTENT.
Age Discrimination in Employment Act, 157 L Ed 2d 1094.
Civil rights and discrimination.
  Age Discrimination in Employment Act, 157 L Ed 2d 1094.
LETTERS OF CREDIT AND CREDIT CARDS.
Finance charge.
  Over-limit fees excluded from definition of finance charge.
    Regulation Z exclusion as reasonable interpretation, 158 L Ed
      2d 450.
Over-limit fees.
  Finance charge defined in Regulation Z as not including.
    Reasonable interpretation of act to exclude, 158 L Ed 2d 450.
Truth in Lending Act.
  Over-limit fees.
    Finance charge defined in Regulation Z as not including.
      Reasonable interpretation of act to exclude, 158 L Ed 2d 450.
LICENSES AND PERMITS.
Adult businesses.
  Ordinances.
    Licensing ordinance.
      Prompt judicial review of administrative decision denying
        license, 159 L Ed 2d 84.
Ordinances.
  Sexually oriented businesses.
    Prompt judicial review of administrative decision denying
      license, 159 L Ed 2d 84.
LIMITATION OF ACTIONS.
Borrowing state statutes of limitation.
  Federal 4 year limitation for claims under enactments made after
    1990.
    Amendment in 1991 to statute allowing action to be
      maintained, 158 L Ed 2d 645.
Federal question.
  Job discrimination.
    Federal 4 year limitation for claims under enactments made
      after 1990 applied where action not maintainable but for
      1991 amendment to statute, 158 L Ed 2d 645.
Habeas corpus.
  Mixed petitions containing exhausted and unexhausted claims.
    Federal district court's failure to give warnings about statute of
      limitations held not to make improper the dismissal of
      mixed petitions that prisoner had filed pro se, 159 L Ed 2d
      338.

LIMITATION OF ACTIONS —Cont'd
Racial harassment.
Federal 4 year limitation for claims under enactments made after
1990 applied where action not maintainable but for 1991
amendment to statute, 158 L Ed 2d 645.

LIMITED PARTNERSHIPS.
Diversity jurisdiction.
Postfiling change in citizenship does not cure lack of
subject-matter jurisdiction that existed at time of filing, 158
L Ed 2d 866.

LOANS.
Student loans.
Bankruptcy.
Dischargeability of student loan debt guaranteed by
governmental unit.
Proceeding to determine dischargeability of debt not a suit
against state, 158 L Ed 2d 764.

M

MEDICAID.
Sovereign immunity.
Consent decree.
Enforcement of decree against state officials not barred by
Eleventh Amendment, 157 L Ed 2d 855.

MEXICO OR MEXICAN LAW.
Carriers.
Federal motor carrier safety administration.
Evaluation by administration of environmental effects of
cross-border operations of Mexican-domiciled carriers not
required under National Environmental Policy Act or Clean
Air Act, 159 L Ed 2d 60.

MINES AND MINERALS.
Grants or patents to land.
Reservation to US of valuable minerals.
Sand and gravel not considered valuable minerals, 158 L Ed 2d
338.

MIRANDA V ARIZONA.
Continuous interrogation of suspect.
Prewarning confession inadmissible, 159 L Ed 2d 643.
Custody.
State court determination of custody for Miranda purposes.
Federal law reasonably applied in court's holding that suspect
not in custody during interrogation, thus suspect not
entitled to habeas relief, 158 L Ed 2d 938.
Interruption of warnings by suspect.
Failure to finish warnings not requiring suppression of physical
evidence, 159 L Ed 2d 667.

INDEX

MIRANDA V ARIZONA —Cont'd
State court determination of custody for Miranda purposes.
Federal law reasonably applied in court's holding that suspect not in custody during interrogation, thus suspect not entitled to habeas relief, 158 L Ed 2d 938.

N

NAME.
Stop and identify.
Statute requiring Terry stop suspect to disclose name does not violated Fourth or Fifth Amendments, 159 L Ed 2d 292.

NATIONAL ENERGY POLICY DEVELOPMENT GROUP.
Federal Advisory Committee Act, 159 L Ed 2d 459.

NATIONAL ENVIRONMENTAL POLICY ACT.
Carriers.
Federal motor carrier safety administration not required to evaluate environmental effects of cross-border operations of Mexican-domiciled carriers by NEPA, 159 L Ed 2d 60.

NEXT FRIEND.
Parent acting as next friend.
Non-custodial father lacked prudential standing to bring suit against daughter's school district to challenge district's requirement that students recite pledge of allegiance, 159 L Ed 2d 98.

O

OFF-ROAD VEHICLES.
Bureau of land management.
Wilderness study areas, vehicle use in.
Federal court's authority to "compel agency action unlawfully withheld or unreasonably delayed" under administrative procedure act, 159 L Ed 2d 137.

ORDINANCES.
Adult businesses.
Licensing ordinance facially valid due to ordinance's assurance of prompt judicial review of administrative decision denying license, 159 L Ed 2d 84.

P

PARTICIPANT OR PARTICIPATION.
ERISA.
Working owner of business qualifies as "participant" in ERISA-covered pension plan if plan covers one or more employees other than owner or owner's spouse, 158 L Ed 2d 40.

PARTIES.
Next friend.
  Religious freedom.
    Non-custodial father could not sue as next friend of daughter to
      bring suit against daughter's school district to challenge
      district's requirement that students recite pledge of
      allegiance, 159 L Ed 2d 98.
Standing.
  Raising constitutional rights of another.
    Non-custodial father lacked prudential standing to bring suit
      against daughter's school district to challenge district's
      requirement that students recite pledge of allegiance, 159
      L Ed 2d 98.

PARTNERSHIP.
Income taxes.
  Withholding of employment taxes.
    Assessment of partnership to extend statute of limitations.
      General partners bound by extension without need of
        separate assessment, 158 L Ed 2d 279.
Taxes.
  Withholding of employment taxes.
    Assessment of partnership to extend statute of limitations.
      General partners bound by extension without need of
        separate assessment, 158 L Ed 2d 279.

PENSIONS AND RETIREMENT.
Amendment.
  Anti-cutback provision of ERISA.
    Amendment to pension plan violated provision by expanding
      types of post-retirement employment that would trigger a
      suspension of benefits already accrued, 159 L Ed 2d 46.
Employee retirement income security act.
  Anti-cutback provision.
    Amendment to pension plan expanding the types of
      post-retirement employment that would trigger suspension
      of benefits already accrued prohibited, 159 L Ed 2d 46.
Participants, who qualifies as.
  Working owner of business qualifies as "participant" in
    ERISA-covered pension plan if plan covers one or more
    employees other than owner or owner's spouse, 158 L Ed
    2d 40.
Post-retirement employment.
  Anti-cutback provision.
    Amendment to pension plan expanding types of
      post-retirement employment that would trigger
      suspension of benefits already accrued prohibited, 159 L
      Ed 2d 46.
Pre-emption.
  HMO's failure to cover certain medical services.
    State court actions alleging that HMO's failure violated state
      statute preempted by ERISA, 159 L Ed 2d 312.

PENSIONS AND RETIREMENT —Cont'd
Employee retirement income security act —Cont'd
Suspension of benefits.
Anti-cutback provision prohibited amendment to pension plan that would trigger suspension of benefits already accrued, 159 L Ed 2d 46.
Working owner of business qualifies as "participant" in ERISA-covered pension plan if plan covers one or more employees other than owner or owner's spouse, 158 L Ed 2d 40.
Pre-emption and pre-emption rights.
Removal of causes.
State court actions alleging that HMO's failure to cover certain medical services violated state statute preempted by ERISA, 159 L Ed 2d 312.
Suspension of benefits.
Anti-cutback provision of ERISA prohibited amendment to pension plan expanding types of post-retirement employment that would trigger suspension of benefits already accrued, 159 L Ed 2d 46.

PLAIN ERROR.
Guilty plea acceptance.
Applicability of plain error rule.
Warnings, failure of district court to give required warnings.
Defendant must show a reasonable probability that, but for court's error, defendant would not have entered guilty plea, 159 L Ed 2d 157.

PLAIN OR COMMON MEANING.
Bankruptcy code.
Attorneys' fees under 11 USCS § 330(a)(1).
Compensation denied to debtor's attorney not employed as a professional person under 11 USCS § 327, 157 L Ed 2d 1024.

PLEA BARGAINING.
Departure from Sentencing Guidelines.
Judge's imposition of sentence exceeding general statutory maximum held to violate defendant's Sixth Amendment right to jury trial, 159 L Ed 2d 403.

PLEDGE OF ALLEGIANCE.
Standing.
Non-custodial father lacked prudential standing to bring suit against daughter's school district to challenge district's requirement that students recite pledge of allegiance, 159 L Ed 2d 98.

POLICE.
Evidence.
Preservation of potentially useful evidence.
Discovery request by defendant.
Effect on subsequent destruction of evidence, 157 L Ed 2d 1060.

POLICE —Cont'd
Good faith.
Preservation of evidence.
Discovery request by defendant.
Effect on subsequent destruction of evidence, 157 L Ed 2d 1060.
Highway checkpoints.
Information-seeking highway stops.
Reasonableness of seizure, 157 L Ed 2d 843.
Preservation of potentially useful evidence.
Discovery request by defendant.
Effect on subsequent destruction of evidence, 157 L Ed 2d 1060.

POLLUTION.
Best available control technology (BACT).
Authority of EPA to determine reasonableness of a state permitting agency's justification for its BACT decision, 157 L Ed 2d 967.
Carriers.
Federal motor carrier safety administration.
Evaluation by administration of environmental effects of cross-border operations of Mexican-domiciled carriers not required under Clean Air Act or National Environmental Policy Act, 159 L Ed 2d 60.
Clean Air Act.
Federal motor carrier safety administration not required to evaluate environmental effects of cross-border operations of Mexican-domiciled carriers by CAA, 159 L Ed 2d 60.
Preemption of rules of regional air-quality management district.
Rules containing emission requirements preempted under § 209(a), which prohibits states and political subdivisions from adopting standards relating to emissions controls, 158 L Ed 2d 529.
Prevention of significant deterioration program.
Best available control technology (BACT).
Authority of EPA to determine reasonableness of a state permitting agency's justification for its BACT decision, 157 L Ed 2d 967.
Construction of major pollutant emitting facilities.
Best available control technology (BACT).
Authority of EPA to determine reasonableness of a state permitting agency's justification for its BACT decision, 157 L Ed 2d 967.
Pre-emption.
Emissions from motor vehicles.
Regional air-quality management district rules preempted by § 209(a) of Clean Air Act, 158 L Ed 2d 529.

POLLUTION —Cont'd
Prevention of significant deterioration program of the Clean Air Act.
Best available control technology (BACT).
Authority of EPA to determine reasonableness of a state
permitting agency's justification for its BACT decision, 157
L Ed 2d 967.

POSTAL REORGANIZATION ACT.
Governmental status of United States Postal Service, 158 L Ed 2d
19.

POSTAL SERVICE.
Monopoly.
United States Postal Service not a person subject to antitrust
liability under the Sherman Act, 158 L Ed 2d 19.
Sherman Act.
United States Postal Service not a person subject to antitrust
liability under the Sherman Act, 158 L Ed 2d 19.

PRE-EMPTION AND PRE-EMPTIVE RIGHTS.
State or local government self-regulation.
Clear intent requirement, 158 L Ed 2d 291.
Telecommunications act of 1996.
Statutes, local laws and regulations prohibiting entities from
providing telecommunications service.
Political subdivisions of state may be prohibited by state
without pre-emption because pre-emption applies to private
entities, 158 L Ed 2d 291.

PREJUDICE OR BIAS.
Habeas corpus.
Requirement, in federal habeas corpus proceedings, of showing of
cause and prejudice with respect to relief from state criminal
conviction or sentence.
Demonstration of cause and prejudice, 157 L Ed 2d 1166.

PRESUMPTIONS AND BURDEN OF PROOF.
Retroactivity.
Foreign sovereign immunities act, 159 L Ed 2d 1.

PRICE CONTROL OR DISCRIMINATION.
Sherman Act.
Foreign trade antitrust improvements act.
Alleged price-fixing excluded from reach of Sherman act by
FTAIA where plaintiff's claim rested solely on independent
foreign harm, 159 L Ed 2d 116.

PRIOR TESTIMONY.
Absent or unavailable witness.
Cross examination as core of trustworthiness, 158 L Ed 2d 177.
Unavailable or absent witness.
Cross examination as core of trustworthiness, 158 L Ed 2d 177.

PRISONS AND PRISONERS.
Claim by state prisoner, for damages caused by acts which if proven would render his conviction invalid.
Favorable-termination requirement not applicable when prisoner's challenge threatens no consequence for the conviction or the duration of sentence, 158 L Ed 2d 32.

PRIVACY.
Damages.
Actual damages must be proved to recover under Privacy Act, 157 L Ed 2d 1122.
Statutory award.
Actual damages must be proved in order to qualify for minimum statutory award under Privacy Act, 157 L Ed 2d 1122.

PRO SE.
Habeas corpus.
Federal district court's failure to give warnings about statute of limitations to prisoner held not to make improper the dismissal of mixed petitions that prisoner had filed pro se, 159 L Ed 2d 338.

PROSPECTIVE OR RETROSPECTIVE MATTERS.
Foreign sovereign immunities act.
Retroactive application of the act, 159 L Ed 2d 1.

PRUDENTIAL STANDING DOCTRINE.
Non-custodial father.
Father did not have prudential standing to bring suit against daughter's school district to challenge district's requirement that students recite pledge of allegiance, 159 L Ed 2d 98.

PUBLIC FUNDS AND MONEYS.
Federal aid to states or other local agencies.
Bribery of officials of entities that receive federal aid.
Federal statute proscribing bribery of officials a valid exercise of Congress' authority under Article I of Constitution, 158 L Ed 2d 891.

PUBLIC LANDS OR PROPERTY.
Bureau of land management.
Off-road vehicle use in wilderness study areas.
Federal court's authority to "compel agency action unlawfully withheld or unreasonably delayed" under administrative procedure act, 159 L Ed 2d 137.
Off-road vehicle use in wilderness study areas.
Bureau of land management.
Administrative procedure act.
Federal court's authority to "compel agency action unlawfully withheld or unreasonably delayed," 159 L Ed 2d 137.

Q

QUALIFIED IMMUNITY.
Bivens action.
Search and seizure.
Warrant invalid due to lack of particularity.
Agent who prepared invalid warrant not entitled to qualified immunity, 157 L Ed 2d 1068.

R

REGULATION Z.
Over-limit fees.
Finance charge defined in Regulation Z as not including.
Reasonable interpretation of act to exclude, 158 L Ed 2d 450.

RELATION BACK.
Equal access to justice act.
Application for fees.
Not substantially justified position of US, allegation required.
Amendment of application after 30 day deadline to include required allegation.
Timeliness preserved by relation back of amendment, 158 L Ed 2d 674.

RELIGIOUS FREEDOM.
Establishment of religion.
State postsecondary scholarship program.
Prohibition against students who receive scholarship funds from pursuing a theology degree not a violation of establishment clause, 158 L Ed 2d 1.
Free exercise.
State postsecondary scholarship program.
Prohibition against students who receive scholarship funds from pursuing a theology degree not a violation of free exercise clause, 158 L Ed 2d 1.
Instruction in religion, generally.
State postsecondary scholarship program.
Prohibition against students who receive scholarship funds from pursuing theology degree not a violation of first amendment, 158 L Ed 2d 1.
Parties.
Standing to sue.
Non-custodial father lacked prudential standing to bring suit against daughter's school district to challenge district's requirement that students recite pledge of allegiance, 159 L Ed 2d 98.
Pledge of allegiance.
Non-custodial father lacked prudential standing to bring suit against daughter's school district to challenge district's requirement that students recite pledge of allegiance, 159 L Ed 2d 98.

RELIGIOUS FREEDOM —Cont'd
Public aid.
State postsecondary scholarship program.
Prohibition against students who receive scholarship funds from pursuing a theology degree not a violation of first amendment, 158 L Ed 2d 1.
Schools and education.
Non-custodial father lacked prudential standing to bring suit against daughter's school district to challenge district's requirement that students recite pledge of allegiance, 159 L Ed 2d 98.
Public aid.
State postsecondary scholarship program.
Prohibition against students who receive scholarship funds from pursuing a theology degree not a violation of first amendment, 158 L Ed 2d 1.
Theological students.
State postsecondary scholarship program.
Prohibition against students who receive scholarship funds from pursuing a theology degree not a violation of first amendment, 158 L Ed 2d 1.

REMOVAL OR DISCHARGE FROM EMPLOYMENT OR OFFICE.
Constructive discharge.
Sexual harassment.
Affirmative defense of employer.
Employer installed a readily accessible, effective policy for reporting complaints and plaintiff unreasonably failed to make use of such procedure, 159 L Ed 2d 204.
Sexual harassment.
Constructive discharge.
Affirmative defense of employer.
Employer installed a readily accessible, effective policy for reporting complaints and plaintiff unreasonably failed to make use of such procedure, 159 L Ed 2d 204.

RESTRAINTS OF TRADE, MONOPOLIES, AND UNFAIR TRADE PRACTICES.
Discovery proceedings.
European Communities, commission of.
Federal district court authorized, under 28 USCS §1782(a), to order discovery requested by private complainant for use in European Commission antitrust proceeding, 159 L Ed 2d 355.
European Communities, commission of.
Discovery proceedings.
Federal district court authorized, under 28 USCS §1782(a), to order discovery requested by private complainant for use in European Commission antitrust proceeding, 159 L Ed 2d 355.

RESTRAINTS OF TRADE, MONOPOLIES, AND UNFAIR TRADE PRACTICES —Cont'd
Foreign state or country.
Foreign trade antitrust improvements act.
Alleged price-fixing activity excluded from reach of Sherman act by FTAIA where plaintiff's claim rested solely on independent foreign harm, 159 L Ed 2d 226.
Person.
United States Postal Service not a person subject to antitrust liability, 158 L Ed 2d 19.

ROADBLOCKS.
Information-seeking highway stop.
Not unreasonable seizure in violation of Fourth Amendment, 157 L Ed 2d 843.

RULES OF CRIMINAL PROCEDURE.
Guilty plea.
Plain error rule.
Applicability in cases involving acceptance of guilty plea.
Warnings, failure of district court to give required warnings.
Defendant must show reasonable probability that, but for court's error, defendant would not have entered guilty plea, 159 L Ed 2d 157.
Plain error.
Guilty plea.
Applicability of plain error rule to acceptance of guilty plea situations.
Warnings, failure of district court to give required warnings.
Defendant must show reasonable probability that, but for court's error, defendant would not have entered guilty plea, 159 L Ed 2d 157.

S

SAND OR GRAVEL.
Public lands.
Grants or patents to land.
Reservation to US of valuable minerals.
Sand and gravel not considered valuable minerals, 158 L Ed 2d 338.

SCHOLARSHIPS.
Religious freedom.
State postsecondary scholarship program.
Prohibition against students who receive scholarship funds from pursuing a theology degree not a violation of first amendment, 158 L Ed 2d 1.

SCHOOLS AND EDUCATION.
Pledge of allegiance.
Non-custodial father lacked prudential standing to bring suit against daughter's school district to challenge district's requirement that students recite pledge, 159 L Ed 2d 98.

SCHOOLS AND EDUCATION —Cont'd
Religious freedom.
Pledge of allegiance.
Non-custodial father lacked prudential standing to bring suit against daughter's school district to challenge district's requirement that students recite pledge, 159 L Ed 2d 98.
Taxes.
Credits.
State statute authorizing state income tax credits for payments funding scholarships to private schools.
Tax injunction act not a bar to federal court suit seeking to enjoin operation of state statute, 159 L Ed 2d 172.

SEARCH AND SEIZURE.
Defective search warrants.
Lack of particularity.
Reasonableness of search, 157 L Ed 2d 1068.
Description or identification.
Warrant, sufficiency of description, generally.
Particularity requirement not met, 157 L Ed 2d 1068.
Disclosure as taking.
Stop and identify statute requiring Terry stop suspect to disclose name does not violate Fourth or Fifth Amendment, 159 L Ed 2d 292.
Highway checkpoints.
Information-seeking highway stop not unreasonable seizure in violation of Fourth Amendment, 157 L Ed 2d 843.
Individualized suspicion.
Special law enforcement concerns justifying some highway stops without individualized suspicion, 157 L Ed 2d 843.
Legality or illegality.
Unlawful search, generally, 157 L Ed 2d 1068.
Name.
Stop and identify statute requiring Terry stop suspect to disclose name does not violate Fourth or Fifth Amendments, 159 L Ed 2d 292.
Privileges and immunities.
Qualified immunity.
Agent not entitled to qualified immunity where particularity requirement of warrant not met, 157 L Ed 2d 1068.
Reasonableness.
Highway checkpoint.
Information-seeking stop not unreasonable, 157 L Ed 2d 843.
Lack of particularity in warrant, 157 L Ed 2d 1068.
Roadblocks.
Information-seeking highway checkpoint not unreasonable seizure in violation of Fourth Amendment, 157 L Ed 2d 843.

INDEX

SEARCH AND SEIZURE —Cont'd

Warrantless search.

Passenger compartment of automobiles.

Search allowed incident to arrest when police officer first made contact with arrestee after arrestee left automobile, 158 L Ed 2d 905.

Presumption against warrantless searches applies to searches which were defective due to lack of particularity in warrant, 157 L Ed 2d 1068.

SELF-INCRIMINATION.

Attorneys at law.

Postindictment questioning.

Knowing and intelligent waiver of Sixth Amendment right to counsel.

Effect of previous interrogation in violation of Sixth Amendment, 157 L Ed 2d 1016.

Description or identification.

Stop and identify statute requiring Terry stop suspect to disclose name does not violate Fourth or Fifth Amendments, 159 L Ed 2d 292.

Police.

Postindictment questioning.

Deliberate elicitation standard.

Determination of whether to suppress self-incriminating statements made in violation of standard, 157 L Ed 2d 1016.

Waiver of privilege.

Postindictment questioning.

Deliberate elicitation standard.

Effect of previous interrogation in violation of standard, 157 L Ed 2d 1016.

SENTENCE OR PUNISHMENT.

Factors in sentencing.

Distinguishing from elements of crime.

Capital offenses and punishment.

Jury decision, rather than sentencing judge sitting alone, required where aggravating circumstance requirement serves as functional equivalent of element of greater offense.

Not retroactively applicable to cases already final on direct review, 159 L Ed 2d 442.

Kidnapping.

Judge's imposition of sentence exceeding general statutory maximum violated defendant's Sixth Amendment right to jury trial, 159 L Ed 2d 403.

SENTENCE OR PUNISHMENT —Cont'd
Mental capacity or condition.
Death penalty, consideration of defendant's mental retardation,
family history, and emotional disturbance.
Certificate of appealability ought to have issued when court of
appeals assessed defendant's Penry v. Lynaugh claim under
improper legal standard, 159 L Ed 2d 384.

SEPARATION OF POWERS.
Mandamus.
Discovery pursuant to Federal Advisory Committee Act, 159 L Ed
2d 459.

SEXUAL HARASSMENT.
Constructive discharge.
Affirmative defense of employer.
Employer installed a readily accessible, effective policy for
reporting complaints and plaintiff unreasonably failed to
make use of procedure, 159 L Ed 2d 204.
Vicarious liability of employer.
Affirmative defense.
Employer installed a readily accessible, effective policy for
reporting complaints and plaintiff unreasonably failed to
make use of such procedure, 159 L Ed 2d 204.

SHERMAN ACT.
Exemptions and exclusions.
Foreign trade antitrust improvements act.
Anticompetitive conduct that causes only foreign injury,
exclusion from Sherman act, 159 L Ed 2d 226.
Foreign trade antitrust improvements act.
Alleged price-fixing activity excluded from reach of Sherman act
where plaintiff's claim rested solely on independent foreign
harm, 159 L Ed 2d 226.
Persons.
Postal service not a person subject to antitrust liability, 158 L Ed
2d 19.
Postal service not a person subject to antitrust liability, 158 L Ed
2d 19.
United States Postal Service not a person subject to antitrust
liability, 158 L Ed 2d 19.

SILENCE.
Evidence.
Continuous interrogation of suspect.
Pre-Miranda warning confession inadmissible, 159 L Ed 2d
643.

SIXTH AMENDMENT.
Deliberate elicitation standard.
Suppression of self incriminating statements made in violation of
standard, 157 L Ed 2d 1016.

SOVEREIGN IMMUNITY.

Bankruptcy.

Student loan debts guaranteed by governmental unit.

Proceeding to determine dischargeability of student loan debt not a suit against state, 158 L Ed 2d 764.

Consent judgments or decrees.

Judicial enforcement of consent decree against state officials not barred by Eleventh Amendment, 157 L Ed 2d 855.

Student loans.

Bankruptcy.

Dischargeability of student loan debt guaranteed by governmental unit.

Proceeding to determine dischargeability of debt not a suit against state, 158 L Ed 2d 764.

SPENDING CLAUSE.

Bribery.

Federal statute proscribing bribery of officials of entities that receive federal funds a valid exercise of Congress' authority under Article I, 158 L Ed 2d 891.

STEWARDSHIP.

Public lands.

Bureau of land management.

Off-road vehicle use in wilderness study areas.

Federal court's authority under administrative procedure act to "compel agency action unlawfully withheld or unreasonably delayed," 159 L Ed 2d 137.

STOP AND IDENTIFY.

Statute requiring Terry stop suspect to disclose name does not violate Fourth or Fifth Amendments, 159 L Ed 2d 292.

T

TAX INJUNCTION ACT.

Arizona statute providing state income tax credit for payments to nonprofit organizations that awarded scholarships to private schools in alleged violation of the establishment clause.

Federal court action challenging state tax credits not barred by TIA, 159 L Ed 2d 172.

TELECOMMUNICATIONS ACT OF 1996.

Statutes, local laws and regulations prohibiting entities from providing telecommunications service.

Pre-emption.

Political subdivisions of state may be prohibited by state without pre-emption because pre-emption applies to private entities, 158 L Ed 2d 291.

THEOLOGICAL STUDENTS.

State postsecondary scholarship program.

Prohibition against students who receive scholarship funds from pursuing a theology degree not a violation of first amendment, 158 L Ed 2d 1.

TIMELINESS.
Equal access to justice act.
Application for fees.
Amendment after 30 day deadline to include required
allegation that US position was not substantially justified.
Relation back of amendment to preserve timeliness of
application, 158 L Ed 2d 674.

TIME OR DATE.
Bankruptcy.
Discharge of indebtedness.
Forfeiture of right to rely on time constraints, 157 L Ed 2d 867.

TRUTH-IN-LENDING ACT.
Finance charge.
Over-limit fees not considered finance charge.
Regulation Z's exclusion as reasonable interpretation of act, 158
L Ed 2d 450.
Over-limit fees.
Finance charge defined in Regulation Z as not including.
Reasonable interpretation of act to exclude, 158 L Ed 2d 450.

U

UNDER GOD.
Addition of words to pledge of allegiance.
Standing to challenge.
Non-custodial father lacked prudential standing to bring suit
against daughter's school district to challenge district's
requirement that students recite pledge of allegiance, 159
L Ed 2d 98.

V

VICARIOUS LIABILITY.
Sexual harassment case under Title VII.
Affirmative defense of employer.
Employer installed a readily accessible, effective policy for
reporting complaints and plaintiff unreasonably failed to
make use of procedure, 159 L Ed 2d 204.

W

WARNINGS.
Guilty pleas.
Plain error review.
Defendant must show reasonable probability that, but for
court's error in failing to give warning, defendant would
not have entered plea, 159 L Ed 2d 157.

WITNESSES.
Good or bad faith.
  Confrontation of witnesses.
    Cross examination as core of trustworthiness, 158 L Ed 2d 177.

WORLD WIDE WEB.
Child online protection act.
  Discretion in granting preliminary injunction against
    enforcement pending constitutionality determination, 159 L
    Ed 2d 690.